The LearnEdge(TM) Perspective

A POWER OF HABIT METHODOLOGY

Bernard Carrier

Gotham Books

30 N Gould St.
Ste. 20820, Sheridan, WY 82801
https://gothambooksinc.com/

Phone: 1 (307) 464-7800

Published by Gotham Books (January 5, 2026)

ISBN: 979-8-3496-9252-9 (H)
ISBN: 979-8-3496-9250-5 (P)
ISBN: 979-8-3496-9251-2 (E)

Foreword

LearnEdge™ represents a revolutionary approach to conducting Software Engineering Economics Modeling (SEEM).

Standing on the shoulders of Dr. Barry Boehm, Walker Royce of Rational explored the application of COCOMOII economic modeling into the Project Management domain. His insights on Software Project Management revealed some additional considerations for technology, scale, quality and process modeling. The next generation cost model required special operational handling.

A key consideration captured by SEEM is required looking closely at what a system is. In essence, a system is comprised of software, hardware and operator(s) to deliver the performance expected. Following the track of COCOMOII created by Dr. Barry Boehm, Dr. Ricardo Valerdi revealed some important insights into quantifying the costs of systems engineering in complex systems. The key considerations relate to the additive, multiplicative and exponential factors applied in the economics modeling approach.

A major contributor in formulating the software costs remained elusive until the work of Dr. Guy Andre Boy revealed in Orchestrating Human-Centered Design how to account for the multiple constraints presented by the software practitioners. An integrated view of software operation and automation can now be introduced.

From a qualitative and quantitative perspective, the work of Capers Jones on estimating software costs not only brought realism to estimating but also brought forward a key measurement to address the complexity of modeling such costs: function point measurement. Backfiring was introduced as a mechanism to trace software engineering economics modeling based on Software Lines of Code (SLOC) versus Function Point (FP).

Building on such revolutionary work, a new insight required to match the two major stages of software development: an engineering stage and a production stage, introduced by Walker Royce. With the advent of the Unified Modeling Language of Rational, such stages are coined Platform Independent Model (PIM) and Platform Specific Model (PSM). A solution coined Model-Driven Architecture was introduced by Dr. Oscar Pastor leading the way to capture both modeling capabilities using a technology coined Integranova Model Execution System (IMES).

Greg Bishop and Cesar Otero of Integranova played a significant role in making LearnEdge™ a reality.

The single element sparsely covered is related to the introduction of “Dynamic Progress Method” for generating the Critical Path Method (CPM). The original work of J. Chris White presents DPM and how such a method will revolutionize resources assignments against project activities. LearnEdge™ embeds each concept introduced by these key contributors. Also, LearnEdge™ offers a mechanism to tailor current “Agile Methodologies” to fit the culture of the organization applying such methodologies.

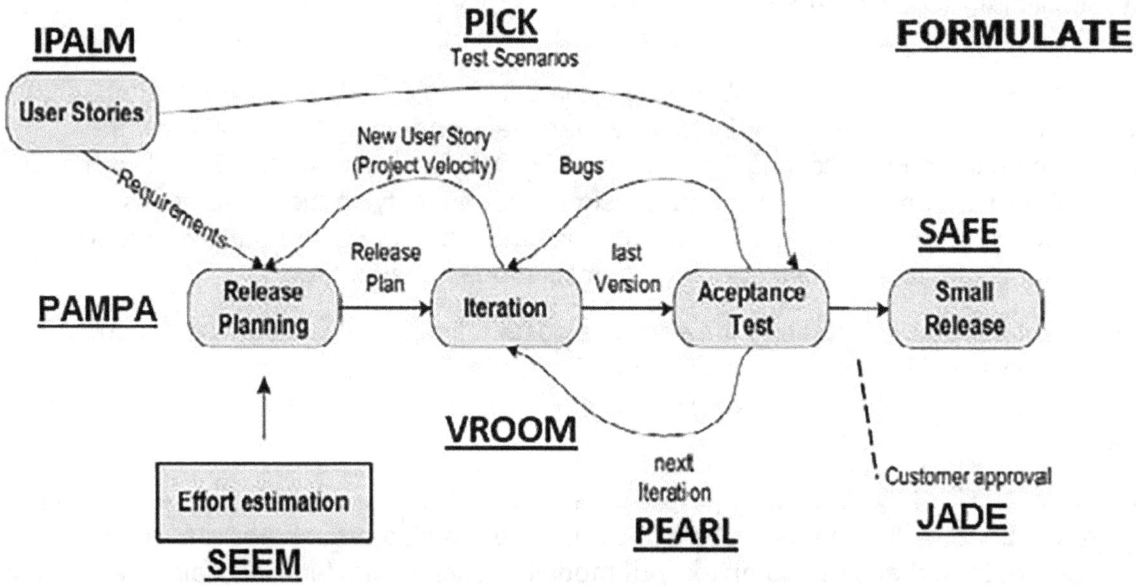

Effort Estimation in **AGIA** *Software Development*

LearnEdge™ (AGIA) is like a High-Speed Train (SEEM) with an 8-cylinder engine (PRODUCTS) fueled by a gas called EFP, delivering its power through a 5-speed transmission system (SAFE). The dashboard (IPALM) offers 9 types of controls (PLASTICS). This vehicle can deliver more than 6 categories of products (POST_TRAIL). Drivers must undergo appropriate training (FEASIBLE) to ensure well-planned delivery (PICK). The route to follow follows a plan (PEARL) called the "Traveling Salesman Algorithm." The roadmap is called "PAMPA."

Preface: A goal driven requirements engineering approach

The book represents a story board. Events and actions are triggered around the key players and the goals pursued. The book introduces two stories: 1. A small project coined The Car Rental Demo. 2. An expert system coined IPALM. One delivers a solution to a non-technical audience and the second one delivers a question-answer environment to support the first one.

What the book elaborates is how to measure both the product aspect of the work and the process aspect of the work using a common measurement coined Effective Function Point. The prologue retraces the history of such. The preface invites the reader to sit in a high-speed train to discover a methodology to let their technological vision come to reality.

The LearnEdge™ workflow picture supports the fact that a project starts and ends. The concept introduced in the book is the fact that 9 parameters dictate the workflow to achieve each goal. The pattern supported meets the Project Management Body of Knowledge (PMBOK) from a functional standpoint and the Baldrige Excellence Framework (BEF) form a performance standpoint: Cost-Schedule-Scope constraints. Kiviat Charts or Radar Charts illustrate the progress. **Project Performance is the focal point of attention.**

There are two stages of exploration: 1. A requirements analysis stage accompanied by Use Cases. 2. A design elaboration stage accompanied by Class Diagrams. The latter is in the appendices. The former is in the main body. **Work Organization is the focal point of attention.**

The 9 parameters cited are related to 9 roles played by the stakeholders. There is a formulation for each role. The book leads the reader towards understanding the formulation related to cost, schedule, and scope constraints. This is illustrated by the IPALM Architecture Reference Model. **Modeling Heuristics and Modeling Language are the focal points of attention.**

LearnEdge™ is about challenging the velocity of knowledge acquisition and understanding. It's about challenging the boundary between semantic and discourse exchanges. What is significant in the methodology is the recognition of the discontinuities that exist in the present development processes, measured by the Effective Progress Management Level (**EPML**) and activity assignments, measured by the Cognitive Function Evaluator Matrix (**CFEM**). Both are covered in Appendix D and B respectively. What LearnEdge™ brings about is a single measurement that bring about our understanding of 9 performance factors:

NOTE:

1. **Terms you should know are listed in Appendix A.**
2. **Tricks of the trade are highlighted in BOLD and listed as Abbreviations in Appendix A.**
3. **Roles and Responsibilities associated with using LearnEdge™ are mapped one on one with the performance factors.**
4. **Key Information related to LearnEdge™ modeling are recorded in Appendix R.**
5. **Proof of concepts approach related to LearnEdge™ is introduced in Appendix S.**

Contents

Table of Figures

List of Tables

Overview

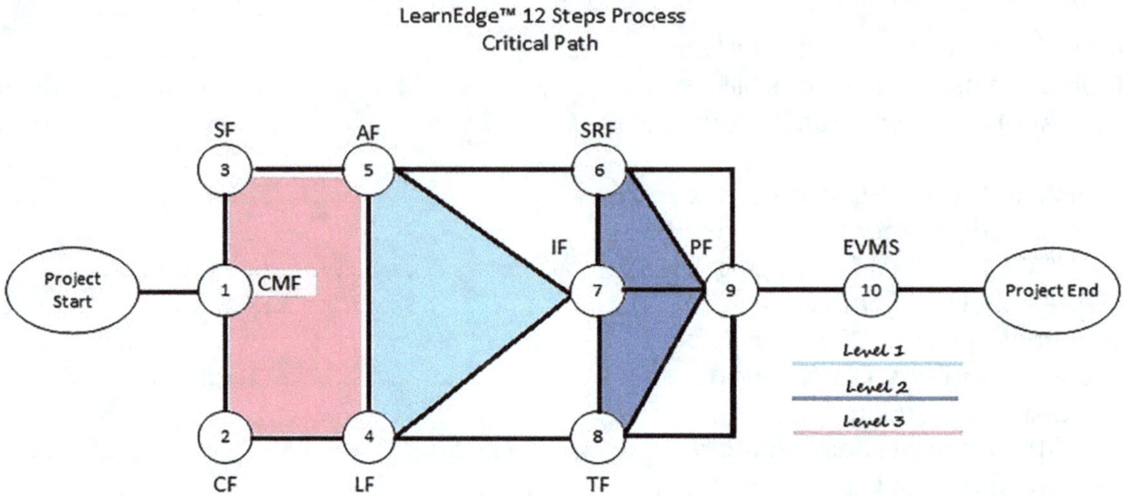

Figure 1 Critical Path

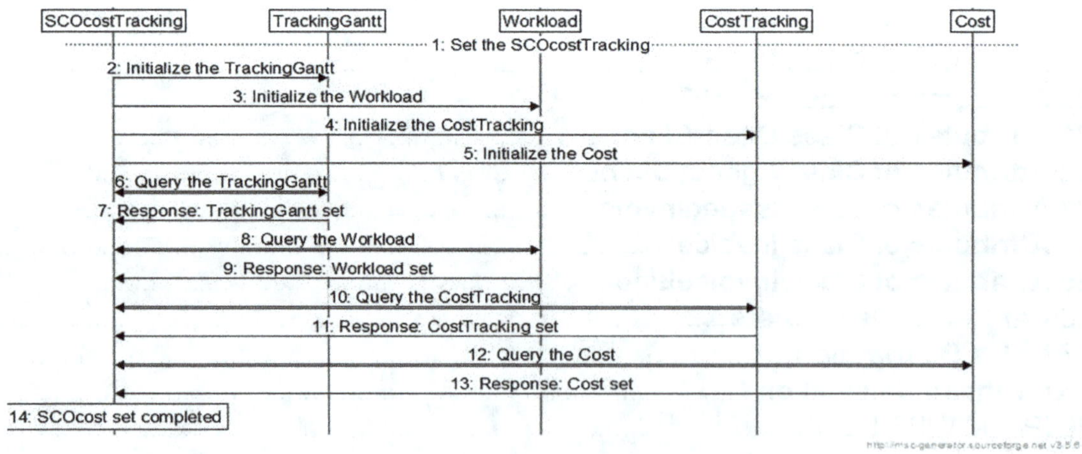

Figure 2 12 Steps Process

The LearnEdge(TM) Capability

The fundamental question to answer is: **What is the problem that LearnEdge™ will effectively solve?**

The answer lies in the state of disarray of the methodologies involved in system/software development:

1. The primary issue is phase discontinuity: the development is broken down in phases with no clear handshake on the functional expansion of needs and wants, such as requirement engineering, architecture design, and implementation.
2. The derived issue is semantic discontinuity: each phase requires a different language to express the functional expansion with no clear transformation rules to confirm either the verification of processes applied, or the validation of results achieved.
3. The resulting issue is scope discontinuity: the complexity of the transformation process from requirements to implementation cannot be represented either by sizing the artifacts generated under each phase or determining the effort required for each.

The vision submitted under this proposal is**: What is unique about the LearnEdge™ solution?**

LearnEdge™ applies an operational approach to system development. Such an approach relies on the application of a single Systems Engineering Economics Model (**SEEM**) integrating three levels of development triple-constraint:

1. The fundamental consideration is the application of the Project Management Body of Knowledge (**PMBOK**) to the scope-schedule-cost constraint balancing act: this is the first level of constraint tackled. The current market in sizing a new development offers two different viewpoints, one from a resulting product generated and one from the functional requirements stipulated. From both perspectives, one cannot track the Work-Breakdown-Structure (**WBS**) throughout each phase in development without experiencing the discontinuities cited above. LearnEdge™ tackles this problem by establishing a **5-WBS** levels System Architecture Framework Evaluation (**SAFE**) process. The tree methodology applied allows for the quantification of the complexity of the processes involved.
2. The derived considerations in evaluating the evolution of product/service development is the considerations related to productivity-quality-risk management: this is the second level of constraint tackled. Given the confidence level achieved in sizing the development

stages, one must account for the development/adaptation effort required under each stage of development, the maintenance/test effort applied during the verification & validation processes, and the impact of the complexity measure against the risk considerations.

3. The resulting considerations expand from the functional assessment to the performance assessment of the development process. The proficiency of the team assigned to conduct the work, the efficiency of the process to bring the cost down, and the capability of processes to demonstrate results as specified under the Baldridge Excellence Framework: (**BEF)** this is the third level of constraint tackled.

What is the mission pursued under the LearnEdge™ vision?

It is to create a seamless integration of the product/service development processes under a single Systems Engineering Economics Model that will allow the application of a Dynamic Progress Methodology (**DPM**) implementation.

Using the standard PERT approach to establish from Optimistic Scenarios down to Pessimistic Scenarios, LearnEdge™ offers distinct dashboards to allow management to monitor and control the three level of triple-constraint seamlessly and dynamically. The scenarios are explored in detail in Appendix E. LearnEdge™ applies a Joint Agile Development Environment (**JADE**) to synthesize the information using radar charts to support any IT project size ranging from small, to large (one year project). LearnEdge™ is a Façade that can be applied under any product/service development effort, whether Model-Driven Architecture (MDA) or Model-Drive Engineering (MDE) based. LearnEdge™ can be delivered as a Software as a Service (SaaS)! LearnEdge™ represents a potential of 40/1 productivity improvement currently demonstrated using a MDA technology. Appendix N and Q provides a development view for small to large projects.

How soon can LearnEdge™ be delivered?

The product is prototyped to the point of requiring a system development house to integrate it as a SaaS solution. The product is trademarked in Canada. With the application of two large projects a year, the Return On Investment will range from 30% to 100% within 5 years or earlier based on the economics assessment.

The key point: the solution is now in the hands of the stakeholders throughout the development process.

The Intelligent Project Assistant in Lifecycle Management (**IPALM**) introduces a project management approach to devising a Model Driven Architecture solution. Both Project Manager and Portfolio Manager can benefit from **IPALM** to measure quantitatively each, and every lifecycle process applied to derive productivity improvement conditions. These conditions offer minimal risk for the performance goals pursued. **IPALM** supports the proposal's effort to clearly delineate the management, technical and financial considerations using a five-level Work Breakdown Structure.

The management model supports the Project Management Body of Knowledge (**PMBOK**) requirements. The technical model supports the Software Engineering Body of Knowledge (**SWBOK**) requirements. The financial model supports the best practices in software engineering modeling.

Appendix G covers a methodology comparison. Appendix H describes the concept of operation. Appendix I elaborates on the knowledge progression. Appendix J presents LearnEdge™ sizing formulations.

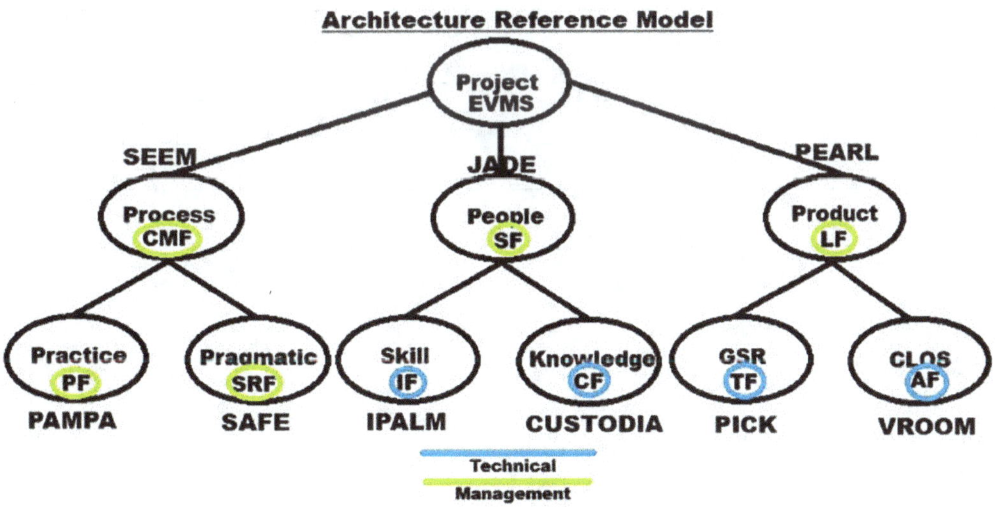

Figure 3 The LearnEdge™ Concept Visualization Stage

Roles and Services mapping

Cross-Ref.	Feasible	Role	Service	Factor	Control
Chapter 4	F	DI	SEEM	SF	Efficiency
Chapter 5	E	CE	CUSTODIA	CF	Competency
Chapter 6	A	SA	AVID	AF	Adaptability
Chapter 7	S	SE	IPALM	IF	Interactivity
Chapter 8	I	RM	SAFE	SRF	Contingency
Chapter 9	B	PM	MOTIF	CMF	Capability
Chapter 10	L	PI	PAMPA	PF	Productivity
Chapter 11		TF	PICK	TF	Quality
Chapter 12	E	SM	PEARL	LF	Dependency

i. Table 1 Roles and Responsibilities

The LearnEdge™ quest for Decision Intelligence

Step1: SITUATION ANALYSIS STAGE

1. **Situation Analysis** We need to be asking the decision questions and connecting all the dots to include outcomes.

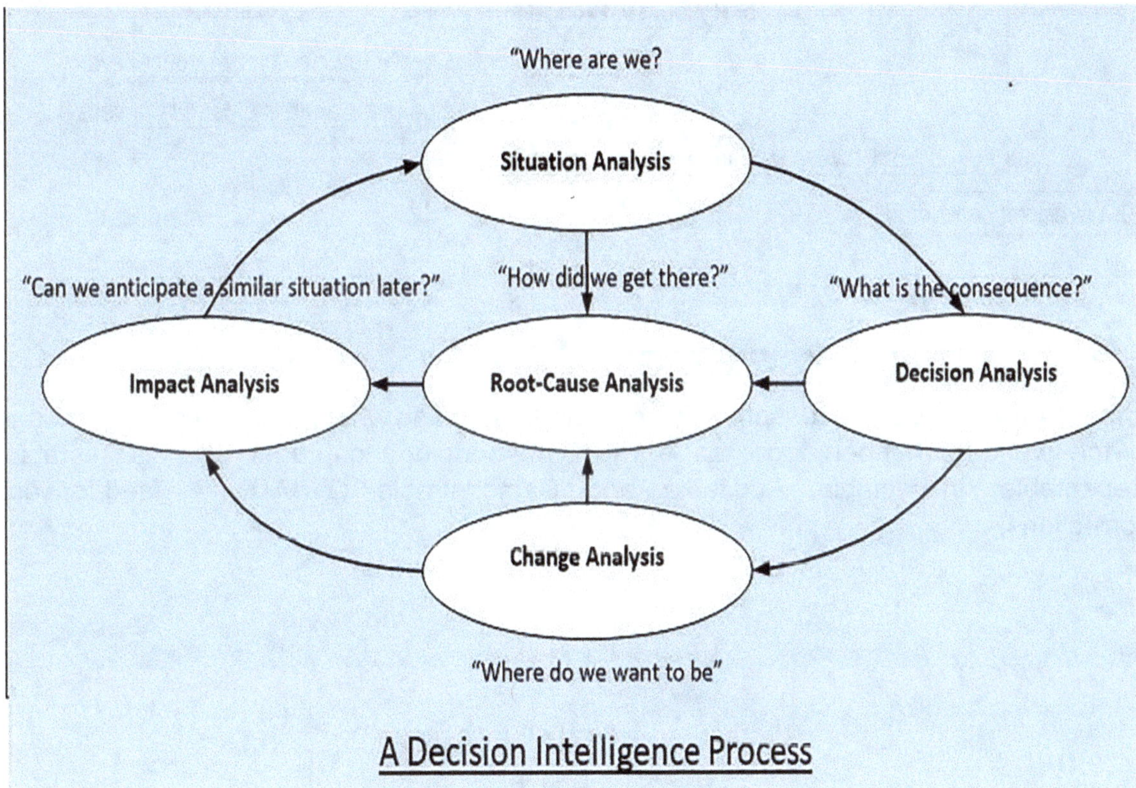

Figure 4 PRISM Model Guy Boy Vision

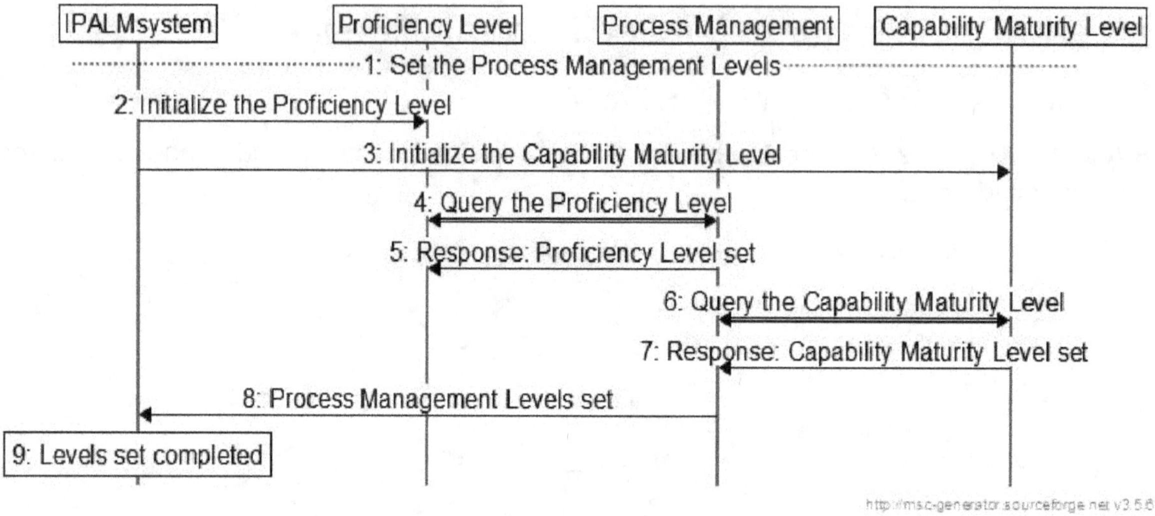

Figure 5 Situation Stage

Step 2: IMPACT ANALYSIS STAGE

2. **Impact Analysis** Causal reasoning is about understanding what things cause other things in the world to happen together. A **PICK** methodology captures what is Testable, Repeatable, Inspectable, Auditable and Demonstrable (**TRIAD**). A feed-forward corrections.

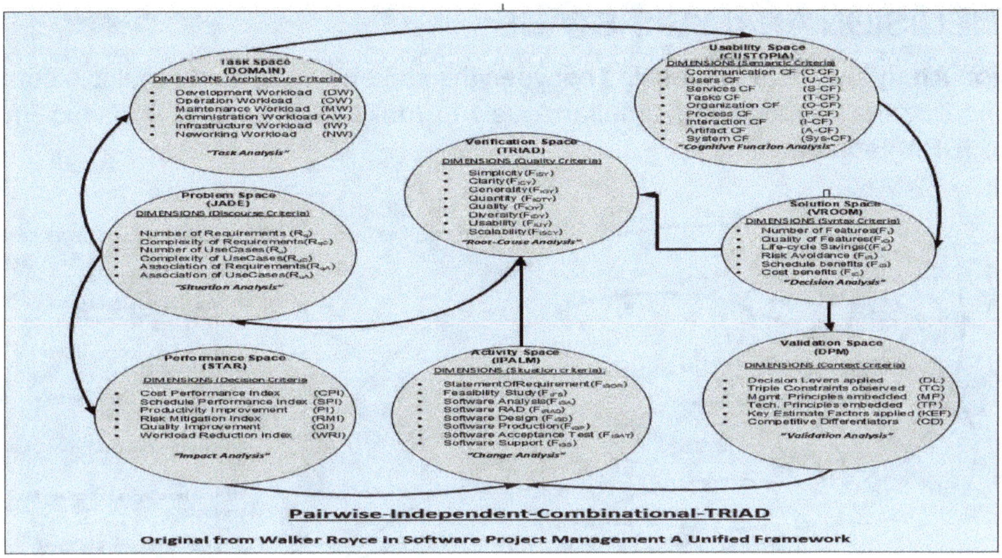

Figure 6 SMART Mode l

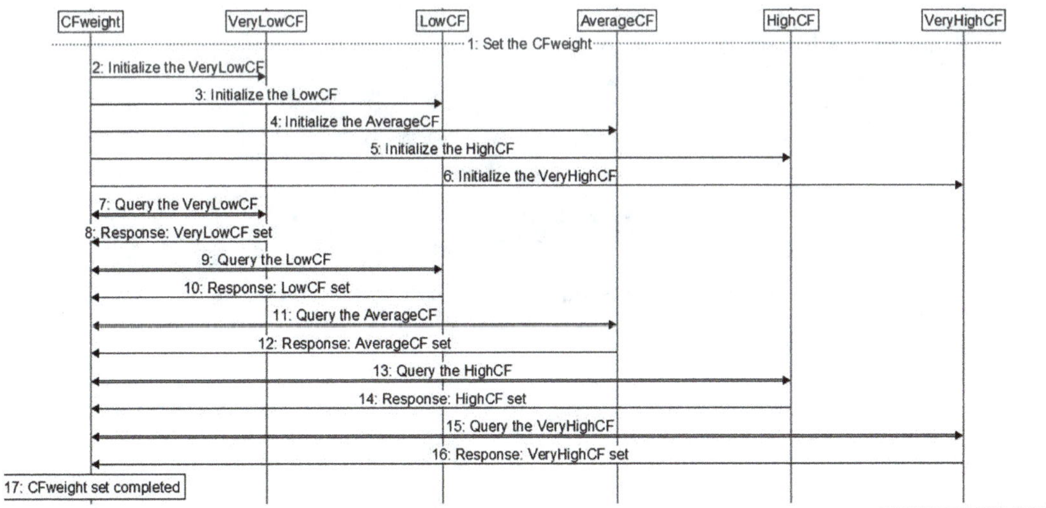

Figure 7 Inspect Stage

Step 3: DECISION ANALYSIS STAGE

3. **Decision Analysis** The relationships between the stakeholders create multiple contextual infusions that they consolidate simultaneously to make decisions, a Dynamic Progress Method (**DPM**) approach.

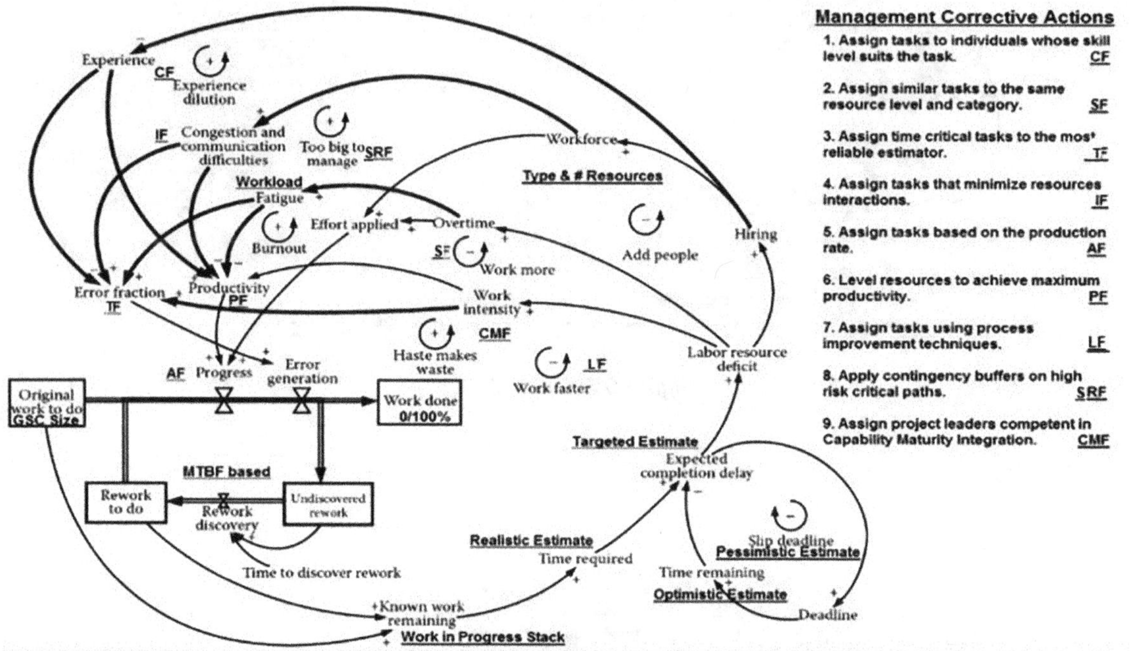

Original from Robert M. Sholtes
in The Dynamic Progress Method

Figure 8 The PEARL Model Chris White vision

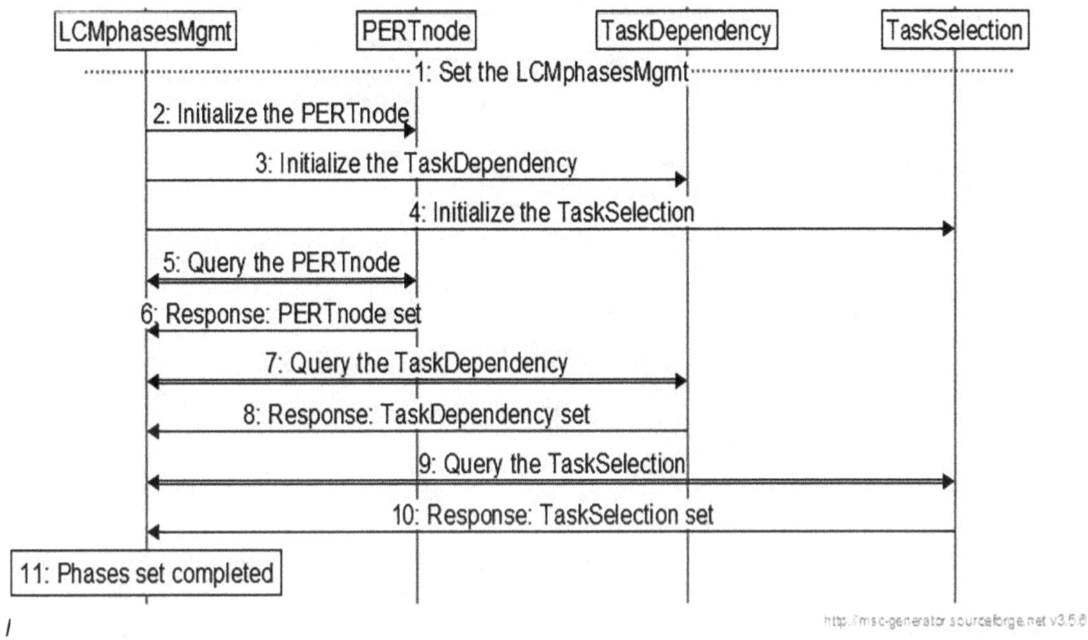

Figure 9 PEARL Actions Stage

Step4: ROOT-CAUSE ANALYSIS STAGE

4. **Root Cause Analysis The** best processes separate tasks into those appropriate for best practices and those appropriate for standard processes, as recommended under the Baldridge Excellence Framework, coined **FRACTALS**.

PMBOK ID	Class	Description	Focus	Method	Dashboard	
1	CostMgmt	Cost Management	Cost Control	Earned-Value	IterationDashboard	[2]
2	OrgMgmt	Resource Management	Resource Control	Human-Centered Design	CFAdashboard	[5]
3	CommMgmt	Communication Control	Interaction Control	JADE	GEMdashboard	[3]
4	QualityMgmt	Quality Management	Quality Control	PICT	SLAdashboard	[4]
5	ScopeMgmt	Scope Management	Productivity Control	IMES	ModelDashboard	[7]
6	IntegrationMgmt	Integration Management	Integration Control	World Modeller	CMMIdashboard	[1]
7	TimeMgmt	Time Management	Schedule Control	YAWL	PIdashboard	[6]
8	RiskMgmt	Risk Management	Risk Control	Tree-Methodology	RiskDashboard	[8]

Figure 10 Baldridge Excellence Framework

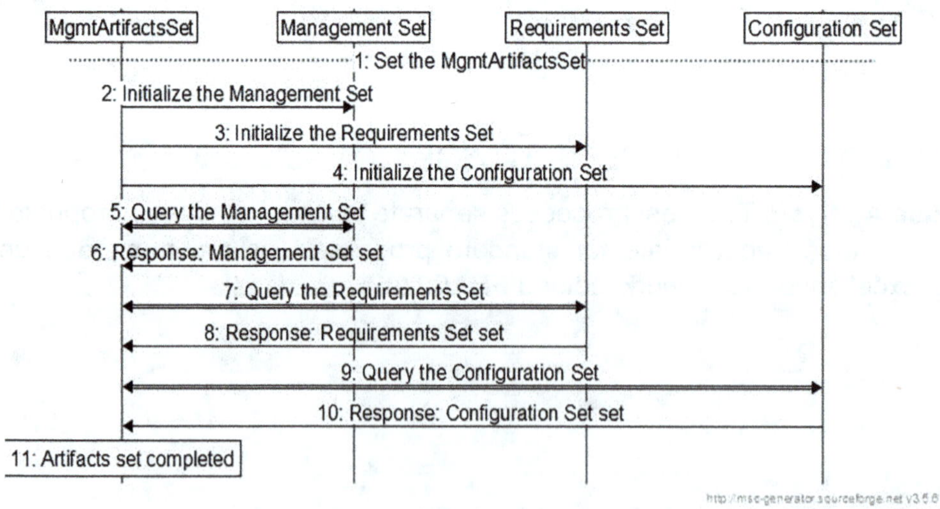

Figure 11 Model Generation Stage

Step 5: CHANGE ANALYSIS STAGE

5. **Change Analysis** Many systems today are built to capture data about the present and the past but have not been mined to understand the cause-and-effect links that could help support decisions about the future. The **CUSTODIA** Model tracks such cause-and-effect links.

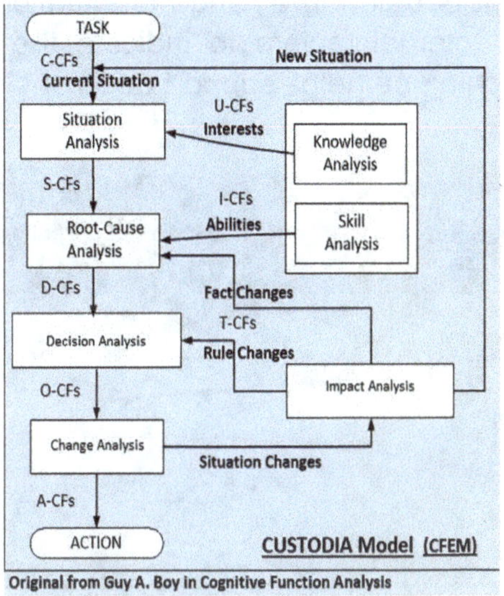

Figure 12 CUSTODIA Model Vision

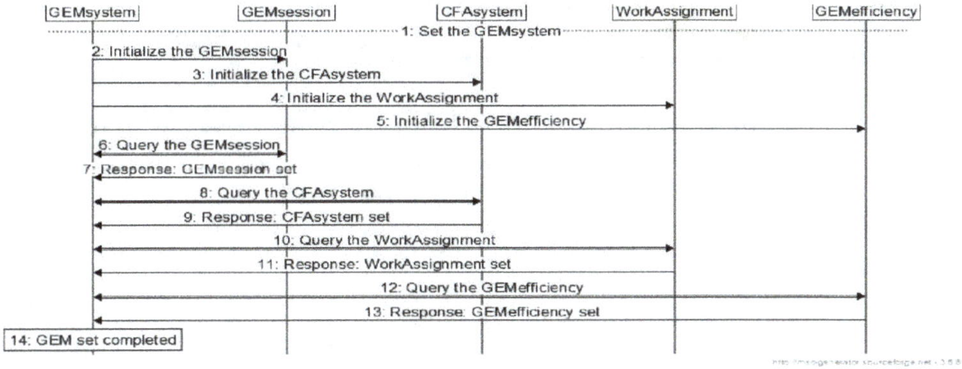

Figure 13 Tasks Stage

6. **TAILOR** A decision tree, coined 5-WBS, is also required to provide semantics, scope, and phase continuity while measuring quantitatively any System Under Study to assess the complexity to make the right decision in a range of situations. The decision tree steps through both external and internal factors to indicate the best decision for multiple combinations of factors. Such a tree helps support decisions about the future.

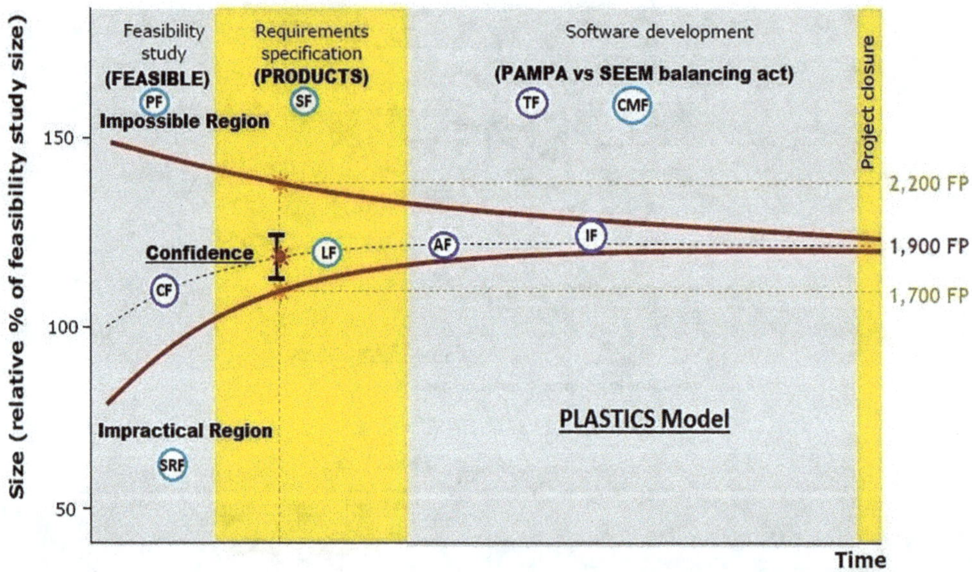

First size estimate of increment 1 – close to the danger zone

Figure 14 PICK Model CMMI Vision

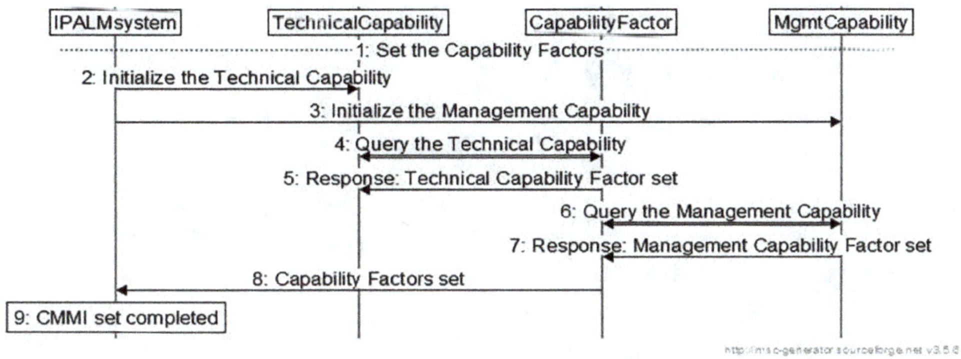

Figure 15 Tailor Stage

MONITORING & CONTROL STAGE

7. **OBSERVE** There are five abilities required to support decision making: Model, Observe, Tailor, Inspect and Formulate (**MOTIF**) the outcomes.

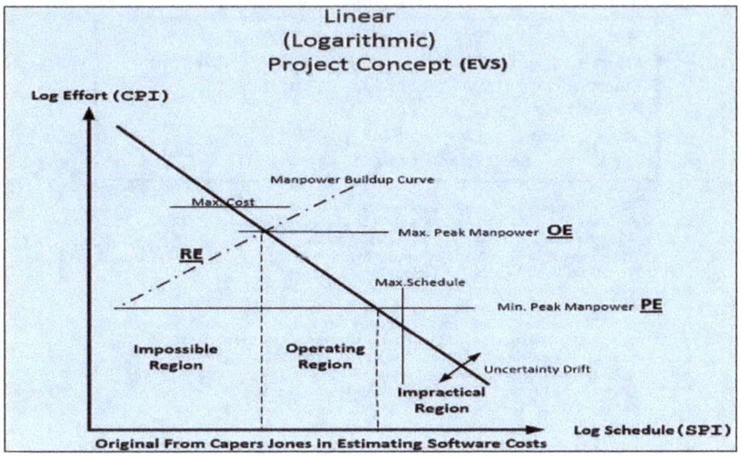

Figure 16 Linear Project Model – Capers Jones Vision

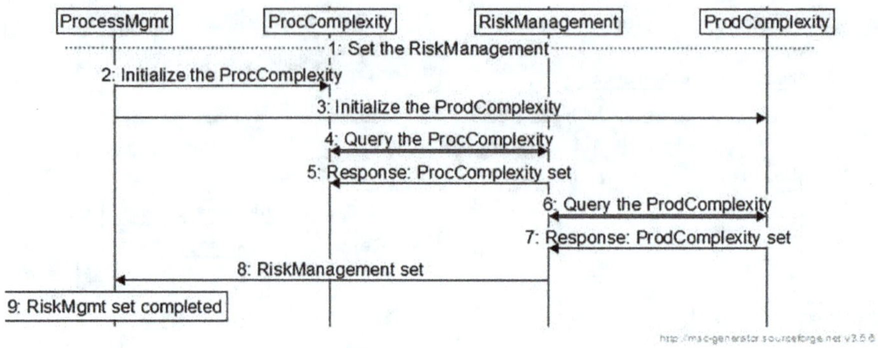

Figure 17 Observe Stage

EARNED VALUE MANAGEMENT STAGE

8. **FORMULATE** There is a need to integrate the process levels, those factors that are inside our control and the externals those factors that are outside our control using a Systems Engineering Economics Modeling approach, coined **SEEM**.

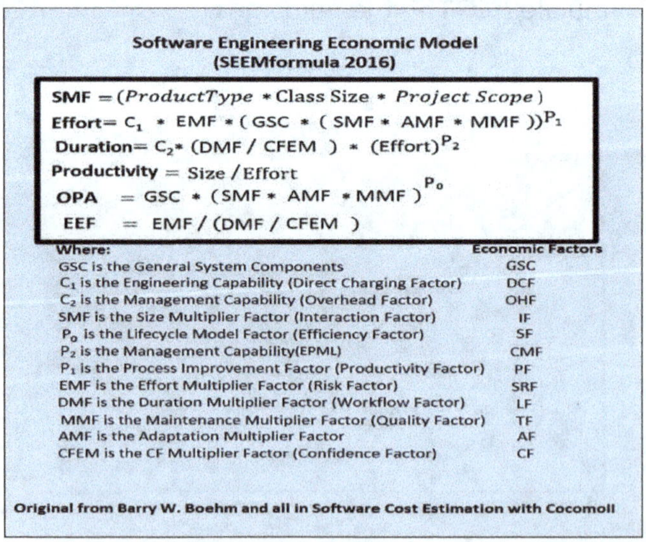

Figure 18 SEEM Model Walker Royce Vision

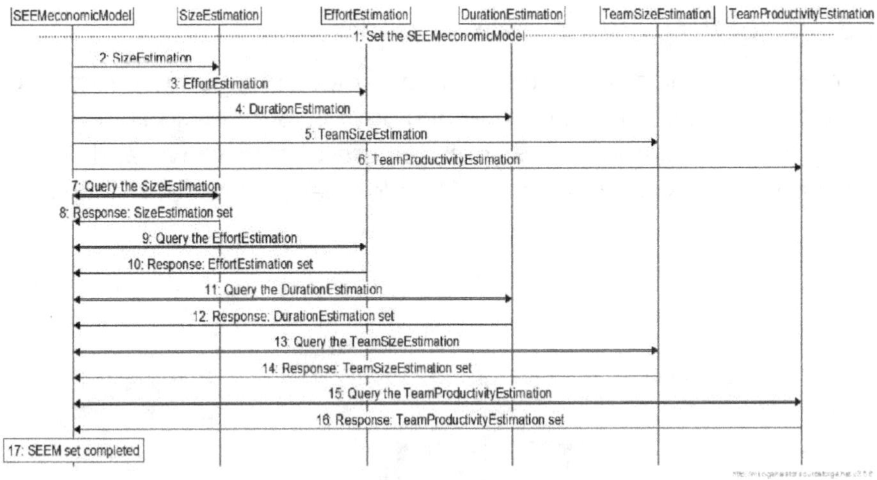

Figure 19 Formulate Stage

IPALM Framework

As a Model-Driven Architecture front-end, **IPALM** not only can measure performance but also can validate the outcomes using a Verifiable Requirements OO Method (**VROOM)** listed in Appendix P. The downstream code generator can then match the Unified Modeling Language specification.

These models can be verified and instantiated by executing a combinational analysis method. This method introduces a Pairwise Independent Combinational KPUs (**PICK**) technique. This technique reduces drastically the number of verification outcomes such as trials, reviews, inspections, analyses, and demonstrations.

IPALM Operational Model Dashboard

With the **IPALM** dashboard, management and executive decisions can weigh the risk factors across all key estimate factors being considered. The Linear Project model will automatically illustrate the best productivity improvement conditions. The Radar Chart model will automatically illustrate the range of variations in the key estimate factors.

Eight Schema Project Performances Balancing

There are often many stakeholders involved in a project to ensure overall success. **IPALM** includes cutting edge project modeling technology in verification languages, to deliver straightforward project management views, architecture design views and detailed component design views captured by the Project Charter, Development Plans, and Architecture Reference Models respectively.

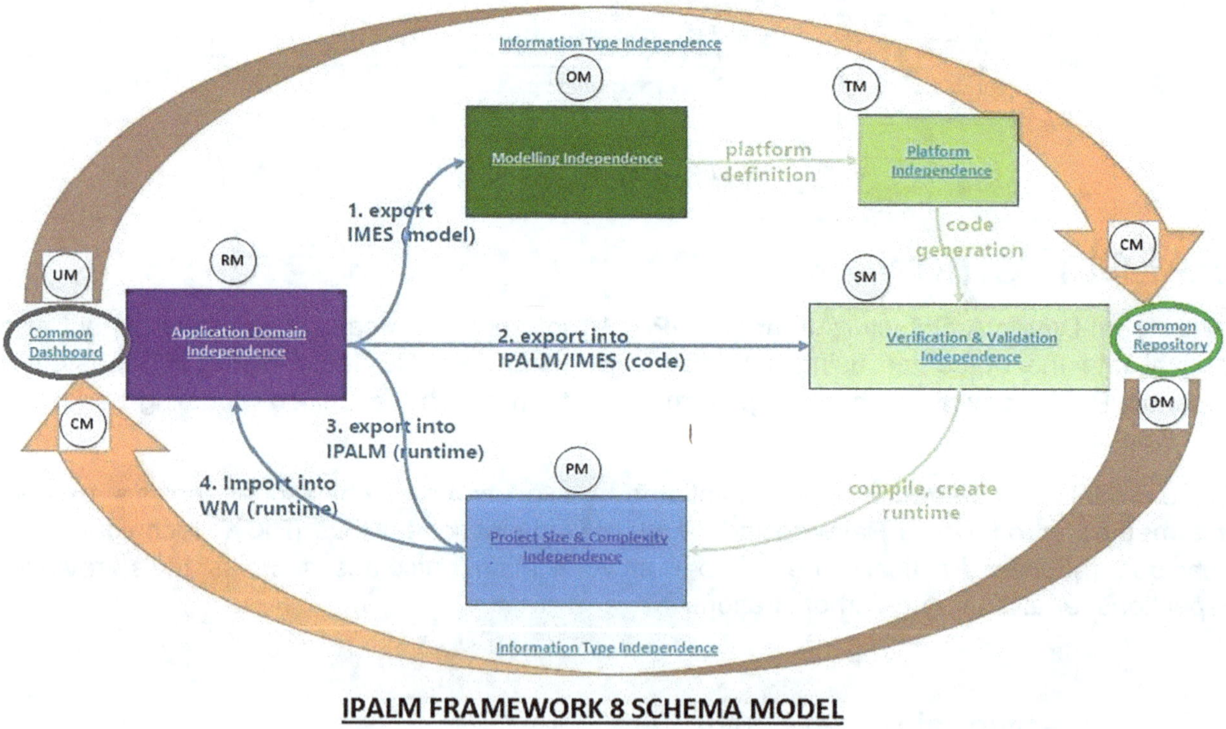

Figure 20PALM Framework Model

Baldrige Performance Framework (BEF) Demonstration

LearnEdge(tm) conducts mission critical operational analyses using a Human Centered Design approach. This approach complements the software engineering methodologies ranging from Spiral, RUP, Agile and more. With **IPALM**, LearnEdge(tm) incorporates CocomoII, and Capers Jones economic analysis techniques to quantitatively measure the outcomes of such methodologies and to predict performance expectations.

LearnEdge(tm) offers the following workshops:

- 2-hour (executive level);
- 2-Day (Executable Architectures);
- 10-day (tailored workshop providing a kick start to your project).

These web-based services provide the best way for your team to learn **IPALM**, quickly and efficiently:

- discover how to develop project management measurement views.
- Exchange with experts who have worked on a diversified set of system architectures and achieve optimal Baldridge Performance outcomes.

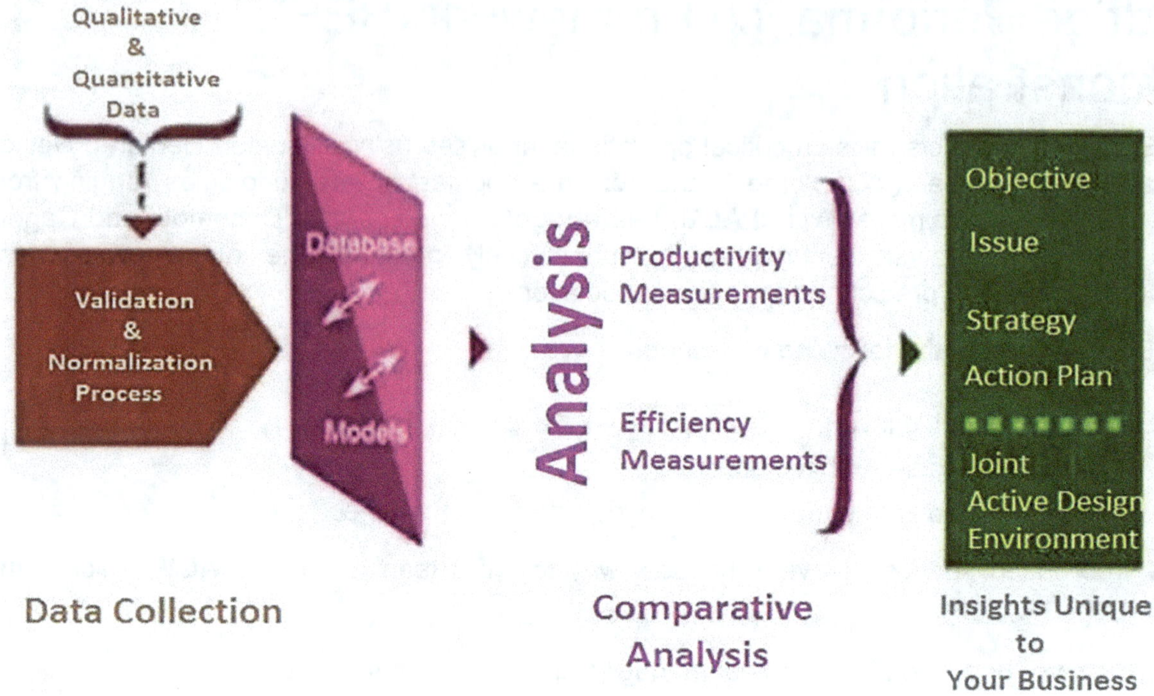

Figure 21 Measurement & Analysis Model – IMES Vision

Chapter 1 LearnEdge™ Concept of operation

1.1 LearnEdge™ operations Overview

What is LearnEdge™ ?

LearnEdge™ is a methodology offering an operational approach to "Application Generation in Action" (**AGIA**), described in Appendix C.

The methodology supports both a language and a notation to elaborate a validated system model of the application under development. Verifiable Requirements in OO Methodology (**VROOM**) Listed in Appendix P covers eight layers of integrated operations:

1. A Situation Analysis layer-based message paradigm approach.
2. A Decision Analysis layer, based on Decision Intelligence paradigm approach.
3. A Context Analysis layer, based on Project Evaluation & Analysis paradigm approach,
4. A Content Analysis layer, based on Cognitive Engineering paradigm approach,
5. A Discourse Analysis layer, based on Joint Active Design Paradigm Approach,
6. A Semantic Analysis layer, based on an Inference-Engine based paradigm approach.
7. A Syntax Analysis layer, based on a Model-Observe-Tailor-Inspect-Formulate paradigm approach.
8. A Lexical Analysis layer, based on Pairwise Independent Combinational Paradigm Approach.

The overall set of layers respond to fundamental questions related to project planning:

1. Who: what are the organizational teams performing the functional areas of the project.
2. Why: what are the goals pursued and associated objectives by team performing the performance areas of the project.
3. Where: what are the areas representing the most risks and how to mitigate such.
4. What: what is the architectural elements required to perform both the functional and performance requirements.

5. When: what is required to conduct Management Corrective Actions throughout the critical path established.
6. How well: what quality plan would best support de the development effort.
7. How much: what Systems Engineering Economics Model would best support the development effort.
8. How soon: what prototyping activities would lead to the most effective delivery of results.

LearnEdge™ embeds Baldridge Excellence Framework and the Project Management Body of Knowledge in its operations.

How does LearnEdge™ tracks performance?

LearnEdge™ tracks nine performance factors using nine services:

	Factors	Services
1.	A Capability Maturity Factor (CMF)	**FEASIBLE**
2.	A Competency Factor (CF)	**JADE**
3.	A Size Efficiency Factor (SF)	**SEEM**
4.	A Total Quality Model (TF)	**PICK**
5.	A System Risk Management Model (SRF)	**SAFE**
6.	A Project Attribute Monitoring Model (PF)	**PAMPA**
7.	A Task Interactivity Model (IF)	**IPALM**
8.	A Lifecycle Model Factor (LF)	**PEARL**
9.	A Model-Driven Architecture Model (AF)	**VROOM**

How does LearnEdge™ assesses performance?

LearnEdge™ breakdown the nine performance factors into three level of constraints:

1. Additive constraints:
    a. Scope oriented: AF
    b. Cost oriented: IF
    c. Schedule oriented: LF
2. Multiplicative constraints:
    a. Scope oriented: PF
    b. Cost oriented: SRF
    c. Schedule oriented: TF
3. Exponential constraints:
    a. Scope oriented: CF
    b. Cost oriented: SF
    c. Schedule oriented: CMF

A single Systems Engineering Economics Model (SEEM) integrates these constraints to achieve a Critical Path Method (**CPM**) delivery using **PEARL**, a dynamic progress method scheduler.

PEARL, a Project Evaluation and Review over the full Lifecycle Model selected tracks both the schedule performance against the CPM as well as the cost performance using the Earned Value Management model factors of ACWP (Actuals), BCWP(Milestones), BCWS (Plan) and BAC (Budget).

The additive nature of the constraints is related to incremental development using a single project size measure coined Effective Function Point (**EFP**). The multiplicative nature of the constraints is related to the impact of process improvement. The constraint is related to a single performance factor coined Effective Progress Management Level (**EPML**). The exponential constraints is related to the organization model presented. A single team size measure coined Cognitive Function Evaluator Matrix (**CFEM**) is related to team effectiveness. Both the cost effectiveness and the capability delivered depend on the **CFEM.**

What are the issues covered by LearnEdge™?

Discontinuities in the various phases of project development leads to low quality and high dependency between functional teams. The following continuity in development phases can be achieved with LearnEdge™:

1. Interactivity to support scope continuity,
2. Timeliness to support phase continuity,
3. Abstraction layering to support production rate continuity,
4. Reactiveness to support risk mitigation continuity,
5. Concurrency to support measurement and analysis continuity,
6. Distributiveness to support low coupling and high cohesion continuity,
7. Dynamic Structuredness to support capability maturity continuity,
8. Communicativeness to support Verification and Validation continuity,
9. Effectiveness to support Earned Value Management continuity.

The net impact of such issues is high coupling and low cohesion between teams.

What values does LearnEdge™ offer?

To meet the specific performance requirements of a project, the following performance criteria apply:

Exponential impact:

1. Capability performance criteria (CMF)
2. Efficiency performance criteria (SF)
3. Proficiency performance criteria (CF)

Multiplicative impact:

4. Contingency performance criteria (SRF)
5. Productivity performance criteria (PF)
6. Total Quality performance criteria (TF)

Additive impact:

7. Interactivity performance criteria (IF)

8. Dependency performance criteria (LF)
9. Production performance criteria (AF)

The net impact of such values is low coupling and high cohesion between teams thus offering effective results.

How does LearnEdge™ delivers such values?

LearnEdge™ follows a Cognitive Engineering pattern for delivering the results expected. The pattern is coined **FEASIBLE:**

F: Formulation of a solution using Semantic Analysis.

E: Evaluation of the solution using Decision Analysis.

A: Agile Adaptation using Context Analysis.

S: Specification of a solution using Content Analysis.

I: Interaction effectiveness using Discourse Analysis.

B. Baldridge framework impact using Performance Analysis

L: Language elaboration using Syntax Analysis.

E: Elicitation of Cognitive Functions using Lexical Analysis

The overall repository of the Knowledge Based capture by LearnEdge™ is coined **CUSTODIA** to highlight the Cognitive Functions (CF) applied:

C: C-CF For Knowledge Base facts information exchange
U: U-CF For Knowledge Base rules information exchange

S: S-CF For Model-Driven Engineering information exchange

T: T-CF For Verification & Validation information exchange

O : O-CF	For Requirements Risk Mitigation information exchange
D: D-CF	For Plan and Performance information exchange
I: I-CF	For Joint Active Design Environment information exchange
A: A-CF	For OO Model-Driven Architecture information exchange

An overall Cognitive Function Evaluation Matrix (**CFEM**) offers a view of the performance of the team assigned on the specific project. A modified Rasmussen's Model elements are captured:

1. Situation awareness: scenario exploration
2. Cooperative work: joint active design
3. Decision making knowledge elicitation
4. Planning and action: decision execution
5. Competence availability: assignment optimization
6. Risk mitigation: application of effective management corrective actions.
7. Architecture complexity evaluation: qualitative measurement of architecture features
8. A Systems Engineering economics modeling optimization: an earned value management methodology

1.2 Motivation for this manual

Einstein once said: "Imagination is more important than knowledge". Imagination leads to creativity. Creativity allows you to master the inspiration that guides you. Such inspiration will lead you to achieve the vision that drives you.

Whether you are Leonardo da Vinci or Picasso, you learn to explore your vision in exploratory steps. These steps might **require iterating** several times to refine a technique that will allow you to have a sense of achieving your objective at a moment of exploring your objective. It might **require incrementing** through these steps prior to achieving some quality results.

The ability to manage the number of steps to achieve your goal is related to **process improvement**.

A mentor for example can propel you ahead by providing you with some valuable life experiences. Process improvement calls for the organization of your work.

The primary aspect of your work is scoping up what you can achieve in the time frame you are allocated. This ability to manage the scope of your work is related to **productivity**. Then, you will achieve the confidence to create your vision at a **production rate** commensurate to your abilities.

1.2.1 The primary concerns at this stage are phase and scope discontinuity. The following considerations will allow you to provide mitigating actions required.

The ability to define a process to apply to achieve some intermediary results calls for a methodology to apply. A methodology offers a guide in defining the activities and tasks required to generate some specific outcomes. A methodology is often accompanied by tools and techniques to apply on each step of an iteration. A methodology relies on a **lifecycle model** of your development effort.

For example, the start can be called inception. The analysis and design stage can be called elaboration. The creating and testing stage can be called construction. Fundamental to the **interactivity** of the methodology is the inclusion of an environment that will assist you in accomplishing the integration of tools and techniques required.

Such an environment will provide a pattern of construction and guidance towards results expected while minimizing the potential errors in handling a technique. The result is **total quality** of work and result.

1.2.2 The primary concerns at this stage are quality and productivity impact on the production rate. The following considerations will allow us to alleviate some of the issues encountered.

In any work, some corrective work is required accompanied by **contingency** actions to mitigate the impact of the errors encountered. The ability to discern the goal pursued and the corrective measures required to realign the work calls for a high degree of competency.

Such a degree of **competency** requires being exposed to numerous scenarios and numerous decision-making actions prior to achieving a reasonable degree of expertise. Tutoring and training both offer some essential support to this path of **self-valuation**.

In addition, a high degree of **self-esteem** can be experienced by achieving the goals pursued in a timely manner. The degree of competency is a measure of your ability to team with partners at work with complementary skills and knowledge while achieving increased **capability** overall.

Teaming effectiveness becomes the norm by which you will be able to assess the full set of outcomes of your effort. You have a sense of **belonging**.

1.2.3 The primary concerns at this stage are the contingency et competency impact on the capability of delivering the results expected.

LearnEdge™ offers a unique pattern of operations coined Model-Observe-Tailor-Inspect-Formulate (**MOTIF**). A single Systems Engineering economics model (**SEEM**) provides an integrated view of all the considerations listed above. A Kiviat/Radar Chart will summarize the observations of progress over time. A total of 9 parameters will be tailored to achieve the performance expected. A Pairwise Independent Combinational KPU (**PICK**) mapping tool allows you to establish the optimal combination of parameters to achieve the goals pursued.
Using the Earned Value Management System (**EVMS**) approach, a single report will provide a view of progress through each iteration. **SEEM** integrates a single formulation to capture progress against the goal pursued. A Project Evaluation and Review over the full Lifecycle (**PEARL**) allows you to create a critical path to the delivery of results consistent with the performance expected.

A System Architecture Feature Evaluation (**SAFE**) accompanies you to establish the best mitigating strategies against the complexity of the project endeavor. A Project Attribute Monitoring and Predicting Agent (**PAMPA**) provides insight into progress required and the impact of corrective actions.

More importantly, as a team, Joint Active Design Environment (**JADE**) supports an integrated approach as a team to accomplish the goal pursued coherently and effectively. **JADE** is accompanied by an Intelligent Project Assistant in Lifecycle Modeling (**IPALM**) to facilitate the demonstration of cost, schedule, and scope constraints handling.

LearnEdge™ orchestrates every operations using a Verifiable Requirements in OO Methodology (**VROOM**) described in the next section. The Object-Oriented language applied is called Visual Prolog. **VROOM** analysis stack occupies 8 layers related to the following layers:

1. Layer 1 Lexical Analysis covered by the **PICK** tool and techniques.
2. Layer 2 Syntax Analysis covered by the **VROOM** tool and techniques.
3. Layer 3 Semantic Analysis covered by **PAMPA** tool and techniques.
4. Layer 4 Discourse Analysis covered by **JADE** tools and techniques.
5. Layer 5 Content Analysis covered by **SAFE** tool and techniques.
6. Layer 6 Context Analysis covered by **PEARL** tool and techniques.
7. Layer 7 Decision Analysis covered by **IPALM** tool and techniques.
8. Layer 8 Situation Analysis covered by **MOTIF** tool and techniques.

VROOM supports Baldridge Excellence Framework (**BEF**) and the Project Management Body of Knowledge (**PMBOK**). A single formulator called **SEEM** integrates each layer per scenario covered.

1.3. An Operational Approach to System Development

Development discontinuities exist at many levels. A prime example, the application of a Virtual Machine applies for Java Development, C Sharp Development, Ruby development and many other languages currently used. The goal pursued is to create an abstraction of both the processing environment and the operating system environment managing time, memory, and disk capabilities. In essence, each of these languages are imperative in nature. You must define the process flow for each class being handled.

The Graphical User Interface allows end-users to operate at a higher abstraction level to deal with word processing, data processing, graphic processing, and many other capabilities. Automation for such operations comes up in macros or some scripting languages.

LearnEdge™ operates at a higher level of language called declarative OO language, more specifically Visual Prolog. Visual prolog offers a **Model-View-Control-Execute** pattern to system development. The view aspect is managed using Form, Dialog, and Window type entities.

The data aspect comes in two categories synthesized under the Knowledge Base: Facts and Rules. A single paradigm describes the key operational concept embedded coined Horn Clause. A Horn Clause encapsulates a Predicate, like a predicate calculus, a clause leading to a goal through matching and unification.

A set of packages form a theory to be validated: pass or fail. Backtracking allows you to go through a set of clauses and backtrack in case of multiple choices or simply failure to proceed forward in the validation process.

The Horn Clause paradigm is ideal for the creation of the next level of abstraction coined Inference Engine. Visual Prolog comes with such an engine coined Prolog Inference Engine (**PIE**). Such an engine allows you to validate either a simple statement or a predicate operating on a knowledge base. This process of consultation allows you to test at the unit level, a predicate.

An application generated under Visual prolog integrates a series of packages, one only controlling the running of the operation. Such a package coined "main" can be declared otherwise by the designer. The main encapsulates the execution predicate called "run". A single package controls the window, menu, and toolbar operation. Under the window capability, a Code Expert allows you to assign specific predicates to support the events selected.

In short, the "view" aspect is managed as an independent feature as a package. A Prolog language header file offers you the list of sub-units related to the program, each contained under their specific package. Such package can be added incrementally or improved/corrected iteratively.

Each package can support the Model-View-Control-Execute pattern. A constructor predicate called "new" is required to create the instance of that class. A dialog and or a form can be integrated to the package under study. Facts can be added as required by the class or the whole application. The operations on that class represented by a predicate declaration provides the full set of controls required. The hierarchical nature of the application and the association nature related to the class under study can be earmarked using various keywords "inherits", "supports", "open" or "export".

The instance of a class can only be declared using the "interfaces" keyword. Otherwise, the class is declared as a procedure. Match and Unify operations happen when a functor type fact is manipulated by a predicate, thus allowing polymorphic operations.

The transformation stack introduced earlier occupies 8 layers related to the following analyses:

1. *Layer 1 Lexical Analysis covered by the **PICK** tool and techniques:*

    a. Associate in pair-wise fashion the relationship between entities.

b. Each entity must be of an independent nature.
c. A combinational relationship between entities.
d. A valid and invalid sampling of the outcomes.

2. *Layer 2 Syntax Analysis covered by the **VROOM** tool and techniques.*

A validated language created with Another Tool for Language Recognition (**ANTLR)**.

3. *Layer 3 Semantic Analysis covered by **PAMPA** tool and techniques.*

A Project Attribute Monitoring and Predicting Agent (**PAMPA**) written in C++.

4. *Layer 4 Discourse Analysis covered by **JADE** tools and techniques.*

A Delphi type communication environnement.

5. *Layer 5 Content Analysis covered by **SAFE** tool and techniques.*

A System Architecture Feature Evaluation (**SAFE**) based on Software Engineering with Formal Metrics.

6. *Layer 6 Context Analysis covered by **PEARL** tool and techniques.*

A Project Evaluation and Review over the full Lifecycle based on **PERT** methodology.

7. *Layer 7 Decision Analysis covered by **IPALM** tool and techniques.*

An Intelligent Project Assistant in Lifecycle Methodology (**PAMPA**).

8. *Layer 8 Situation Analysis covered by **MOTIF** tool and techniques.*

The use of signaling methodology provides a means to establish the interdependence between features by the implemented by the services integrated. LearnEdge™ covers text, graphic, formula. database and knowledge base.

LearnEdge™ asserts information to be recorded in the Knowledge Base and then recovered using a retract predicate when needed back. The user "consult" the knowledge base during the Inference Engine interactions.

In essence, each pack is compiled individually or collectively to generate the application. Once generated, each predicate is implemented in accordance with the class declaration and the interface declaration. The implemented portion of the package creates the supported inheritance hierarchy of the application declared in the interface.

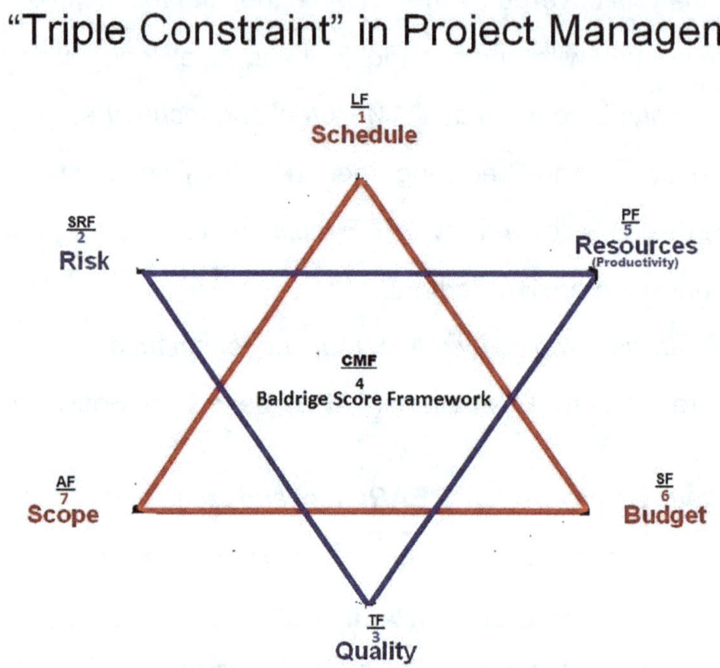

Figure 22 IPALM STAR Parameterized Model

The formulation of the LearnEdge™ model follows the following parameterized model:

S = [A, G, I, L, E, S, T, A, R, **P, O,-S, N]**

AGILE

A::=The analysis conducted on the success or failure of the application.

G::= Logical Guards, e.g. AND, OR, XOR, NOT) before or after the events called up.

I::= The backtrack inference engine applied on clauses.

L::= Links between nodes based on the events considered.

E::= Events responded to via the GUI.

STAR

S::= The simulation of the network to establish the range in performance.

T::= The local test carried out on the predicate or theory (set of predicates) under observation

A::=The actions conducted given the event selected.

R::= The results achieved on executing the predicate or the theory

POS'N

P::= The predicate node considered.

O::= The objective pursued under each package associated with a theory.

S::= Solution provided: goal.

N::= Network of packages established.

In essence, the core network is comprised of vertices (Nodes), links, events, guards, and actions. The additional elements form an overlay to control the execution, the simulation, the analysis, the test, and the reporting required.

LearnEdge™ follows a Cognitive Engineering pattern for delivering the results expected. The pattern is coined **FEASIBLE**:

F: Formulation of a solution using Semantic Analysis.

E: Evaluation of the solution using Decision Analysis.

A: Agile Adaptation using Context Analysis.

S: Specification of a solution using Content Analysis.

I: Interaction effectiveness using Discourse Analysis.

B. Baldridge framework impact using Performance Analysis

L: Language elaboration using Syntax Analysis.

E: Elicitation of Cognitive Functions using Lexical Analysis

A network of operations linking 12 nodes will suffice to demonstrate operational success.

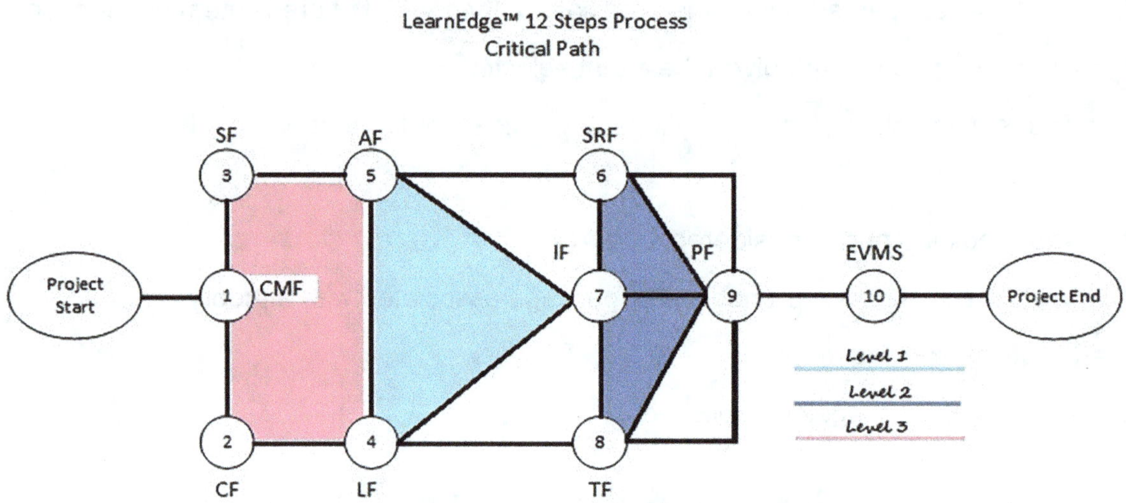

Figure 23 IPALM FEASIBLE RANGE

LearnEdge™ follows a Cognitive Engineering pattern for delivering the results expected. The pattern is coined **FEASIBLE,** where Node 1 and Node 12 are the Start and End respectively:

F: *Formulation of a solution using Semantic Analysis*:

Node11 to Node 12 transition for the Earned Value Management actions.

E: *Evaluation of the solution using Decision Analysis:*

Node 2 to Node 4 transition for the Efficiency Analysis actions.

A*: Agile Adaptation using Context Analysis:*

Node 4 to Node 5 transition for the Capability and Risk Mitigation actions, and

Node 4 to Node 6 transition for the Capability and Dependency Analysis actions, and Node 4 to

Node 7 transition for the Capability and Productivity Analysis actions.

S*: Specification of a solution using Content Analysis:*

Node 3 to Node 4 transition for the Capability and Cognitive Engineering actions.

I*: Interaction effectiveness using Discourse Analysis:*

Node 5 to Node 8 transition for the Contingency and Quality Analysis actions.

Node 6 to Node 8 transition for task and resource assignment actions *B:*

B*aldridge framework impact using Performance Analysis:*

Node 10 to Node 11 transition for system acceptance test to delivery actions

Node 11 to Node 12 transition for Earned Value Management analysis reporting actions.

L*: Language elaboration using Syntax Analysis:*

Node 7 to Node 9 transition for **MOTIF** modeling actions

Node 8 to Node 9 transition for **IPALM** modeling actions *E:*

E*licitation of Cognitive Functions using Lexical Analysis:*

Node 8 to Node 10 transition for Quality and Interactivity tradeoffs and

Node 9 to Node 10 transition for **PICK** and **VROOM** modeling tradeoffs.

A network of operations linking these 8 **FEASIBLE** features will suffice to demonstrate operational success using 12 transitions covering the full lifecycle of the project. This network is applied to generate the Schedule and the Critical Path using the Critical Path Method (**CPM**).

The following section will demonstrate the mapping between the Interaction Box representation of Predicates against Cognitive Functions required to establish the Cognitive Function Evaluator Matrix (**CFEM**).

Chapter 2 Mapping LearnEdge™ Against an Expert System

The Natural Language Processing applied with LearnEdge™ is coined VROOM and the Knowledge Base is coined SAFE!

Mapping LearnEdge(tm against an Expert System Technology applies to a Visual Prolog Inference Engine (**PIE**) perspective.

IPALM Framework

IPALM Framework *(FocusOfAttention)* CFEM (Assignments)	People *(R&Rs)* WHO	Data *(Capabilities)* WHAT	Time *(Events)* WHEN	Network *(Workflows)* WHERE	Motivation *(Goals)* WHY	Function *(Features)* HOW	Budget *(Allocations)* HOW Much	Performance *(Metrics)* HOW Well	Demonstration *(Iterations)* HOW Soon
Objective/Scope Business View Role:Owner	Organizational Policies	Business Concepts	Business Events	Feasibility Study	ROI	Business Process	Business Case	EPML	IPALM System
Enterprise Model Conceptual View Role:Business Analyst	Organizational Structure	Business Model Classes	Enterprise Events	Requirements	EVS	Enterprise Process	Project Charter	Earned Values	PAMPA/SEEM
System Model Logical View Role:Designer	Organizational Workflows	System Model Classes	System Events	Design	Throughput, Response time	System Process	Work Package	Efficiency	CFA/GEM
Technology Model Architectural View Role:Builder	Organizational Infrastructure	Component Model Classes	Component Events	Implementation	Reliability	Component Process	Engineering Charge Order	Productivity	IMES
Release Model Build View Role:Support	Organizational Stakeholders	Deployment Model Packages	Deployment Events	Deployment	Maintainability	Deployment Process	Production Charge Order	Quality	Service Level Agreement
Rasmussen'sModel Functional View Role:User	Human-Centered Design	8-Schema Architecture Model	Decision Events	Active Design	Operability	Cognitive Engineering	Integral Engineering Charge Order	CFFM	IPALM System

Figure 24 IPALM Knowledge Base

The rationale for such a mapping is related to the value to interface with LearnEdge™ as a Consultation Facility

(**Who|What|When|Where**) and as an Explanation Facility (**Why**).

LearnEdge™ goes beyond the basic W5 questions, the basis of planning, by also tackling such questions as:

How, How Much, How Well, and How Soon, the basic H4 questions

The W5H4 paradigm spreads over 12 iterations (the Project Development Framework) allows LearnEdge™ to provide the stakeholders an integrated view of the development plan. Appendix T explores Natural Language Processing in order to sharpen "Critical Thinking".

The expert system technology supported under LearnEdge™ incorporates the following expert system aspects, coined **FEASIBLE**:

1. **F**ormulation: Heuristics are applied to arrive at a solution quickly and efficiently using SEEM.
2. **E**licitation: Explanations are given to explain how to arrive at a conclusion using CUSTODIA.
3. **A**daptation: Inference is supported to provide alternative path to that conclusion applying AVID.
4. **S**pecification: The solution can be provided in different ways depending on the needs and wants by applying IPALM.
5. **I**nteraction: Knowledge and Answers can be acquired over time using JADE.
6. **B**usiness Decisions: The process and product management are integrated to reach a common goal by applying a MOTIF pattern.
7. **L**ocalization: The system can search using Deductive/Inductive Reasoning a solution throughout the solution tree being explored using PAMPA.
8. **E**valuation: The system provides a dynamic progress methodology capability to assess various combinations of solutions using PICK and

9. PEARL: The system applies the Project Evaluation and Review Technique (**PERT**) to establishing a critical path method (**CPM**).

Roles and Services mapping

Cross-Ref	Feasible	Role	Service	Factor	Control
Chapter 4	F	DI	SEEM	SF	Efficiency
Chapter 5	E	CE	CUSTODIA	CF	Competency
Chapter 6	A	SA	AVID	AF	Adaptability
Chapter 7	S	SE	IPALM	IF	Interactivity
Chapter 8	I	RM	SAFE	SRF	Contingency
Chapter 9	B	PM	MOTIF	CMF	Capability
Chapter 10	L	PI	PAMPA	PF	Productivity
Chapter 11		QM	PICK	TF	Quality
Chapter 12	E	SM	PEARL	LF	Dependency

i. Table 2 Roles and Responsibilities

IPALM Scenarios Parameters

Table 3 IPALM Scenarios Parameters

DPM Facets	IB	Policy	Pl.	Proficiency	Availability	Productivity	Quality	Complexity	Production	Project Work to Do (Hrs)	Actual Resource Hours
IPALM Factors	IF	CMF	EF	CF	WF	PF	QF	RF	AF	Pessimistic Expected Optimistic	(Hrs/Day)
LOW	0.9	0.9	0.9	0.9	0.9	0.9	0.9	0.9	0.9	406 500 600	3
MEDIUM	0.95	0.95	0.95	0.95	0.95	0.95	0.95	0.95	0.95	1620 2000 2320	5
HIGH	1	1	1	1	1	1	1	1	1	6467 8000 9067	8

		PHASES	Risk Level
IF =	6.01%		
CMF =	3.66%		
		Inception	High
EF =	7.45%	Elaboration	Medium
CF =	7.08%	Construction	Low
WF =	30.22%	Transition	Low
PF =	8.53%		
QF =	9.68%		
RF =	14.50%		
AF =	12.87%		

Table 4 Phases Distribution

Formulas

(1) Team Size = Effort / Duration
(2) Production = Project Size / Duration
(3) Productivity = Production / Team Size
(4) Overhead Factor = (CMF+QF+WF+RF)/(AF+PF+EF+CF+IF)
(5) Duration = Work to Do / Completion Rate

(6)Completion Rate = Effective Resource Hours

(7)Effective Resource Hours = #Resources *Actual Resource Hours

(8) Productivity*PI*Policy

(9)Proficiency * Availability * Quality * Risk * Production*Interaction

Let us consider specific Cognitive Functions examples:

1. CF: Staff qualification will result in a scheduled decrease or increase and in cost increase or decrease, conversely.
2. WF: Staff or other external resources availability will result in schedule increase or decrease.
3. RF: Staff work assignment complexity will result in schedule increase or decrease.
4. QF: Staff commitment to quality level will result in schedule increase or decrease.
5. AF: Staff commitment to production level (e.g. 32 FPs per week) will result in schedule increase (Pessimistic) or decrease (Optimistic);
6. CMF: Staff number changes or overtime level approval will lead to fatigue, complexity and recovery time increase, thus impacting productivity.
7. PF: Resource productivity increases or decreases represent direct feedback to overmanning and overtime approval.
8. IF: Team size assignments will result in schedule or cost pressure changes.
9. EF: Changes in project scope, and introduction of process automation or artifact generation will result in schedule and cost pressure changes.

Pairwise Independent Combinational KPU (PICK)

1. Number of resources
2. Resource proficiency distribution
3. Resource availability distribution
4. Resource productivity distribution
5. Process Improvement distribution
6. Process complexity distribution
7. Product quality distribution
8. Product production distribution
9. Project work to do distribution
10. Project policy distribution
11. Project infrastructure interaction distribution
12. Project size distribution

Chapter 3 LearnEdge Power of Habit 12 steps

LearnEdge™ Introduction: The Sea Travel Analogy **Output: Issues and Solutions Table**

To travel at sea is an act of faith in your naval instruments to confidently set your course of actions. As business manager, you are the captain of a cruise ship. Your cargo and your passengers are the products or services that you proudly present to each of your potential investors. Such products and services augment the value added of your company. At the same time, you understand the drive of your service providers to explore new destinations and the product manufacturers to be reaching out as vast a market as possible. Success in your endeavor brings a smile to everybody's face. Challenges fuel the energy to achieve some high level of capabilities: predicting risks and making effective decisions.

The LearnEdge(tm) Inc. Professional Inviter approach **Output: Power of Habits Charts**

When a ship is about to sail, you can hear from miles or kilometers away the joyous sound of the horn announcing some imminent departure. In the language of business, you are embarking on a **Project Charter** phase whereas the commitment to travel is signed as a contract between the sponsor and the service and product providers. This situation is as **close to action** as any business manager would wish to be. Prior to engaging in such a trip, here are the three aspects that the captain must be most concerned about: how long the trip will be, how much it will cost to supply the ship and what size of crew can carry the workload required. These three business considerations form the basis of any project triple-constraint restrictions. The captain has a **Project Plan** in place with a firm budget to allocate, **a follow-up** to the commitment to perform.

Interestingly enough, prior to sailing, the travel sponsor had to go through a market validation to **qualify** the ship for the kind of trip pursued. For each trip, a **Strength-Weakness-Opportunity-Threat (SWOT) Chart** is prepared to assess the financial, technical and management aspects of the overall proposed trip. Given that most destinations were reached during some previous travel explorations, your ship log would record precisely the kind of expected performances required and the kind of operational readiness you must be. To achieve a high degree of confidence, such a captain conducts **a feasibility study** to assert with a low degree of risk that such destination is worth exploring for. You are ready to **invite** your guests onboard for an enjoyable trip with a high degree of **acceptance criteria** under any **travel scenarios**. Some dynamic process evaluation must be performed to assess the range of opportunities.

IDEA Process – Smart goals achieved through power of habits activities Output: SMART Goals Graphs

The IDEA validation process allows for the measurement and analysis of the following:

1. During the **Qualify Phase**, a Statement of Requirements is explored by the participating stakeholders; Sponsor's areas of "**Attention**" are captured in the **SWOT Analysis**.
2. During the **Invite Phase**, an assessment of product, process and resource's ability to perform is assessed; Sponsor's key "**Interests**" are captured in the **Feasibility Study**;
3. During the **Close to Action Phase**, a contract, commitment to perform, must be signed between each stakeholder; Sponsor's key "**Decisions**" are captured by the **Project Charter**.
4. During the **Follow-up Phase**, the scope, financial, schedule, quality, risk and stakeholder's activities to perform are set; Sponsor's project "**Execution**" is captured by the **Project Plan**.

LearnEdge Power of Habit 12 steps:

1. Follow a plan (**JADE**).
2. Set quality goals (**PICK**).
3. Apply Management Corrective Actions (**SAFE**).
4. Establish a work pattern (**MOTIF**).
5. Establish an economy of scale (**EVMS**).
6. Categorize the problem.
7. Research similar problems.
8. Prepare a domain architecture (**VROOM**) .
9. Analyze generic facets of the domain (**IPALM**).
10. Verify processes for process improvement (**PAMPA**).
11. Apply a dynamic progress method (**PEARL**).
12. Summarize results with a Systems Engineering economics model (**SEEM**).

Chapter 4 Systems Engineering Economics Model (SEEM)

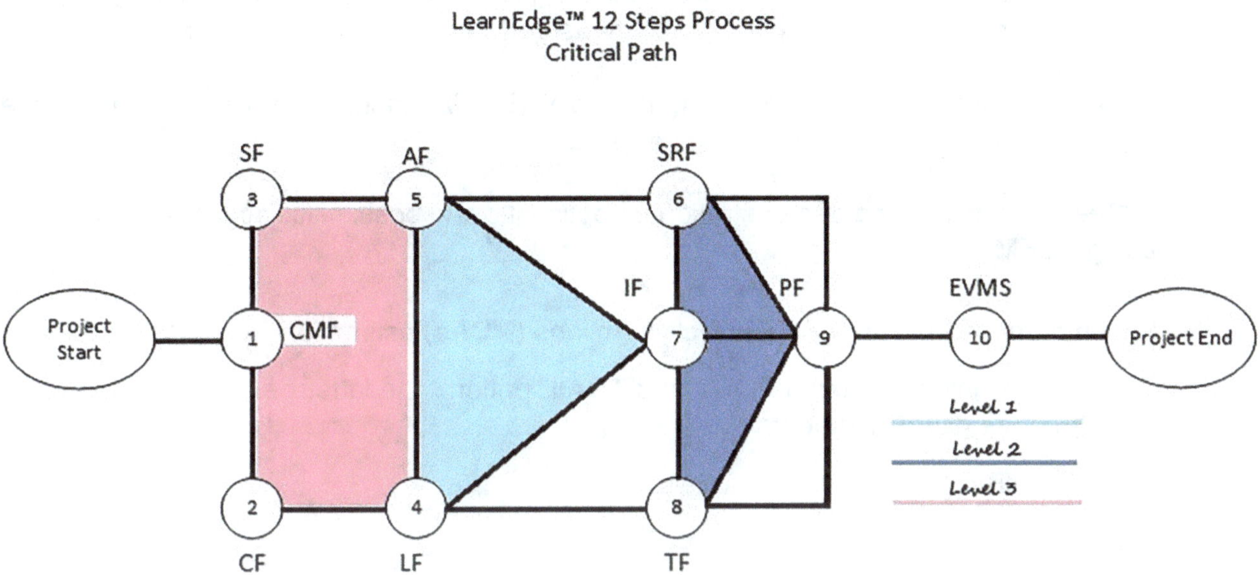

Figure 25 Critical Path

Underneath the PIE engine sits an Economic model called **SEEM** a parameterized model of a scenario being explored. The following core project considerations will be accounted for:

- Project Sizing from the lowest Work Breakdown Structure (**WBS**) element to the highest.
- Effort Estimation accounting for project architectural complexity, production rate and overhead considerations.
- Total Project Duration accounting for Process Improvement considerations, Capability Maturity Considerations and management overheat considerations.
- Total Team Size Estimation using the Communication Model called **JADE,** given the ratio of concurrent activities and serial activities.

- Production Rate consideration for each iteration assessed and the overall project traceability.
- Productivity considerations given the project size under consideration and the team size.
- Cognitive Function Evaluation Matrix factor (**CFEM**) consideration given the estimated effort multiplier factor measured and the estimated duration multiplier factor considered.
- Effective Progress Management Level (**EPML**) factor consideration given the Process Improvement policies applied.

See appendix E for a demonstration on optimistic and pessimistic scenarios estimation using SEEM.

1. Recommended Management Corrective Actions (**MCAs**) estimation.

The total work assignments follow a **POST** and **TRAIL** pattern, the latter being the lowest Work Breakdown Structure (**WBS**) element:

P: Product sizing breakdown of models.

O: Class Object Sizing Average.

S: Project Scope sizing, very small to very large projects

T: TRAIL WBS element sizing

T: Total System Integration classes.

R: Reporting classes.

A: Agent class to track layers and partitions.

I: Interaction classes

L: Logic handling classes

Chapter 5. A Cognitive Engineering Approach to Architecture Exploration

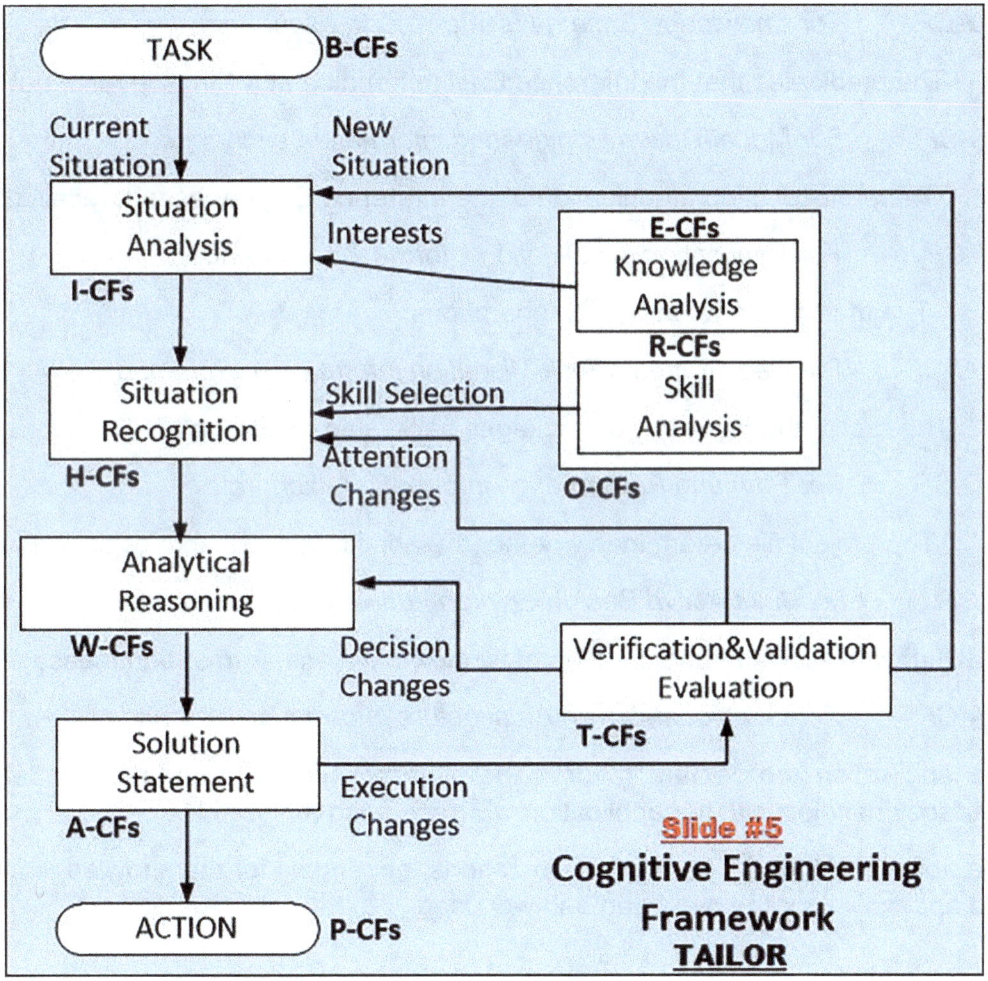

Figure 26 IPALM Cognitive Engineering Model

The overall repository of the Knowledge Based capture by LearnEdge™ is coined **CUSTODIA** to highlight the Cognitive Functions (**CF**) applied:

C: *C-CF* *For Knowledge Base facts information exchange*

The facts that the Inference Engine handles, at a Class level or not.

U: *U-CF* *For Knowledge Base rules information exchange*

The predicates that the Inference Engine handles at a Class level or not.

S: *S-CF* *For Model-Driven Engineering information exchange*

The protocol of communication of the Inference Engine: assert, recall, consult.

T: *T-CF* *For Vérification & Validation information exchange*

The matching and unification operations

O : *O-CF* *For Requirements Risk Mitigation information exchange*

The root of the hierarchy of packages generated based on an IE design.

D: *D-CF* *For Plan and Performance information exchange*

The project file determines whether the application: console or a window.

I: *I-CF* *For Joint Active Design Environment information exchange*

The GUI design allows for the creation of windows, dialogs, forms, and message boxes.

A: *A-CF* *For OO Model-Driven Architecture information exchange*

The application architecture records the hierarchy of the application under study. All interfaces handled with the application will trace such a hierarchy.

See appendix H for the concept of operations, appendix I for the knowledge assessment and appendix J for the overhead and workload.

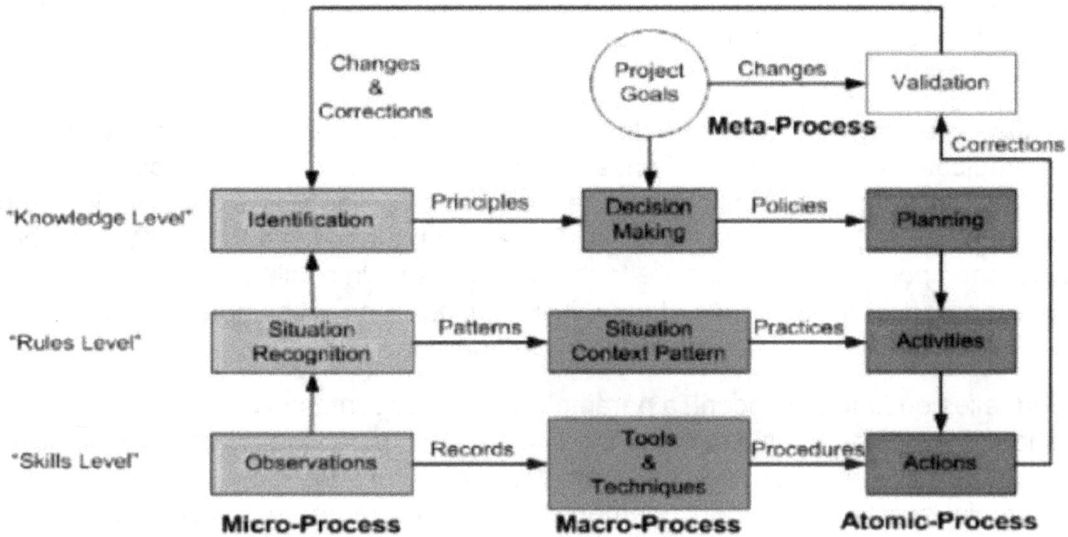

Figure 27 Rasmussen Model

An overall Cognitive Function Evaluation Matrix (**CFEM**) offers a view of the performance of the team assigned on the specific project. A modified Rasmussen Model elements are captured:

1. Situation awareness: scenario exploration
2. Cooperative work: joint active design
3. Decision making knowledge elicitation.
4. Planning and action: decision execution
5. Competence availability: assignment optimization
6. Risk mitigation: application of effective management corrective actions.
7. Architecture complexity evaluation: qualitative measurement of architecture features
8. A Systems Engineering economics modeling optimization: an earned value management methodology

The **CUSTODIA** Knowledge Base follows the Horn Clause formulation of any predicate. The class implemented in this fashion is related to a package. Each of the classes from a hierarchy will use the “inherits” keyword. The class with an interface is tagged with the name of the interface. An interface using the keyword “supports” integrates other classes. The keyword “open” links other classes

For each clause in a predicate, an Interaction Box pattern serves as a basis of tracing the goals pursued. A predicate is made up of a series of goals. In that sense, a predicate represents a theory to be demonstrated. The basic component of an Interaction Box is a node with four ports. The entry to the node is the Call or Redo ports. The exit to the node is a Predicate succeed or fail ports. The succeed port carries a message to the next clause. On a failed clause, the control goes back to the redo port of the previous clause. This backtracking technique is unique to Prolog. Clauses are recorded in a stack fashion in the knowledge base.

Visual Prolog relies on functor concept, a parameterized representation of facts to apply matching and unification of the parameters. On a call, the clause must match the parameters of the functor. On processing the call, the clause must unify with the parameter. This is a distinct set of operations of Prolog. The clause does not conduct numerical operations; it unifies the parameters linked to the functor. A type conversion is required for the actual numerical operation.

A predicate can be either deterministic or not. Deterministic predicates do not backtrack, they are executed once, and do not produce alternate solutions, like a procedure call. Non-deterministic predicates backtrack to alternate paths. Alternate paths are defined by multiple clauses having the same name and number of arguments.

A unique symbol in prolog called cut “!” is used just like any other goal in a predicate. There are three instances when a cut is necessary:

1. When you want to execute only one clause of a predicate.
2. When you want to limit a program’s search through facts in the knowledge base.
3. When you must handle exceptions conditions. Cut is used in conjunction with fail.

To exclude other paths, each clause within the predicate must contain the cut as one of its goals.

Whereas fail backtracks to cause the next iteration of the loop to occur, a recursive predicate calls itself. Interaction boxes for recursive predicates are nested. For example, the factorial predicate is a good example of a recursive predicate. List handling is another good example of recursive predicate.

It is possible to add and remove clauses at run-time using the following evaluable predicates:

1. asserta(clause) adds a clause to the beginning of the knowledge base.
2. assertz(clause) adds a clause to the end of the knowledge base.
3. retract(clause) removes a clause from the database.

Hash Tables provide a method for speeding up access to the database. A hash table lets you store information in groups called buckets. The hash table provides you with quick access to any bucket within the table. Hash table can use references to a list of buckets. Also, a hash table can use linked lists.

Binary trees can also be created to store information in hierarchical order. Because information is in a hierarchy, you can employ non-sequential search strategies. Binary trees are made up of nodes and branches. The first node in a binary tree is called the "root node". Branches point to the nodes that are subordinate to the current node, thus forming a layered hierarchy. In a binary tree, each node has exactly two branches. Depth first search and breadth first search are two kinds of search strategies that you can employ. Both strategies can be implemented with lists that control the order in which nodes are searched. A tree is balanced if all its branches extend to the same level.

Chapter 6 VROOM Design and Implementation Strategy

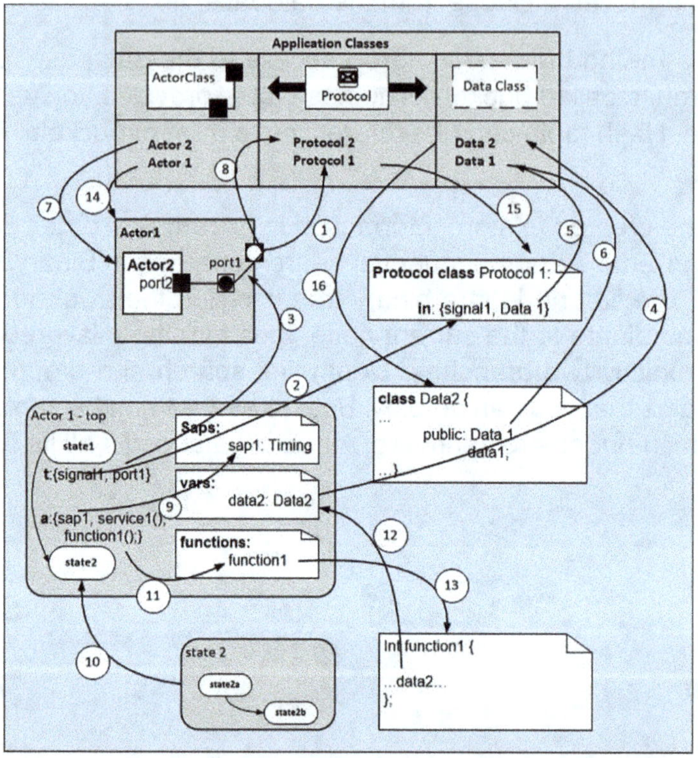

Figure 28 Verifiable Requirements in OO Methodology

Semantic, Scope and Phase discontinuities

Discontinuities are intrinsic to the nature of system development process. For example, the requirements definition, the architecture specification, and the production activities are characterized by different thought process and different verification criteria. A simple classification scheme differentiates four commonly encountered discontinuities:

- Scope discontinuities are caused by lack of formal coupling between the representations at different levels of detail, such as functional capabilities versus primitive data type manipulation.
- Semantic discontinuities are caused by a lack of formal coupling between the representation of data structures versus functional behavior definition.
- Phase discontinuities are caused by lack of formal coupling between requirements, design and implementation representation.
- Team discontinuities are caused by the lack of formal resources and tasks assignment over the full lifecycle of the development.

Seet appendix P for the language syntax validated using ANTLR (Another Tool for Language Recognition).

Typically, a system modeler captures the functional capabilities of the system under study and the interactions with the adjacent environment. This is coined the system boundary setting stage. By applying multiple set of scenarios, the model evolves as a prototype, covering all interfaces requirements.

Operational approach to Phase and Semantic continuity

The use of a single phase, independent set of modeling abstractions eases many development problems related to requirements traceability, and iterative development issues. A Model-Observe-Tailor-Inspect-Formulate (**MOTIF)** is applied throughout the development effort.

The operational approach treats Requirements definitions and Design specifications as programs written in a very high-level modeling language transforming declarative statements into executable statements written is Visual Prolog.

All the infrastructure interfacing, such as windows services and GUI considerations, are compiled and executable. Verification of an executable model is carried out by compiling the feature and running it. The executability of the models means that they can be used for early prototyping of the features under study.

This the foundation for the Application Generation in Action paradigm supported by LearnEdge™.

The language supported by LearnEdge™

With the modeling language implementation, three development interfaces are presented to the modeler:

- Single Phase Interface, the Estimation Phase, supports requirements, Design, Test model abstractions.
- Operational model interface supports both new and legacy interfaces integration.
- Virtual Machine interface supports the executable specifications of the model.

In LearnEdge™, the overall development environment is coined JADE (Joint Active Development Environment).

Feasibility heuristics embedded provides an integrated mechanism apply a customer focus approach to system development by considering the human interactions.
The LearnEdge™ Application Framework (LEAF) relies on the relationship between eight economic factors coined FEASIBLE. The pair-wise association between each aspect covered by PICK (Performance Intelligence in Communicating Knowledge) allows the team to explore twelve steps of development described under IPALM (Intelligent Project Assistant in Lifecycle Modeling). The application of PICK allows the analyst to generate a SEEM (Systems Engineering Economics Model) scenarios: Optimistic Estimates, Realistic Estimates and Pessimistic Estimates.

There are eight aspects of human-centered design coined FEASIBLE:

- Formulation: A clear and unambiguous statement of wants and needs in both functional and performance requirements.
- Evaluation: A specific, Measurable, Auditable, Repeatable, Time-bound (SMART) set of criteria for system acceptance.
- Adaptation: A balanced development process to achieve optimum cost-schedule-scope triple-constraint requirements.
- Specification: A phase independent operational approach-based sets of models.

- Interaction: An integrated environment delivering model and test generators in a coherent and consistent manner.
- Business vision: A business case driven system development.
- Localizations: Risk mitigation techniques prioritized based on a measured system architecture complexity assessment.
- Élicitation: A Joint Active Développent Environnent (**JADE**) technology.

Chapter 7 Intelligent Project Assistant in Life cycle Modeling

IPALM Framework

IPALM Framework *(FocusOfAttention)* CFEM (Assignments)	People *(R&Rs)* WHO	Data *(Capabilities)* WHAT	Time *(Events)* WHEN	Network *(Workflows)* WHERE	Motivation *(Goals)* WHY	Function *(Features)* HOW	Budget *(Allocations)* HOW Much	Performance *(Metrics)* HOW Well	Demonstration *(Iterations)* HOW Soon
Objective/Scope Business View Role:Owner	Organizational Policies	Business Concepts	Business Events	Feasibility Study	ROI	Business Process	Business Case	EPML	IPALM System
Enterprise Model Conceptual View Role:Business Analyst	Organizational Structure	Business Model Classes	Enterprise Events	Requirements	EVS	Enterprise Process	Project Charter	Earned Values	PAMPA/SEEM
System Model Logical View Role:Designer	Organizational Workflows	System Model Classes	System Events	Design	Throughput, Response time	System Process	Work Package	Efficiency	CFA/GEM
Technology Model Architectural View Role:Builder	Organizational Infrastructure	Component Model Classes	Component Events	Implementation	Reliability	Component Process	Engineering Charge Order	Productivity	IMES
Release Model Build View Role:Support	Organizational Stakeholders	Deployment Model Packages	Deployment Events	Deployment	Maintainability	Deployment Process	Production Charge Order	Quality	Service Level Agreement
Rasmussen'sModel Functional View Role:User	Human-Centered Design	8-Schema Architecture Model	Decision Events	Active Design	Operability	Cognitive Engineering	Integral Engineering Charge Order	CFEM	IPALM System

Figure 29 IPALM process framework

Application Intelligence with IPALM

1. Motivation for an Intelligent Project Assistant in Lifecycle Modeling
   The link between systems engineering and project management triple-constraints of cost, schedule and scope is recognized but not very well understood.
   IPALM addresses this issue by using a value-based approach based on an Effective Function Point (EFP) measure.
2. Fundamentals of systems engineering
   Systems engineering is an interdisciplinary approach and means that focuses on defining customer's needs, integrating stakeholder's requirements, and realizing a successful system within the context of the customer's environment.
3. Systems Engineering Heuristics
   A Dynamic Progress Method (DPM) is applied to extract the value and ranges of eight control factors for the successful delivery of a system, coined PLASTICS:
   - Productivity factor.

- Lifecycle factor.
- Architecture factor.
- System Development Risk factor.
- Total Quality factor.
- Confidence factor.
- Systems Engineering Economics factor
- Interactions Factor

4. Development Principles Integrated
    - Based on the development process on an architecture-first approach.
    - Establish an incremental and iterative lifecycle process.
    - Establish a changé management environnement.
    - Establish a configurable process that is economically scalable.
    - Instrument the process for objective quality control and process assessment.
    - Emphasize component-based development to reduce management complexity.
    - Capture design artifacts using Model-Driven Architecture notation.
    - Establish an operational approach to integrate and validate early the stakeholders' wants and needs.
    - Establish a legacy round-trip engineering environment to enable teams to spend more time on engineering.
    - Plan an intermediate release in groups of usage scenarios with evolving and traceable level of detail Chapter 6 VROOM operational approach

See appendix O for the IPALM WBS applied for and appendix Q for the MDA demonstration.

Chapter 8. A Risk Mitigation Approach to Architecture Exploration

In architecture exploration, you go through four stages of evaluation coined **AVID**:

1. **A**daptation stage: given an established architecture, which areas would be impacted?
2. **V**alidation stage: which new requirements would impact the current architecture?
3. **I**nvention stage: which new development would impact the current architecture?
4. **D**evelopment stage: which new development methodology would impact the current architecture?

LearnEdge™ integrates two methodologies to capture changes and the impacts thereof:

1. Provide you with the means to establish a Systems Engineering Process Architecture (**SEPA**), a process data flow mechanism.
2. Establish a Dynamic Progress Methodology (**DPM**) to incorporate Management Corrective Actions (MCAs), a process control flow mechanism. DPM applies Program Evaluation & Review Technique (**PERT**) to establish the total schedule and the associated Critical Path.

See appendix K for the monads (lowest WBS elements) and appendix L for the tree methodology applied.

Many techniques can be applied to detect defects in a design, for example peer review, formal metrics evaluation triggered by the number of interfaces associated with the system, either internal or external. Assigning a variable called K tracking the number of changes or defects and a variable M tracking the total number of features. The internal count can be formulated as **(K*K-1)/2** under PICK count; and the external count can be formulated as **K* (M-K)**. Features count can be tracked using Use Cases while defect count can be tracked using Test Cases. The Message Sequence Chart (**MSC**) mechanism applied by LearnEdge™ offers a visual means to conduct such an activity.

To establish the degree of effort required during the development effort, empirically the number of communications required can be determined as to extract the maximum number of full-time personnel required. Historically, a record of time spent on serial activities, time spent on concurrent activities, and time spent on group activities can be tracked using time sheets records. The total count would reflect the team total timeline on the project. The formula to establish the total team participants is based on the ratio (R) of serial and concurrent activity against the group activity: **$N_{max} = [(R_c-R_s)/R_g]1/2$.** For the mathematically inclined, such a formula peaks. Consequently, the selection of ratio can be established given the average group sessions using recommended, for example 18-20 minutes per day to carry on Management Corrective Actions. In short, the impact of a **JADE** environment on the team size has a significant impact on the total effort carried out.

Another important observation into the realm of entity relationships, using Normal Form for the Knowledge Base, the combinational complexity increases significantly whether it's a 2-way, 3 way or N way relationships. The combinational count would follow this formula where M is the number of features and N the relationship factor: **$_NC^M = M!/N! * (M-N)!$** where "!" implies factorial count. The application of the Third Normal Form for example would reduce duplication significantly.

As a final point on the count measures, the application of **SAFE** allows a designer to establish both the complexity of development affecting the size of a project and the quality of the results affecting the number of testcases required. LearnEdge™ tracks all these considerations.

Chapter 9. An Application Generation in Action (AGIA) Invention

When dealing with **AVID** development phases discontinuity, the application of **PEARL** establishes a critical path for a project covering nine project constraints at three levels of considerations:

1. Additive level covering architecture component sizing, **GUI** design sizing and process activities assignment sizing. A first estimate of the Production Rate can be established.
2. Multiplicative level covering the Systems Engineering Process Architecture (**SEPA**) component development practices related to quality management, risk management and productivity. The impact of Management Corrective Actions (**MCAs**) on the Production Rate can be established.
3. Compounded level covering "Orchestrating Human Centered Design" brings out such concepts as:
    a. organizational integration and optimization using **IPALM**, to assert the overall effort of a project.
    b. risk mitigation using complexity measurement using **SAFE**,
    c. Dynamic Progress Method (DPM) encapsulated in **PEARL** supporting Management Corrective actions (**MCAs**), and to assert the overall schedule of a project.
    d. Scenario based **AVID** development operational approach using **VROOM**.
    e. Authority sharing using a **JADE** environment.
    f. Project culture integration and evolution using **CUSTODIA** knowledge base.
    g. Combinational optimization of interrelationships using **PICK**.
    h. The integration of an Earned Value Management System (**EVMS**) offers the ability to establish a Systems Engineering Economics Model to assert the overall cost of a project.

See appendix C for the strategy of implementation, appendix F for the checklist, appendix G for the positioning and appendix M for the vision.

Underneath the PIE engine sits an Economic model called **SEEM** a parameterized model of a scenario being explored. The following core project considerations will be accounted for:

2. Project Sizing from the lowest Work Breakdown Structure (**WBS**) element to the highest.

3. Effort Estimation accounting for project architectural complexity, production rate and overhead considerations.

4. Total Project Duration accounting for Process Improvement considerations, Capability Maturity Considerations and management overheat considerations.

5. Total Team Size Estimation using the Communication Model called **JADE,** given the ratio of concurrent activities and serial activities.

6. Production Rate consideration for each iteration assessed and the overall project traceability.

7. Productivity considerations given the project size under consideration and the team size.

8. Cognitive Function Evaluation Matrix factor (**CFEM**) consideration given the estimated effort multiplier factor measured and the estimated duration multiplier factor considered.

9. Effective Progress Management Level (**EPML**) factor consideration given the Process Improvement policies applied.

10. Recommended Management Corrective Actions (**MCAs**) estimation.

The total work assignments follow a **POST** and **TRAIL** pattern, the latter being the lowest Work Breakdown Structure (**WBS**) element:

P: Product sizing breakdown of models.

O: Class Object Sizing Average.

S: Project Scope sizing, very small to very large projects

T: TRAIL WBS element sizing

- T: Total System Integration classes.
- R: Reporting classes.
  - A: Agent classes track layers and partitions.
- I: Interaction classes
- L: Logic handling classes

Chapter 10 Project Attributes Monitoring and Predicting Agent

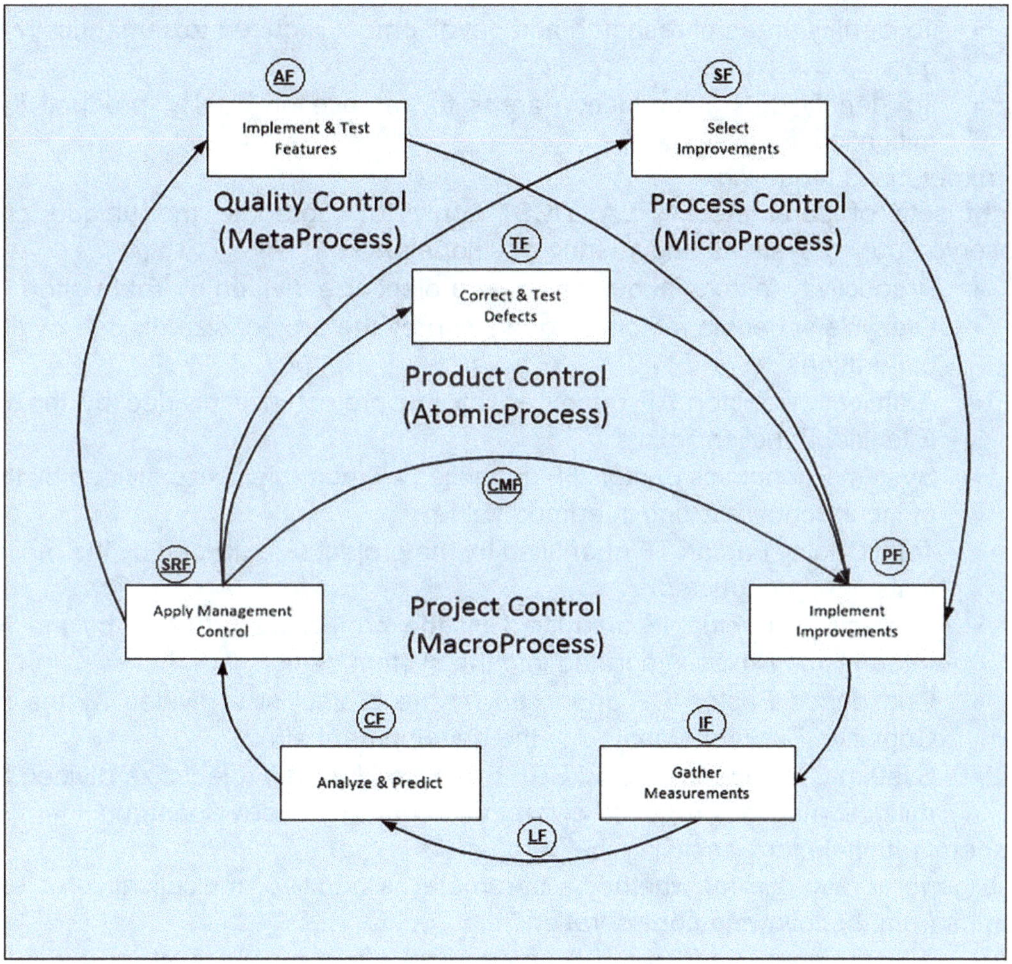

Figure 30 Project Monitoring and Predicting Agent Model

PAMPA Overview

1. Objective pursued
    - To achieve a balanced approach throughout the lifecycle of development.
    - To separate architectural specifications from system production.
    - To identify areas of research and development required to semantically bridge the gap.
    - To identify during production areas to improve on quality, productivity and risk mitigation.
2. Parameterized Modeling
   Eight sets of parameters (**PLASTICS**) apply to aggregate the unique phenomena observed during systems engineering development:
    - Productivity factor: PF quantified as project size divided by Team effort.
    - Lifecycle schedule factor: LF quantified by the project size divided by the number of iterations.
    - Architecture factor: AF quantified by the project size divided by the number of Effective Function Points.
    - System Economics Factor: SF quantified by the project size divided by the number of increments resulting in earned value.
    - Total Quality Factor: TF quantified by the project size divided by the maintainability tests to be conducted
    - Interactivity Factor: IF quantified by the project size divided by the number of Interactions Boxes integrated into the system design.
    - Confidence Factor: CF quantified by the project size divided by the number of Cognitive Functions applied in the development effort.
    - System Contingency factor: SRF quantified by the project size divided by the risk mitigation actions required given the complexity of development.
3. General rationale for classifying the parameters
   The general rationale for whether a parameter is additive, multiplicative or exponential comes from the following considerations:
    - A parameter is additive if it has a local effect on the system under study. For example, Effective Function Point (**EFP**) count, Use Cases and Test Cases count.

- A parameter is multiplicative if it has a global effect on the system under study. For example, changes and defects count for maintainability assessment, risk mitigation steps for complexity reduction.
- A parameter is exponential if it has a compounded effect across the lifecycle of the system under study. For example, capability maturity assessment, economic efficiency assessment.

See appendix S for the Process Improvement criteria.

Chapter 11 Pairwise Independent Combinational KPU (PICK) Testing

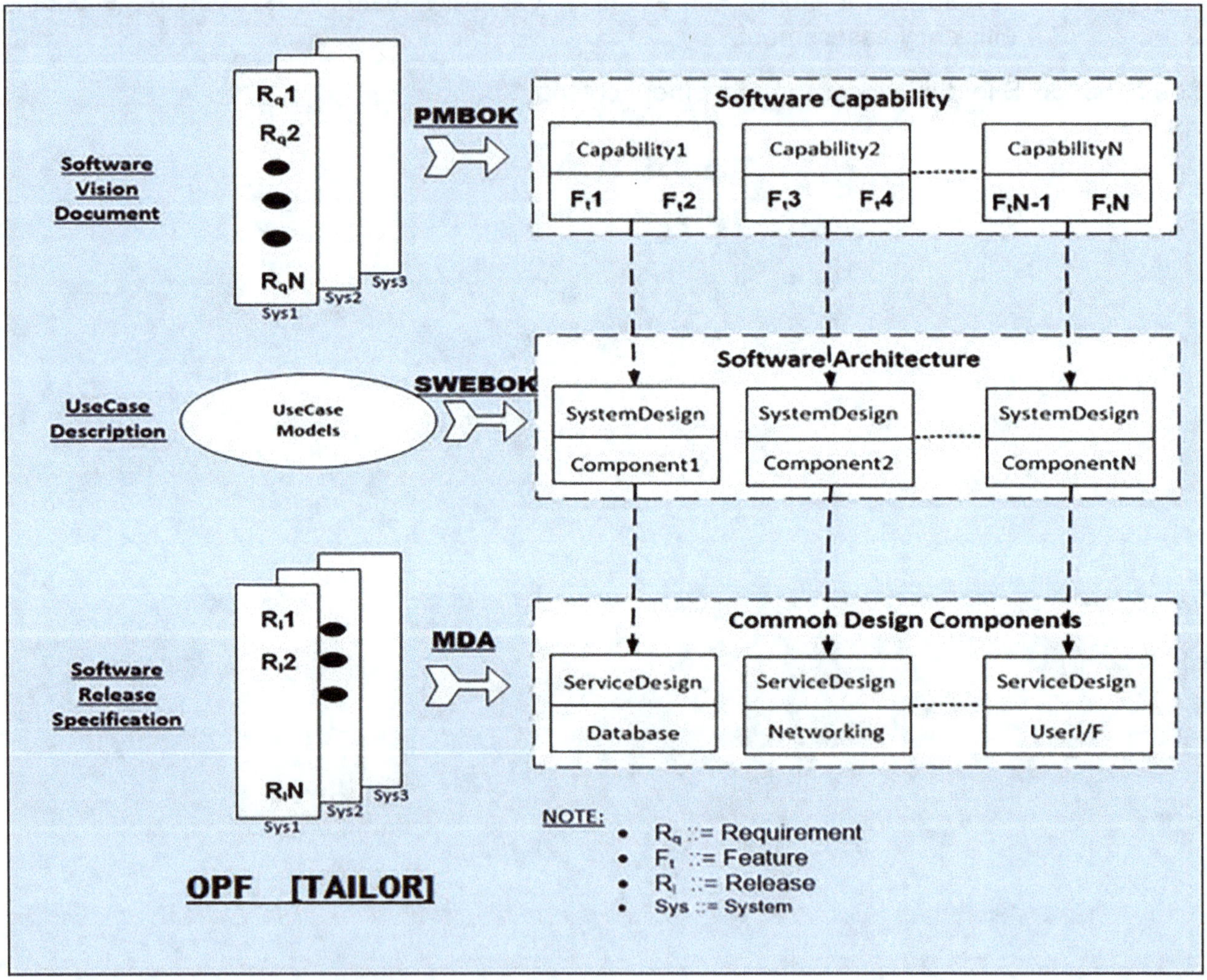

Figure 31 Performance Intelligence in Communicating Knowledge

Pairwise Independent Combination KPU Testing (PICK)

PICK overview

From an O-O perspective, an application integrates a set of active classes, components and subsystems. Each entity possesses a set of attributes to ensure uniqueness for identification purposes. Each entity or cell possesses a set of services to exhibit its behavior or to enable communication. In essence, a pair-wise relationship exists between any cells contained within the application being generated.

See appendix S for the proof of concept.

From an implementation perspective, there is a single call to create an executable process of that application. The remaining features of the application are dynamically linked as a library for each feature. As a design rule, each service possesses a single-entry point and a single exit point. This is the most important design consideration to consider for a performance assessment.

PICK establishes the optimal pair-wise dependencies between these cells. From the outcomes of such an optimization, LearnEdge™ applies the PEARL algorithm to establish the global schedule for the project using the Critical Path Method.

Baldrige Excellence Framework

LearnEdge™ maps the development process applied using the Baldrige Excellence Framework to establish a balance pace in the development effort. The overall framework acts as a pattern coined FRACTALS:

1. Project Focus considerations, e.g. leadership, strategy, workforce, operation, result and customer.
2. Project Results considerations, e.g. management and technical sets of the Work Breakdown Structure (**WBS**).
3. Project Assignment considerations e.g. Resource and Task assignment applied using Dynamic Progress Method. (**DPM**)
4. Project Control considerations e.g. Quality Control, Process Control and Products Control managed with Project Attributes Monitoring and Predicting Agent (**PAMPA**).

5. Project Team building considerations e.g. Sizing of the Effective Progress Management Level (**EPML**) and the Cognitive Function Evaluator Matrix (CFEM).
6. Project Adaptation considerations e.g. The integration of the Enterprise Environment Factor
7. Project Lifecycle selection considerations e.g. Project Management Body of Knowledge (**PMBOK**) standard

Systems Engineering Project Architecture

The overall project architecture applied with LearnEdge™ is coined SEPA:

- At the root, the performance specifications follow the workflow of the Baldrige Excellence Framework (**BEF**).
- Branching from the root base**,** IPALM expands the LearnEdge™ workflow entities to cover Process Development, Resources Development and Products Development.
- Under Process Development, IPALM covers the best practices and pragmatics applied for risk mitigation.
- Under Resources Development, IPALM covers the engineering skills and knowledge required to effectively conduct the work.
- Under Products Development, IPALM covers the Generic System Requirements (**GSR**) and the Class of Systems under study.

Chapter 12 Project Evaluation, Analysis & Review over the LCM (PEARL)

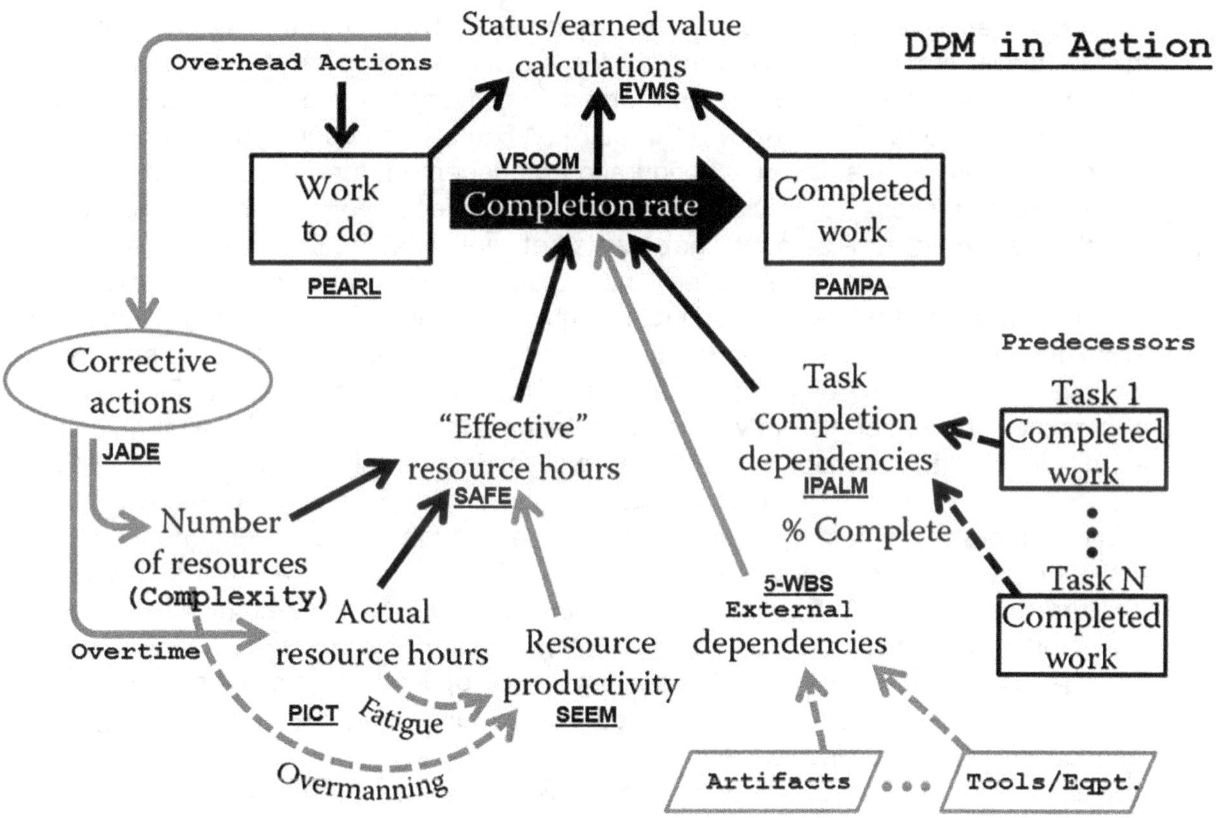

Figure 32 Dynamic Progress Method Model

Pearl Overview

1. Project Evolution
   A project naturally evolves from a statement of requirements (SOR) to a feasibility study (FS) down to an architecture analysis to create a boundary around the system under study and the environment where it will operate.
   Progress is achieved by partitioning the requirements by prioritizing use cases based on the complexity and the risk mitigation policies in place. From an iterative perspective, each checkpoint and milestones will be earmarked by delivery of a prototype or a specification depending on the Work Breakdown Structure (**WBS**) agreed upon. Changes are inherent for these iterations of software Configuration management form an essential part of the development process to track the changes or defects encountered throughout the development process. A semantic gap exists between what the user's expect as outcome and developer can map to the system under study. How can you bridge that gap?
2. A common frame of reference: Verifiable Requirements in OO Methodology (**VROOM**)
   From the principle called Architecture First, it's common sense to integrate all stakeholders to have a single view of the architecture of the system under study. From a user's perspective, the earlier a prototype can be provided, the earlier the designer can establish a baseline in the development effort as well as establishing a change management process. It's primordial that the architectural development principles will play an important role in establishing a common frame of reference throughout the development effort.
3. From the architectural reference model, LearnEdge™ applies a System Architecture Feature Evaluation (**SAFE)** algorithm to assess the least complex architecture based on the Work breakdown structure agreed upon. LearnEdge™ applies a Performance Intelligence in Knowledge **(PICK**) assignment for optimal project nodes relationships. LearnEdge applies an optimal resources assignment using the Systems Engineering Economics Modeling (SEEM) algorithm for the best scenario selection. LearnEdge™ applies a Project Attribute Monitoring and Predicting Agent (PAMPA) algorithm to establish the Effective Process Management Level required to achieve the goals pursue.
4. From the Cognitive Engineering Framework established, a maximum team size was evaluated against the tasks sequencing applied under a PEARL estimation. As a result, the Critical Path Method was applied to establish the total schedule. The net impact I to obtain the total scope of the project and as a result the expected productivity and complexity assessment.

DPM Steps

Step 1: A detailed discussion is applied to gather the core project requirements at the executive level using a Decision Intelligence methodology.

Step 2: Feasibility Study of the initial requirements and prototyping specifications for the optimal solution.

Step 3: Presentation of the optimal solution and discussion on the impact of constraints, assumptions and policies to devise alternate solutions.

Step 4: Establishment of trade-off criteria to assess the technical, managerial and financial impact of the solutions highlighted.

Step 5: Production of a Prototype illustrating the optimal solution capabilities.

Step 6: Selection and recommendation for the implementation of the optimal solution, given the current project context.

Step 7: A development plan is delivered that includes project management, requirements management, configuration management, quality management and system management; and,

Step8: Project Charter generation, including all stages of development, such as requirements stage, engineering stage, production stage and testing stage, See Appendix C

Step 9: Training and Workshop by LearnEdge(tm) in response to Joint customer's deployment plan.

LearnEdge™ Differentiators

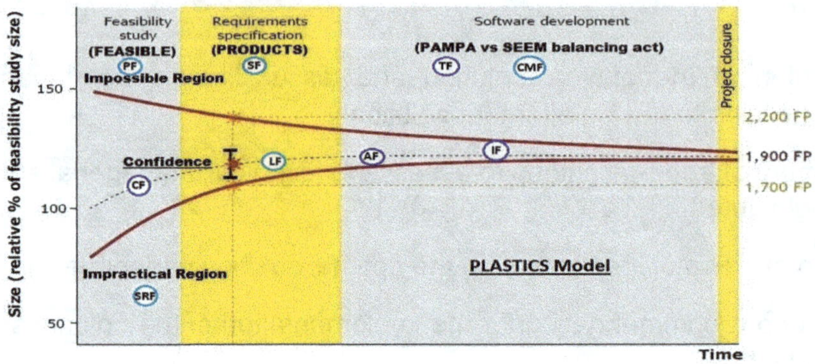

First size estimate of increment 1 – close to the danger zone

Figure 33 PICK Model CMMI Vision

1. Completion rate assessment based on Effective Function Point measurement and Effective Labor Hour.
2. A modeling language supporting three layers of scope assessment: functional, non-functional and performance requirements.
3. A three-layer triple-constraint performance model capturing performance goals under one Systems Engineering Economics Model.
4. A development scheduler based on Dynamic Progress Method to assess the impact of Management Correction Actions (MCAs).
5. A five-layer Work breakdown structure to track the full sets of charts of accounts to assess development complexity quantitively.
6. A Systems Engineering economics model demonstrating the allowable operating regions to minimize risk and improve productivity.
7. A joint active development environment allowing stakeholders to apply an operational approach to system development using cognitive engineering.

8. A verifiable requirement in OO methodology representation to establish scope, phase and semantic continuity throughout the development lifecycle.
9. The application of Baldrige Excellence Framework capturing ten system development principles.
10. A development model capturing both the Critical Path Method for scheduling estimation and Earned Value Management for budget estimation.
11. An Application Generation in Action implementation strategy to facilitate prototyping and effectively track the requirements traceability.
12. A common measurement and analysis method to ensure continuous process improvement.

IPALM Project Statistics

Table 5 IPALM Project Statistics

Project Name	Total FP Count	CRUD Count	HV Count	HV%	Total LOC Count	BL Count	PM Count	PM%
Add	241	94	84	0.348548	191308	60925	130383	0.681534
AdventureWorks	229	135	0	0	218511	80620	137891	0.631048
Alm	5772	2072	2374	0.411296	266986	112921	154065	0.577053
BibleInstituteSystem	444	172	153	0.344595	259253	91537	167716	0.64692
CarRentalDemo	841	245	414	0.492271	396681	107916	288765	0.727953
Cfa	241	94	84	0.348548	191308	60925	130383	0.681534
ExpenseReport	367	117	159	0.433243	211325	73122	138203	0.653983
Gem	354	185	45	0.127119	405053	164715	240338	0.59335
Lss	192	115	0	0	193524	67256	126268	0.652467
MDAproject	2195	1117	231	0.105239	688076	126268	561808	0.816491
Northwind	349	213	0	0	272353	102830	169523	0.622439
OpenPPM	1816	1092	0	0	1051931	448303	603628	0.573829
Pampa	875	452	51	0.058286	530974	219597	311377	0.586426
Seem	1074	444	189	0.175978	714192	250953	463239	0.64862
IPALMv0.1	4336	1554	1702	0.392528	1375389	623998	751391	0.546312
IPALMv0.4	6772	2126	3273	0.483314	2553960	1090165	1463795	0.573147
IPALMv0.7	6763	2065	3308	0.489132	2513833	1076683	1437150	0.571697
IPALMv0.7.3	7155	2236	3413	0.477009	2617924	1153836	1464088	0.559255

IPALMv0.7.5	7147	2256	3300	0.461732	2755999	1207801	1548198	0.561756
IPALMv0.	715	227	326	0.4561	27682	12180	15502	0.5599

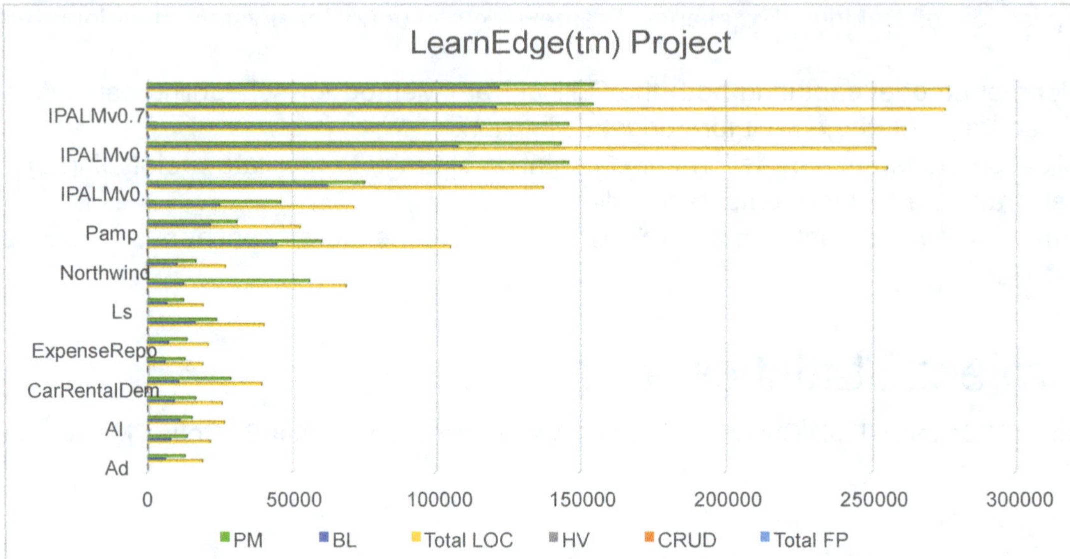

Figure 34 IPALM Projects Statistics

The Car Rental demo represents a small size two weeks project in the spectrum of project sizes. IPALM represents a six months large project size. Both were created by the writer for demonstration purposes.

Principles Embedded in IPALM Manifesto

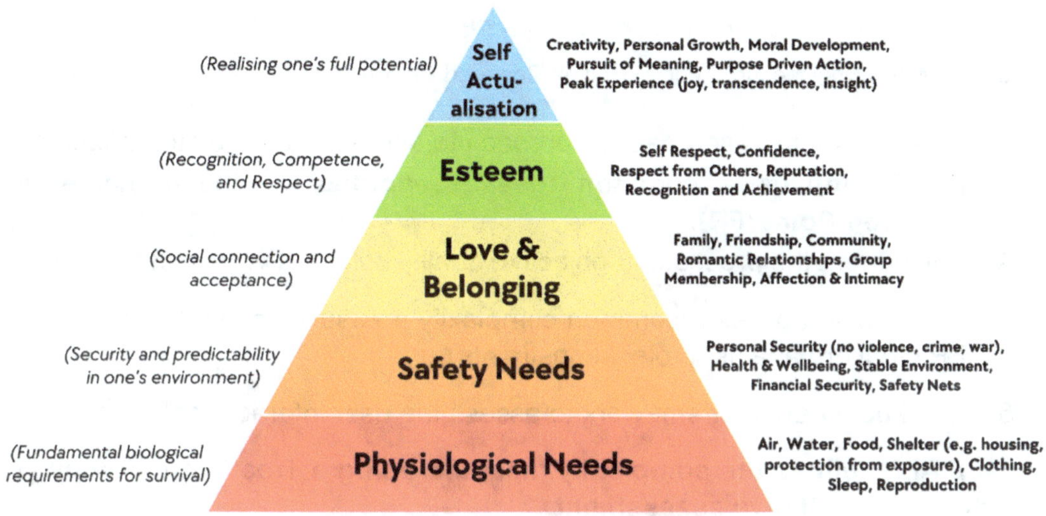

.

Figure 35 IPALM Maslow Hierarchy

Principles of Modern Project Management embedded

IPALM (Intelligent Project Assistant in Lifecycle Management) is based on the following project management principles:

1. "Establish a quantifiable Problem-Solving process to extract the best development scenarios."

   IPALM relies on the MDA methodology called IMES (Integranova Model Execution System) to derive each component of the IPALM framework.

2. "Base the process on an Architecture-first approach."

IPALM refines the project estimates using a framework-based approach matching each Key Estimate Factor (KEF):

a. Project Framework Earned Value Plan.
b. Process Framework Capability Maturity Plan;
c. Product Framework Productivity and Quality Plan.
d. Cognitive Engineering (People) Human Centered Design Plan.

3. “Use a demonstration-based approach to assess intermediate artifacts.”
   IPALM applies a common measure across all these elements, called Function Point (FP).
4. “Instrument the process for objective quality control and process assessment.”

   IPALM also applies a common complexity measure coined UTOPIA to adjust the FP measure against project constraints.

5. “Provide a general framework to assess the user interactions”

IPALM refines the complexity measure using a Tree Methodology (TM) thus providing a quantitative assessment.

6. “Provide a general framework to assess the complexity of the WBS, OBS”

IPALM applies a Cognitive Function Evaluator Matrix (CFEM)to evaluate the Organization Policies in place

7. “Provide a general framework to answer questions such as: who, what, when, where and why?”

IPALM extracts the Process Improvement, the Capability Maturity, and the Productivity from a Linear Project Concept

8. “Establish a changé management environnement.”

   IPALM incorporates Risk Management, Complexity Assessment, and Schedule Compression consideration using the Effort Adjustment Factor, the Size Adjustment Factor and the Duration Adjustment Factor respectively.

9. "Plan intermediate releases in groups of usage scenarios with evolving levels of detail."

IPALM can be tailored and calibrated to account for new or existing projects thus applying a PERT method

10. "Establish a configurable process that is economically scalable."

IPALM demonstrates the impact of methodology selection such as RUP, DSDM, Agile, CMMI (see Appendix G)

11. "Establish an iterative life-cycle process."

IPALM is a project management framework generated with IMES.

12. "Transition design methods to emphasize a Maslow Hierarchy based development."

IPALM is based on the MOTIF pattern for the design methods for each iteration.

The themes presented are very varied to be able to respond to an unknown demand. At the core, the demonstrators rely on the fact that graphic, textual, and data information represent the significant contribution of exchanges. What LearnEdge™ adds is the mathematical and logical contribution to support the concepts promoted by LearnEdge(tm).

For example, every project is based on three constraints: cost, schedule, and requirements. Each of these constraints is mathematically formulated by LearnEdge(tm). When you balance these three constraints, you obtain an optimization point for the success of your project. Your human resources are allocated in an optimal way. This is the fundamental principle supported by LearnEdge(tm).

Appendix A Glossary and Abbreviations

Glossary

Actor

A role played by any person, organization, or system that interacts with an application but is external to it. Actors are modeled on use-case diagrams.

Alpha Testing

A testing period in which pre-release versions of software products, products that are often buggy, are released to users who need access to the product before it is to be officially deployed.

Analysis

This is an approach to modeling in which the goal is to understand the problem domain. Modeling patterns are applied to describe a solution to a domain problem.

Architectural Modeling

High-level modeling of the technical domain whose goal is to provide a common overall vision of the problem domain. Architectural models provide a base from which detailed design will begin.

Artefact Reuse

The reuse of previously created development artefacts: Use Cases, standards documents, domain-specific models, procedures and guidelines, and other applications.

Beta Testing

Testing used as a follow up to Alpha Testing to ensure that the software meets as many user's needs as possible prior to product release.

Build

This is the process to create a software product, using a known baseline of base source code. This is the act of compiling and linking source code in compiler languages.

Capability Maturity Model Integration

A strategy that describes the key elements of an effective software process, as defined by the Software Engineering Institute (SEI).

Cause

This is the basis for an action, or a decision given a situation.

Change

This is a transition from one situation to another, a different situation from a previous one. This is also the observed effect of an action or a decision on the current situation.

Competency

Knowledge and skills required to mitigate the impact of changes and defects encountered

Component

Small-scale, cohesive software items such as user interface widgets, that are reused when building applications.

Component Reuse

The reuse of pre-built, fully encapsulated components in the development of an application.

Contingency

Actions required to mitigate the impact of the errors or complexity of operations encountered

Critical Path

In a project network diagram, it is the series of activities that determines the earliest completion of a project. The Critical Path for a project will change from time to time as activities are completed ahead of or behind schedule.

Data Dictionary

This is a repository of information. The repository describes the layout of a database, the layout of a flat file, the layout of a class, and any mapping among the three.

Data Flow

In a process model, a data flow represents the movement of information from a source process to a destination process.

Decision

This is the selection of an option to solve a problem, given a set of selection criteria.

Defect

This is the inability of your application to completely and effectively meet your user's needs.

Deliverable

This is any document or system component that is produced during the development of a system.

Dependency

Assignment of resources to tasks related to the sequence of activities planned under a project plan

Design

A style of modeling with the goal of describing how a system will be built based on the defined requirements. Design applies design patterns

to deliver the design components.

Design Pattern

This is a modeling pattern that describes a solution to a domain problem.

Detailed Design

This is a style of modeling, which focuses on the design of a single piece of software by expanding the data processed, and associated algorithms on the data.

Domain Architecture

This is a collection of high-level models that describe the problem domain.

Efficiency

Actions to optimize the decisions taken to reach the goals and objectives pursued

Feasibility Study (FS)

This is a document that addresses three main issues:

`□ Can the system be built?

`□ Can you afford to build the system? and

`□ Can you maintain and support it?

Framework

This is a reusable application frame that can be extended or tailored to produce custom applications.

Guideline

This is a description of how something should be done. Guidelines are recommended steps.

Impact

This is the anticipated effect of an action or decision on the current situation.

Impact Analysis

A determination of how the application will be affected by a given change. Your analysis should describe the modifications that need to be made to the models, documentation, and source code.

Integration

This is the process of combining different activities, programs, or hardware components into a functional system or subsystem.

Interactivity

The communication decisions made to facilitate concurrency in operations as opposed to serialization of operations.

Key Process Area (KPA)

This is an issue that must be addressed to achieve a specific CMM maturity level.

Life Cycle Process Pattern

This is a process pattern that depicts a software life cycle process, often made up of a collection of phases, stages, and activities.

Mechanism

This is process by which something is done or comes into being. **Meta-language**

A language used to describe other languages using an Extended Backus-Naur Form (EBNF) notation.

Method

This is the procedures and techniques characteristic of a particular discipline, or field of knowledge.

Methodology

In the context of systems development, this is the collection of techniques and approaches that you take when creating a system.

Metrics Measurement

This is the process of collecting, summarizing, and acting on measurements to potentially improve both the quality of the software and the actual software process.

Model

This is an abstraction describing a problem domain and/or a solution to a problem domain.

Notation

This is a set of symbols that are used in the drawing of models.

Pattern

This is the description of a general solution to a common problem or issue from which a detailed solution to a specific problem may be determined.

Policy

This is a directive of the activities required to achieve a process goal.

This set of information represents what constitutes an activity.

Practice

This is the method of procedure used in a specific field of knowledge.

Principle

This is the rule or standard, a fixed or predetermined policy or mode of action.

Problem

This is a situation that presents risk, uncertainty, and complexity in conducting the actions required.

Procedure

This is a series of steps to be followed to perform a given task. This set of steps represents how an activity shall be done.

Process

This is a series of activities in which one or more input events are used to produce one or more outcomes.

Process Checklist

This is a qualitative means to indicate that an activity should be completed while working on a defined process.

Process Pattern

This is a pattern that describes a proven, successful approach and/ or series of activities for developing software.

Production

Decisions made to increase production of deliverables based on the environment assigned or the resources assigned

Productivity

Decisions made to reduce the number of tasks and activities in conducting the processes called up in a project plan

Prototyping

This is an iterative process to generate prototypes, a mock-up of a portion of the application, in which users are actively involved in the mocking up of the user interface for an application.

Release

This is a version of an application or component that has been made available for use by its developers.

Reliability

This is the likelihood of a system or component functioning over a given period under specified conditions without defect.

Reusability

This is the ability of a design or a code to be usable again in another application or system.

Rule

This is an authoritative direction for procedure.

Situation

This is a position or status with regard to conditions and attendant circumstances. This is also a combination of circumstances at a given moment.

Standard

This is a directive of what activities must be conducted, as defined by a standard office such as IEEE, to achieve a process goal.

Technique

This is the systematic procedure by which a complex task is accomplished.

Version

This is one or more revision to a deliverable resulting in a new version.

List of Acronyms

AU Application Usage

CE Cognitive Engineering

CES Cognitive Engineering System

CFA Cognitive Function Analysis

CFEM Cognitive Function Evaluator Matrix

CLUE Generic Language Usage Exchange

CM Configuration Management

CMMI Capability Maturity Model Integration

COCOMO Constructive Cost Model

CPC Concurrent Project Context

CPM Critical Path Method

CR Change Request

CS Control System

DAG Database Access Generator

DD Detailed Design

DE Development Engineering

DOMAIN Development-Operation-Maintenance-Admin-Info-Network

DUE Development Usage Exchange

ECT Earliest Completion Time

EPML Effective Progress Management Level

EPN Expanded Petri-Net

ES Expert System

EST Earliest Service Time

GLUE Generic Language Usage Exchange

GUI Graphical User Interface

IE Interaction Engineering

IEEE Institute of Electrical & Electronics Engineers

IM Infrastructure Management

ISE Integrated System Environment

ISO International Standard Organization

KPA Key Process Area

LAN Local Area Network

LST Latest Service Time

MM Maintenance Management

MTBF Mean Time Between Failures

MTTR Mean Time To Repair

OBS Organization Breakdown Structure

OPEN Object-oriented Process, Environment and Notation

OS Operating System

OSI Open System Interconnection

P&P Policy & Procedure

PAMPA Project Attribute Monitoring and Prediction Associate

PDL Program Design Language

PE Product Engineering

PERT Program Evaluation and Review Technique

PI Process Improvement

PIE Prolog Inference Engine

PM Project Management

PMI Project Management Institute

PP Payback Period

PRB Project Repository Broker

PRM Programmer Reference Manual

PS Prototyping System

PSS Performance Support System

QA Quality Assurance

QC Quality Control

QM Quality Management

RA Risk Analysis

RAD Rapid Application Development

RAM Responsibility Assignment Matrix

ROI Return On Investment

ROOM Real-time Object-Oriented Methodology

RTM Requirement Traceability Matrix

S&P Standard & Procedure

SAP Service Access Point

SAT System Acceptance Test

SBS System Breakdown Structure

SCP System Change Proposal

SDP Software Development Plan

SE Software Engineering

SEES Software Engineering Exploration System

SEP Software Engineering Process

SEPA Software Engineering Process Architecture

SHEF Software Hierarchy Estimating Form

SIU System Interaction Usage

SM System Management

SLOC Software Lines of Code

SMART Specific, Measurable, Accurate, Realistic, Time Bound

SPD System Product Description

SPP Service Provisioning Point

SPR System Problem Report

SQL Structured Query Language

SRD System Requirement Document

SWOT Strength-Weakness-Opportunity-Threat

UA User Agent

UAG User Agent Generator

UM User Manual

UML Unified Modeling Language

VD Vision Document

VDD Version Description Document

VIU Visual Interaction Usage

V&V Verification & Validation

VM Virtual Machine

VME Virtual Machine Environment

WBS Work-Breakdown Structure

LearnEdge™ Curriculum 2025

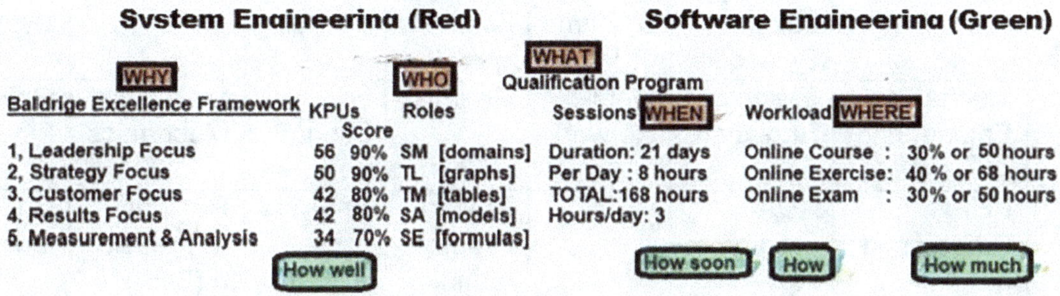

System Eng.	AC Motor design	Aeronautics Formula	Physics	Aero Dynamics	Air Propulsion	RADAR System	Antenna Design
System Eng.	Tablet System	Turbine Design	Automation	Business Process Modeling	Cellular Network	Parabolic Antenna	Telecommunication
System Eng.	Cognitive Engineering	Cognitive Science	Reliability and Availability	Operating System	Combustion Model	Thermodynamics	Fiber Optic communication
System Eng.	Router Network	Early Warning System	Computer Science	DC Motor Design	Desktop Computer	Diesel Engine	Digital Electronics
System Eng.	Electricity	Electromagnetic Radiation	Electronics	Interface Emulator	Combustion Engine	Control System	Engineering Physics
System Eng.	Fluid Dynamics	Fluid Mechanics	Vibration	Optics	SONAR System	Systems Engineering	Guidance System

System Eng.	Distributed Computing	Embedded Java Bytecode	Embedded System	Voice Recognition	Laptop System	Chemical Engineering	Industrial Conttol System
System Eng.	Mechanical Engineering	Electrical Engineering	Mobile Network	Chemistry	HDL Language	Solid Mechanics	Optical Fiber
Software Eng.	PHP Progamming	ADA programming language	PERT	Phyton Programming	Analysis of Algorithms	Regular Expression (BNF)	Critical Path Method
Software Eng.	SmallTalk Language	Software Engineering	Operations Research	Graphic Design	SQL Language	Scalable Vector Graphic	Symbol Table
Software Eng.	Compiler/Interpreter	RIS Assembly Language	Unified Modeling Language	VHDL	Gantt Chart	Visual Basic Language	Visual Prolog
Software Eng.	Extended Backus Naur Form	Extensible Application Markup Language	Complexity	GREP	ASP.NET	Engineering Economics	YAWL
Software Eng.	ANTLR	APL Programming	Architecture Analysis and Design	Human Centered Design	Lexical Analysis	Operating System	Estimator/Evaluator
Software Eng.	C/C++ Programming Language	LEX/YACC	NETBEANS	Logic	MAKE	Mnemotechnics	Visual Studio

Software Eng.	Abstract Data Structure	Software Simulation	Gaussian Process Simulator	Reliability and Availability	C# Programming Language	Parsing	VROOM
Software Eng.	Java Language	Data Mining	ML Programming Language	Ruby Programming	Semantic Analysis	Hardware Emulation	Combination Analysis

Table 6 Knowledge Progression Unit (KPU)

Appendix B Cognitive Function Evaluation Matrix

Part I Compounded Factors Considerations

a. LearnEdge™ Introduction
b. A joint active design environment
c. A built-in Systems Engineering economics model

Part II Multiplicative Factors Considerations

d. A built-in System Architecture Evaluation
e. Resource and task assignment based on Performance Intelligence Communication of Knowledge
f. A measurement and analysis capability based on Project Attributes Monitoring and Predicting Agent

Part III Additive Factors Considerations

g. A built-in Verifiable Requirements in OO Methodology (**VROOM**)
h. An integrated Project Evaluation, Analysis and Review over the full lifecycle (**PEARL**)
i. An intelligent Project Assistant in Lifecycle Management (**IPALM**)

Part IV Effective Process Management Levels

j. A Dynamic Progress Methodology (DPM) model
k. A risk mitigation strategy based on Management Corrective Actions (**MCA**)
l. An Application Generation in Actions Environment

CFEM Formulation

CFEM = $\sum \quad (RoleKDUs * RoleFactors)$/ Total KDUs

Appendix C Application Generation in Action

AGIA Development Framework.

IPALM Framework

IPALM Framework *(FocusOfAttention)* CFEM (Assignments)	People *(R&Rs)* WHO	Data *(Capabilities)* WHAT	Time *(Events)* WHEN	Network *(Workflows)* WHERE	Motivation *(Goals)* WHY	Function *(Features)* HOW	Budget *(Allocations)* HOW Much	Performance *(Metrics)* HOW Well	Demonstration *(Iterations)* HOW Soon
Objective/Scope Business View Role:Owner	Organizational Policies	Business Concepts	Business Events	Feasibility Study	ROI	Business Process	Business Case	EPML	IPALM System
Enterprise Model Conceptual View Role:Business Analyst	Organizational Structure	Business Model Classes	Enterprise Events	Requirements	EVS	Enterprise Process	Project Charter	Earned Values	PAMPA/SEEM
System Model Logical View Role:Designer	Organizational Workflows	System Model Classes	System Events	Design	Throughput, Response time	System Process	Work Package	Efficiency	CFA/GEM
Technology Model Architectural View Role:Builder	Organizational Infrastructure	Component Model Classes	Component Events	Implementation	Reliability	Component Process	Engineering Charge Order	Productivity	IMES
Release Model Build View Role:Support	Organizational Stakeholders	Deployment Model Packages	Deployment Events	Deployment	Maintainability	Deployment Process	Production Charge Order	Quality	Service Level Agreement
Rasmussen'sModel Functional View Role:User	Human-Centered Design	8-Schema Architecture Model	Decision Events	Active Design	Operability	Cognitive Engineering	Integral Engineering Charge Order	CFEM	IPALM System

Figure 36 Zachman Framework

Use Case primary purpose is to specify what features belong to what actors (user interacting with the system under study). Actors are shown as little stick characters. Use Case capture features, in oval shape, using a rectangle. A Use case has a name related to the actor role. Features are services provided. You may have multiple actors sharing the same Use case. The variants, or refinements, will be demonstrated by the inherited Use case.

Use cases are accompanied by Use Case Descriptions, one for each service provided. These constitute Story Points.

There is at least one Use Case per system and subsystem and component. In other words, the Use case follows a tree hierarchy consistent with the system hierarchy. The key concern is to capture end-user's requirements while interacting with those entities.

The vertical blocks in a Use case would capture the Policies and Procedures required to run that specific business operations. The Actors would capture the Roles and Responsibilities of the staff interacting with the system. The services listed would capture what features can be automated!

OIDs on the other hand capture the class interactions. These occur at the Architectural level, not the Requirements level. The class/classes required to deliver the features identified under the Use case are clustered by Use case service name. The Actors in the OID are the classes of the Object Model. The arrow in the OID indicates the Association between classes.

The Logic Flow on the left of the diagram indicates the overall Functional Model considerations (transactions) between classes. The time consideration is running downward. A convention will be required to avoid conflict between logic flow (instantaneous) and time flow on the diagram! Message drop/errors are earmarked with a *.

From Cognitive Engineering perspective is comprised of three axes coined 7-A (People), 8-S (Product) and 7-I (Process), described below. This is the Cognitive Engineering Framework embedded within LearnEdge™ !

VROOM to IPALM mapping

Table 7 VROOM to IPALM mapping

VROOM Model Map	**IPALM Breakdown (8-S)**		**EFP Ratio**
	Activity	**Model**	%
System	Performance Model	(**PM**)	7
Architecture	Open Architecture Model	(**OM**)	11
Protocol	Communication Model	(**CM**)	5
Database	Data Tracking Model	(**DM**)	7
Functional	Transformation Model	(**TM**)	3
Risk	Risk/Complexity Model	(**RM**)	11

Interaction	User Interaction Model (**UM**)	7
Dynamic	State Transition Model (**SM**)	7
	Sub-Total	**58%**
	Requirements creep	
	Number of iterations (3)	
	Implement changes (7% Each)	21%
	Validate changes (7% Each)	21%
	Sub-Total	42%

Orchestrating Staff Performance

LearnEdge™ establishes a balance between management and technical activities by applying a fix overhead ratio accounting for the full suite of the main stake holders for ultimate "Velocity".

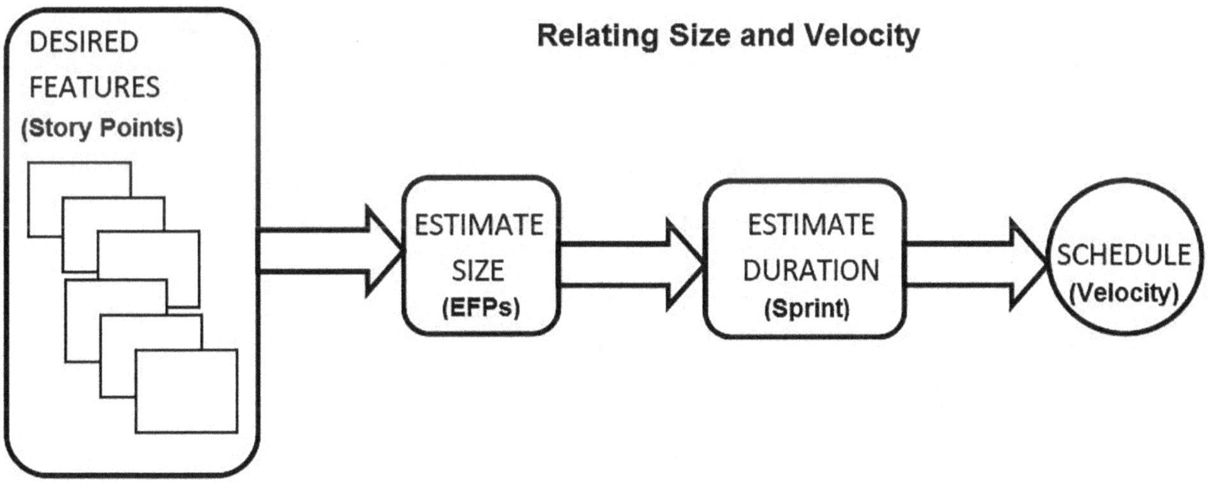

Figure 37 IPALM Agile model

Also, LearnEdge™ maintains an in-scope and out of scope baseline by applying the following methodology:

1. The Tree Methodology for complexity assessment
2. Case-Base Reasoning approach by implementing a goal-driven system to cover a full suite of scenarios and,
3. A fully implemented Cognitive Engineering Framework .

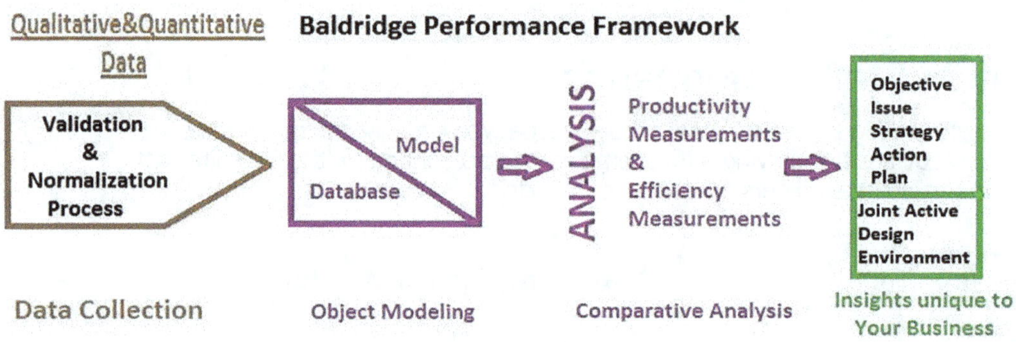

Figure 38 IPALM Effective Function Point Measurement

Four Management Models applied within LearnEdge™

Architecture-Oriented team characterized as:

a. Stable team;
b. Specialized knowledge;
c. High Integrity of the architecture;
d. Clear definition and stability of components interfacing;
e. Complex iteration planning;
f. Simplified integration; and,
g. Ease of component sharing and reuse.

Feature-Oriented team characterized as:

a. Unstable team;
b. Broader knowledge;
c. Low integrity of the architecture;
d. Instability of component interfacing;
e. Simple iteration planning;
f. Complex integration; and,
g. Difficult component sharing and reuse.

Component-based team characterized as:

a. Integrity of software architecture;
b. Ease of component sharing and reuse;
c. Reduced complexity of components; and,
d. Ease of identification of quality levels.

Activity-based team characterized as:

e. Streamlining of testing effort;
f. Streamlining of code review;
g. Ease of reporting;
h. Logical grouping of task;
i. Fewer build and iteration problems; and,
j. Logical link to CPM.

Appendix D Effective Progress Management Level

Effective Progress Management Level

Management Corrective Actions

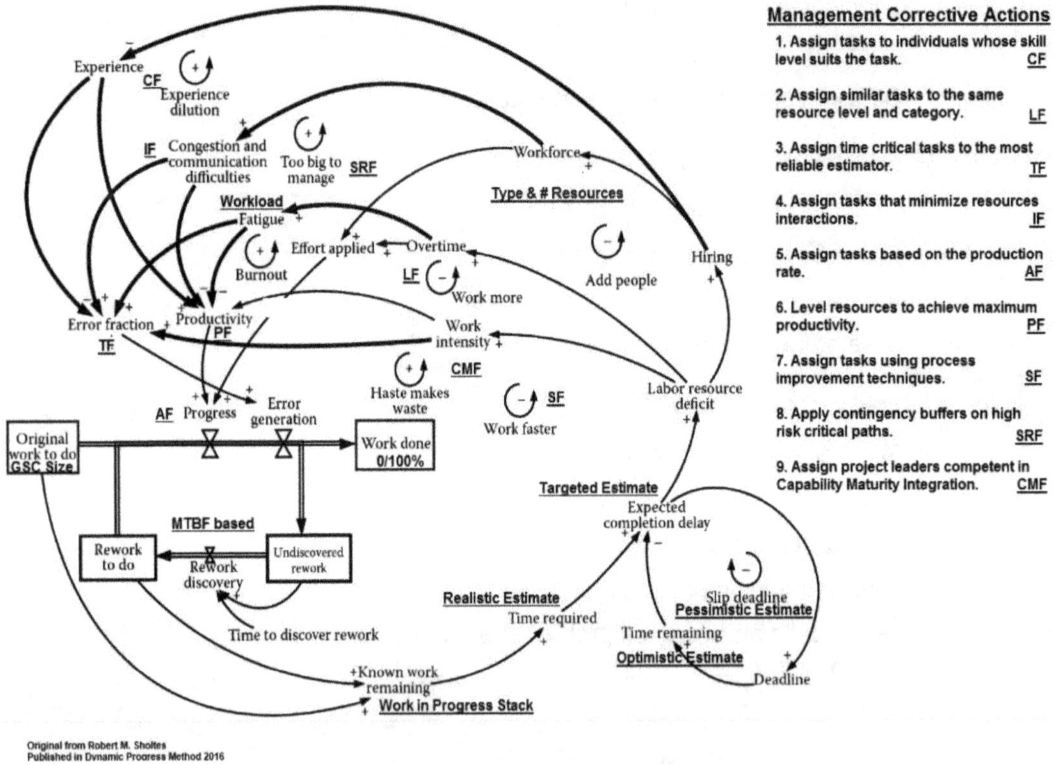

Figure 39 IPALM Management Corrective Actions

EPML Formulation

EPML = $\sum \quad (RoleMCAs * RoleFactors)$/ Total MCAs

Appendix E Systems Engineering Economics Model Scenarios

Optimistic Scenario

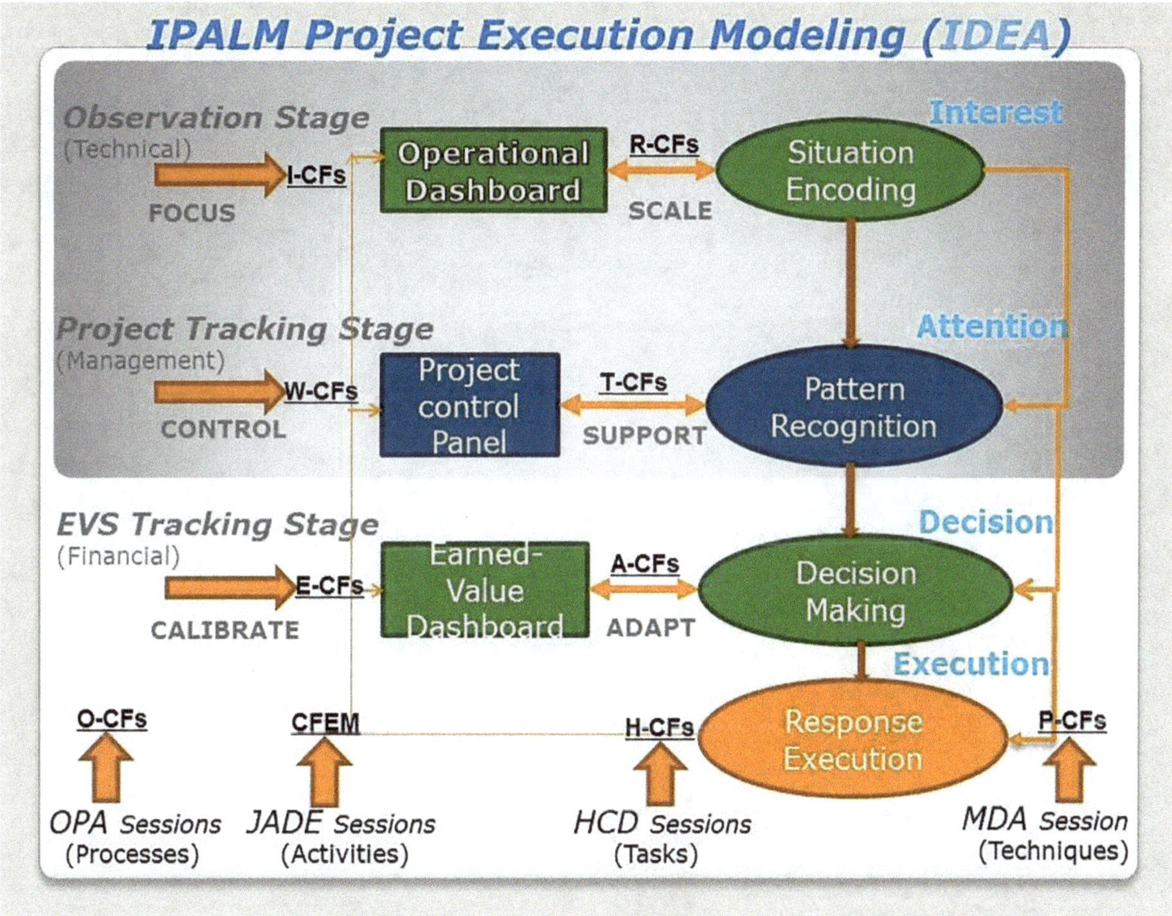

Software Engineering Economic Model (SEEM) Process

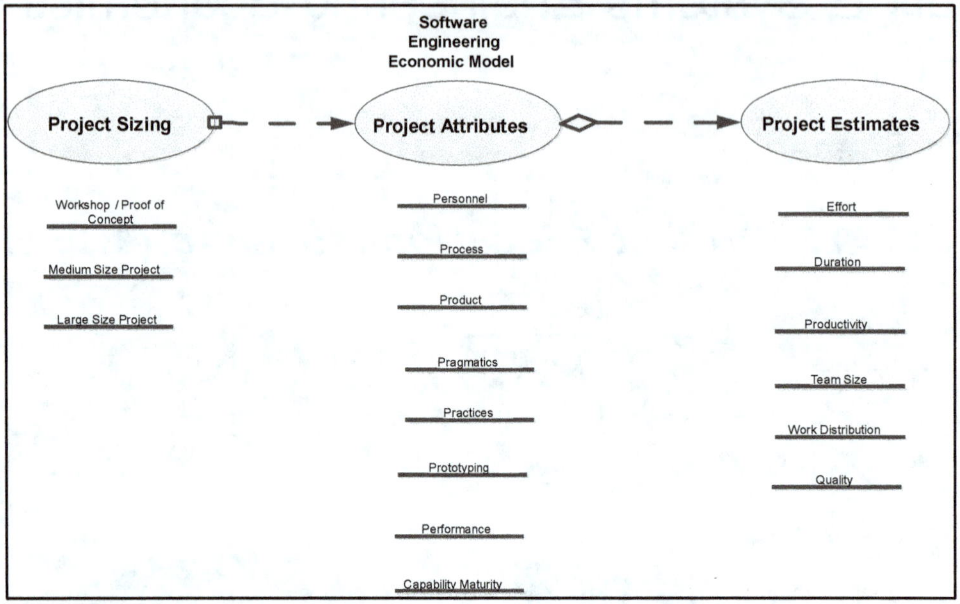

Linear Project Concept

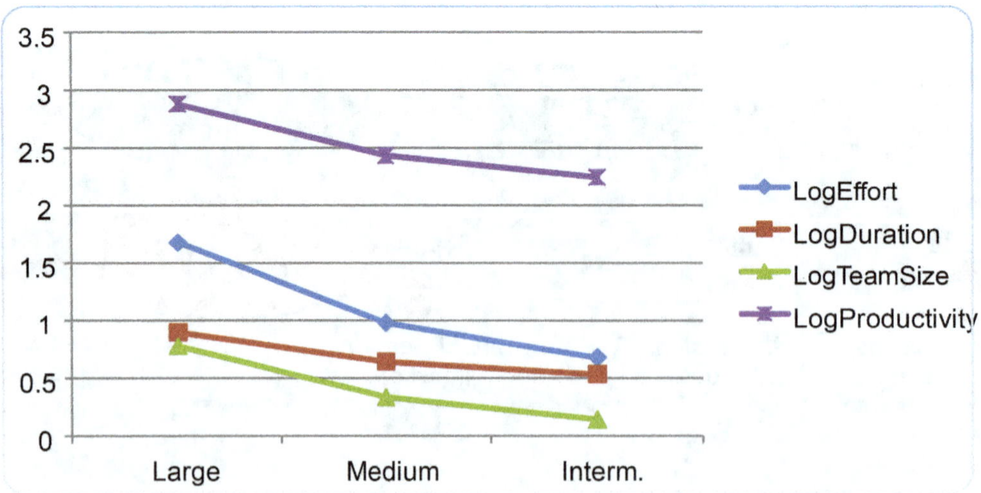

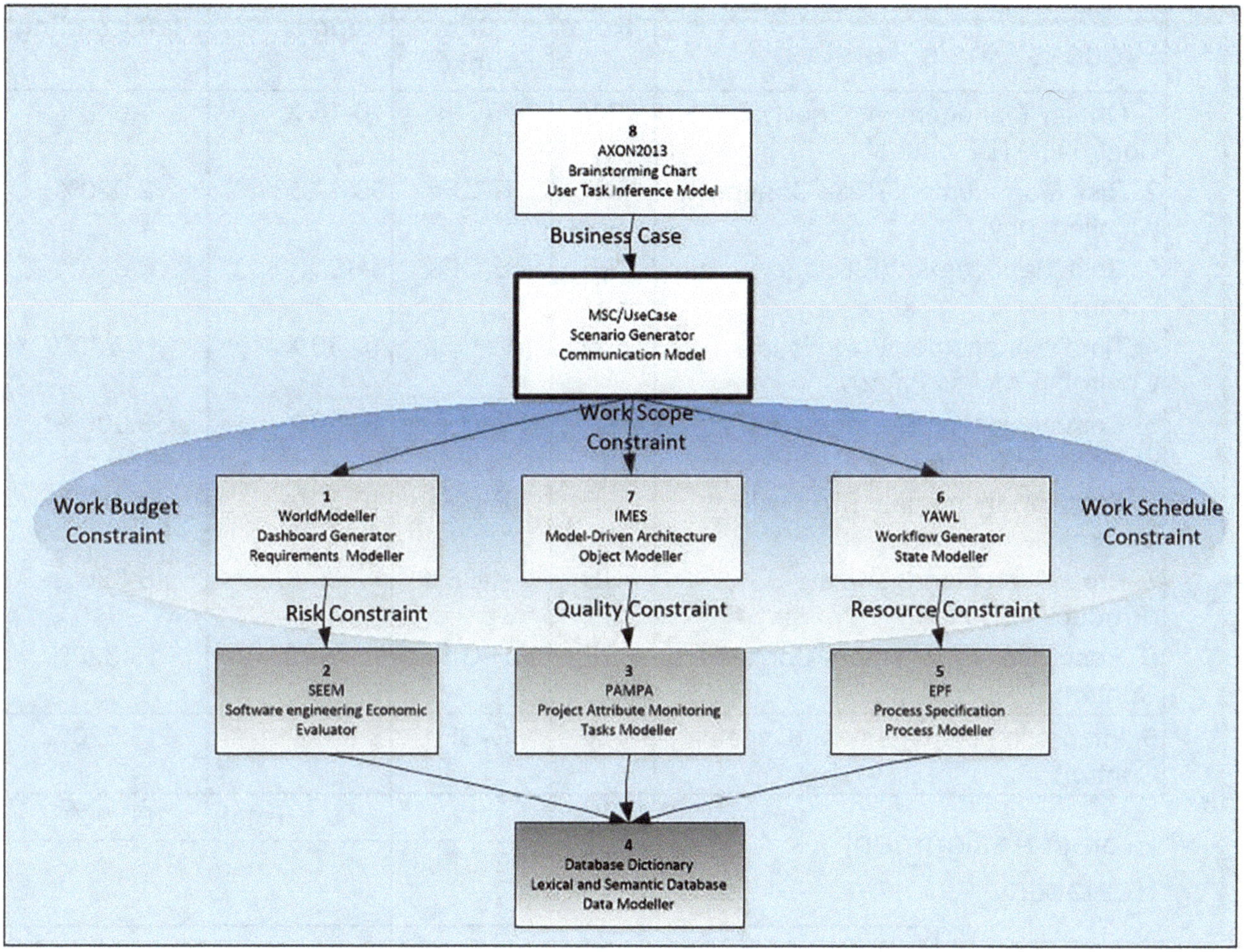
8
AXON2013
Brainstorming Chart
User Task Inference Model
Business Case
MSC/UseCase
Scenario Generator
Communication Model
Work Scope Constraint
Work Budget Constraint
1
WorldModeller
Dashboard Generator
Requirements Modeller
7
IMES
Model-Driven Architecture
Object Modeller
6
YAWL
Workflow Generator
State Modeller
Work Schedule Constraint
Risk Constraint
Quality Constraint
Resource Constraint
2
SEEM
Software engineering Economic Evaluator
3
PAMPA
Project Attribute Monitoring
Tasks Modeller
5
EPF
Process Specification
Process Modeller
4
Database Dictionary
Lexical and Semantic Database
Data Modeller

Process Goals Pursued	Role	CFs Applied	Range	Staff Loading
1. Quality Management(Quality Control) [MTBF based]	QM	T-CFs	10-15 X	1.640%
2. Risk Management (Risk Control) [Contingency]	RM	R-CFs	90%-95%	2.920%
3. Cost Management(Efficiency Control)	SC	E-CFs	5-10 X	6.640%
4. Time management(Workload Control) [Process Improv.]	SM	W-CFs	10-30 X	19.240%
5. Communication Management (Interaction Control)	SA	I-CFs	10-20 X	9.600%
6. Scope Management (Productivity Control)	SE	P-CFs	10-30 X	25.000%
7. Production Management (Production Control)	SD	A-CFs	10-30 X	8.320%
8. Resource Management(Confidence Control)	CE	H-CFs	10%-25%	13.320%
9. Integration Management (Capability Control)	PM	O-CFs	2-3 X	13.320%
			Total:	100.000%
Project Assignment Scalability:		B-CFs		

1. Number of FPs per class	32
2. FSP Throughput per month	128
3. Number of timeboxes (TB) per month	2

	4. Component size assigment in FPs(1 TB)			64	
	5. Project Scope Assignment (in FPs)			640, 1280, 6400, 12800	
Applicable Projects	**Type**	**Size (FPs)**	**Staff(Max)**	**AvgDuration**	**MaxCost ($US)**
1. Workshop	Demo	32-64	1 FSPs	1-2 weeks	$14,080.00
2. Small Application	Small	320-640	2 FSPs	5-10 weeks	$140,800.00
3. Average business App.	Medium	1280-2560	5 FSPs	2-4 months	$563,200.00
4. Distr. Enterprise App.	Large	3840-7680	5 FSPs	6-12 months	$1,689,600.00

Note: (1) A **Timebox** represents a two-week effort or 64 FPs at $220/FP

(2) By applying a **Group Elicitation Method**, 5 **Timeboxes** can be assigned independently (320 FPs)

Overhead Ratio Goals Pursued:

1. Development %: SA + SE + CE + SD = 56.24%
2. Overhead %: PM + QM + SM + RM + SC = 43.76%
3. Overhead Ratio: Overhead/Development 0.778094
4. Charging Rate: Development+Overhead 1.778094

PMBOK ID	Class	Description	Focus	Method	Dashboard	
1	CostMgmt	Cost Management	Cost Control	EarnedValueMethod	IterationDashboard	[2]
2	OrgMgmt	Resource Management	Resource Control	CognitiveFunctionMethod	CFAdashboard	[5]
3	CommMgmt	Communication Control	Interaction Control	AgileDesignMethod	GEMdashboard	[3]
4	QualityMgmt	Quality Management	Quality Control	CombinationalMethod	SLAdashboard	[4]
5	ScopeMgmt	Scope Management	Productivity Control	ModelDrivenMethod	ModelDashboard	[7]
6	IntegrationMgmt	Integration Management	Integration Control	DecisionEngMethod	CMMIdashboard	[1]
7	TimeMgmt	Time Management	Schedule Control	DynamicProgressMethod	PIdashboard	[6]
8	RiskMgmt	Risk Management	Risk Control	GenericTreeMethod	RiskDashboard	[8]

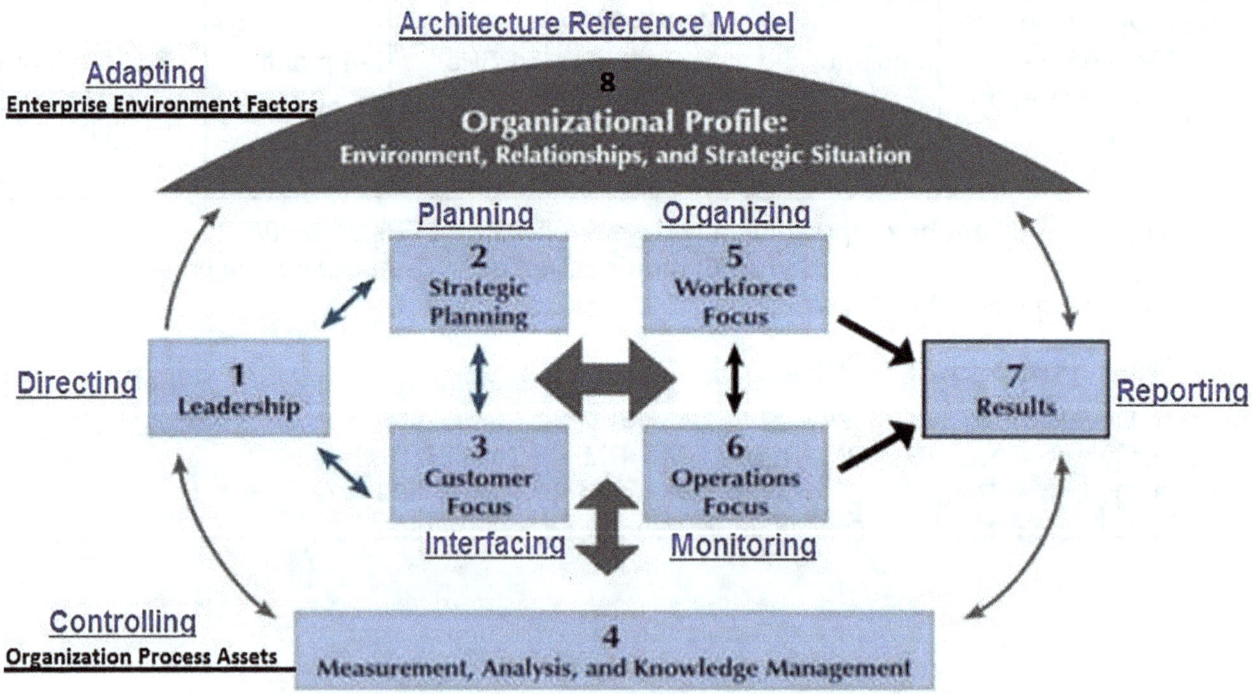

Best Practices embedded with project attributes

Attributes (Focus of Attention)	***Key Practices Description***	***8 Schema Model used*** **[PRODUCTS]**	***Staff Loading***
Confidence Control	Human-Centered Design Control	Usability and EfficiencyModel [UM]	HSL/HF
Total Quality Control	Data Tracking control	Data Tracking Quality Model [DM]	TSL/TF
Efficiency Control	Cost tracking and control	Cost Data Model [CM]	ESL/EF
Workload Control	Workload tracking and control	Solution Workflow Model [SM]	WSL/WF
Interaction Control	Communication interaction control	Open Architecture Model [OM]	ISL/IF
Risk Control	Risk control	Risks Model [RM]	RSL/RF
Productivity Control	Productivity estimation and control	Productivity Model [PM]	PSL/PF
Production Control	Production estimation and control	Transaction Model [TM]	ASL/AF
Organization Control	Capability maturity assessment	Capability Maturity Model [CMM]	OSL/OF
Performance Control	Baldrige Performance assessment	Badrige Performance Model [BM]	BSL/BF

Model	Actor	Goals	Focus of Attention	Staff Loading
UM	CE [DC]	Resource Control	Scalability and diversity impact analysis with process reuse	HCD SL
DM	QM [OH]	Quality Control	Issues and Actions tracking and analysis	Total Quallty SL
CM	SC [OH]	cost Control	Artifact Set Cost tracking and analysis	Efficiency SL
SM	SM [OH]	Schedule Control	Goal-driven workflow analysis for effort control	Workflow SL
OM	SA [DC]	Comm. Control	Correct or change the economic model using SMF/DMF/EMF	Interaction SL
RM	RM [OH]	Risk Control	Risk Mitigation Analysis	Risk SL

PM	SE [DC]	Scope Control	Team/Individual productivity analysis using SCRUM and PI	Productivity SL
TM	SD [DC]	Production Control	Artifact Set Generation	Artifact SL
CMM	PM [OH]	Performance Control	Project goals tracking and analysis	Organization SL

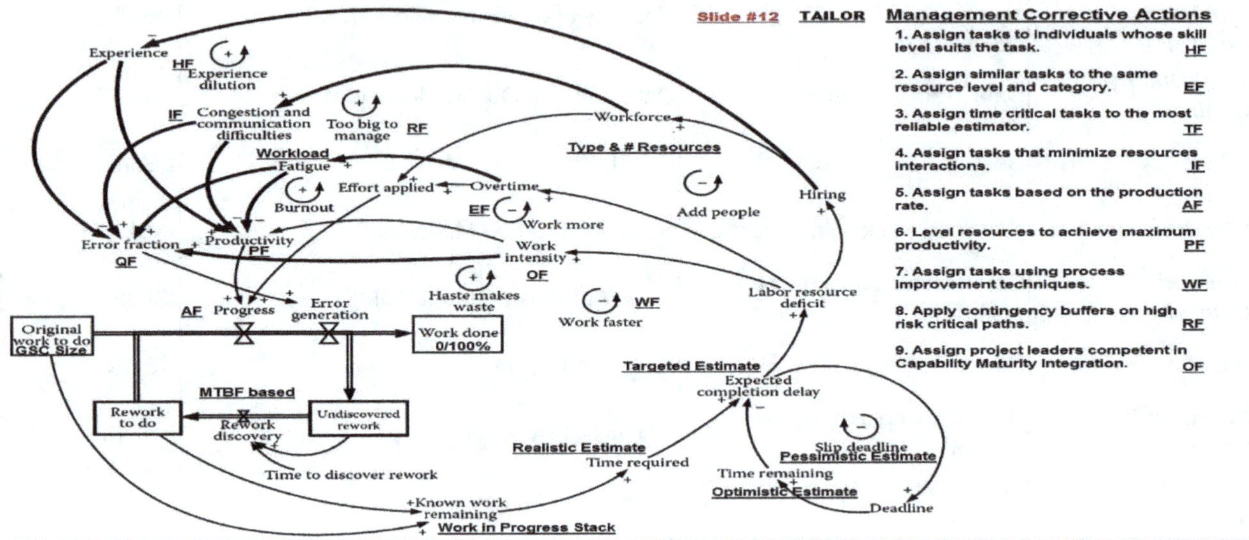

SEEM Task Loading Scenarios

Activity Type	**Tasks Staff Loading Formula**											**Total**
ArtifactSet Factor (Production Control) Production Mgmt	**ASL =**	**Forms +** 18%	**Reports +** 15%	**Algor. +** 20%	**Classes +** 6%	**Tables +** 23%	**Agents +** 7%	**Links +** 6%	**Services** 5%			100%

Productivity Factor (Productivity Control) Productivity Mgmt	**PSL =**	**PM +** 6%	**RM +** 15%	**OM +** 20%	**DM +** 6%	**UM +** 28%	**CM +** 7%	**TM +** 6%	**SM +** 6%	**BM** 6%		100 %
Workflow Factor (Schedule Control) Time Mgmt	**WSL =**	**PM +** 10%	**SM +** 10%	**SC +** 5%	**SA +** 25%	**SE +** 10%	**RM +** 5%	**CE +** 10%	**QM +** 10%	**SD** 15 %		100 %
Interaction Factor (Project Control) Integration Mgmt	**ISL=**	**P_CF +** 7%	**O_CF +** 13%	**W_CF +** 12%	**E_CF +** 26%	**R_CF +** 27%	**H_CF +** 10%	**A_CF** 5%	**B_CF** 5%	**I_CF** 5%	**T_CF** 5%	100 %
Org. Capability Factor Capability Control) Project Mgmt	**OSL =**	**PF +** 12%	**OMF +** 7%	**WF +** 13%	**EF +** 26%	**RF +** 14%	**HF +** 10%	**AF +** 8%	**BF** 10%	**IF** 10 %	**TQF** 10%	100 %
Risk Variance Factor (Risk Control) Risk Mgmt	**RSL =**	**PF_V +** 12%	**OF_V +** 7%	**WF_V +** 13%	**EF_V +** 26%	**RF_V +** 14%	**HF_V +** 10%	**AF_V +** 8%	**BF_V** 10%	**IF_V** 10 %	**TF_V** 10%	100 %
Total Quality Factor	**TSL =**	**CPLX +**	**IF +**	**FEA +**	**COV +**	**REL +**	**Root-Cause**	**PI**	**OH**	**DC**		

(Quality Control) Quality Mgmt		11%	25%	15%	7%	12%	10%	10%	5%	5%		100 %
Cost Factor (Cost Control) Cost Mgmt	**ESL =**	**AA +** 5%	**AC +** 10%	**AD +** 15%	**AT +** 20%	**AM +** 15%	**AF +** 10%	**AS +** 10%	**AP +** 10%	**AO** 5%		100 %
HCD Proficiency Factor (Confidence Control) Resource Mgmt	**HSL =**	**PAMPA +** 10%	**JADE +** 10%	**PICK +** 10%	**MDA +** 10%	**HCD +** 10%	**ANTLR +** 10%	**SEEM +** 10%	**YACC +** 10%	**DPM +** 10 %	**DI** 10%	100 %
Baldrige Perf. Factor (BPF Control) Decision Intelligence	**BSL =**	**Lever +** 12%	**External +** 26%	**Interm +** 30%	**Outcome** 32%							100 %

NOTE: Ratio of time spent on an activity related to a goal associated with a performance factor

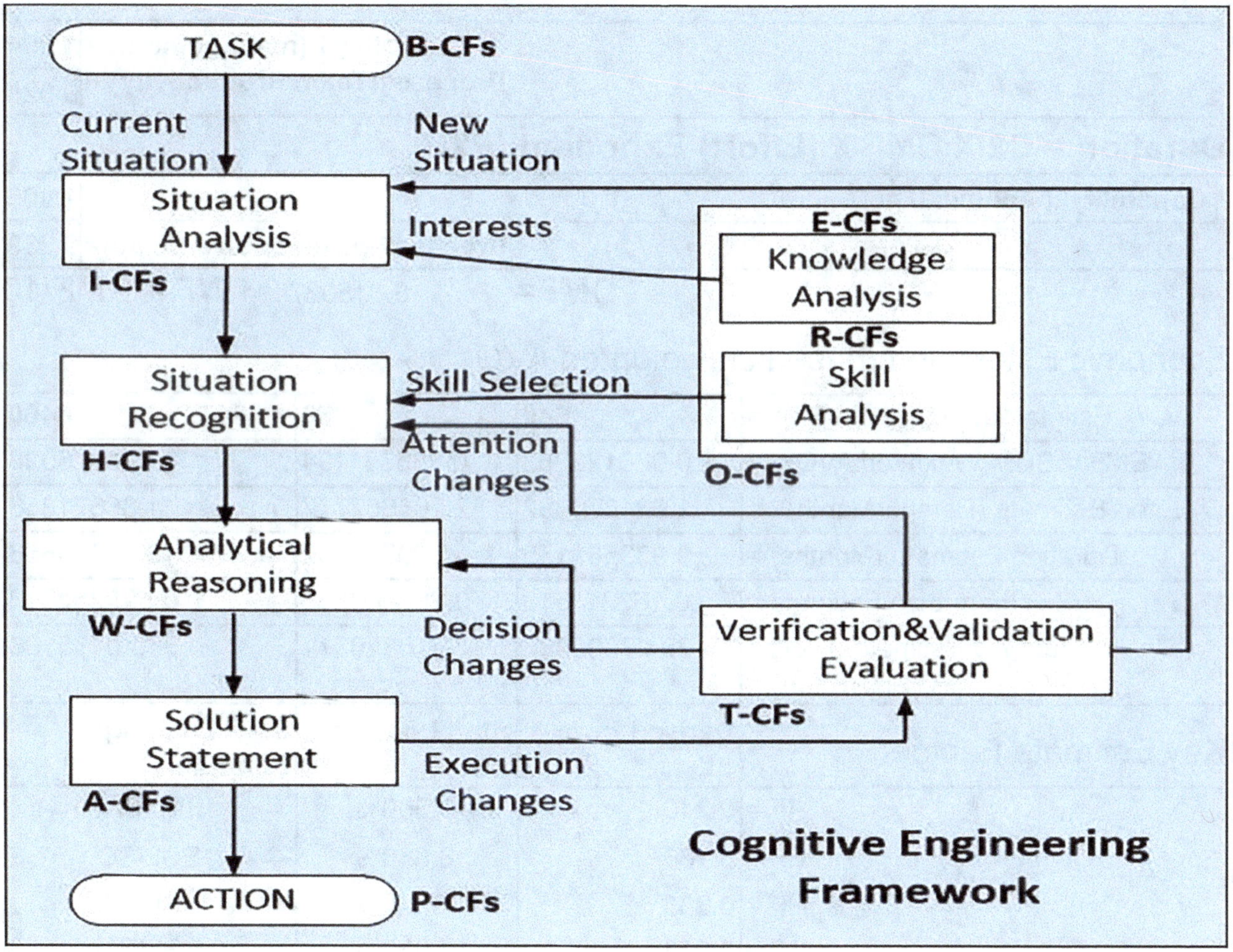
TASK
B-CFs
Current
Situation
New
Situation
Situation
Analysis
Interests
I-CFs
E-CFs
Knowledge
Analysis
R-CFs
Situation
Recognition
Skill Selection
Skill
Analysis
H-CFs
Attention
Changes
O-CFs
Analytical
Reasoning
W-CFs
Decision
Changes
Verification&Validation
Evaluation
T-CFs
Solution
Statement
Execution
Changes
A-CFs
Cognitive Engineering
Framework
ACTION
P-CFs

SEEM Economic Analysis Formula

Effort = C1 X EMF X (GSC X (SMF +MMF + AMF+IMF)) Exponent (P1)	
Capability1 (management) =	1.094
Process1(Team Productivity) =	0.625
Duration = C2 X DMF X (Effort) Exponent (P2)	
Capability2(technical) =	1.406
Process2 (Project Size Scale)=	0.333

DMF= 6.015037594 **WF =** DMF/10

Economic Estimation (based on weighted AVG)

Estimated Adjustment Size =	**640**	**1280**	**6400**
EMF = SUM(Weighted AVG) =	0.026120253	0.035551194	0.043426528
Effort Estimate (Person-Month) =	1.621276832	2.206652777	11.36671356
Duration Estimate (Months) =	9.933587155	11.00745932	18.99984656
Team Size Estimate =	0.163211618	0.200468856	0.598252913
Productivity Estimate (Project Size/Effort) =	394.7505987	290.0320371	563.0475306
Key Estimate Factors	**Derived from SL**	**Staff Loading %**	**Staff Loading Formula**
IF =	0.240	9.600%	ISL/SA
EF =	0.166	6.640%	ESL/SC
HF =	0.333	13.320%	HSL/CE
RF =	0.073	2.920%	RSL/RM
TF =	0.041	1.640%	TSL/QM
PF =	0.625	25.000%	PSL/SE

WF=	0.481	19.240%	WSL/SM
AF =	0.208	8.320%	ASL/SD
OF =	0.333	13.320%	OSL/PM
Total	2.500	100.000%	

Software Engineering Economic Model
(SEEMformula 2016)

$$\textbf{GSC} = (ProductType * \text{Class Size} * Project\ Scope)^{P}$$

$$\textbf{Effort} = C_1 * EMF * (GSC * (SMF * AMF * MMF))^{P_1}$$

$$\textbf{Duration} = C_2 * DMF * (Effort)^{P_2}$$

$$\textbf{Productivity} = Size / Effort$$

$$\textbf{OPA} = SMF * AMF * MMF$$

$$\textbf{EEF} = EMF / DMF$$

Where:	**Economic Factors**
GSC is the Generic System Components	GSC
C_2 is the Engineering Capability (Direct Charging Factor)	DC
C_1 is the Management Capability (Overhead Factor)	OH
SMF is the System Multiplier Factor (Interaction Factor)	IF
P is the Lifecycle Model Factor (Efficiency Factor)	EF
P_2 is the Management Capability (Capability Maturity Factor)	CMF
P_1 is the Process Improvement Factor (Productivity Factor)	PF
EMF is the Effort Multiplier Factor (Risk Factor)	RF
DMF is the Duration Multiplier Factor (Workflow Factor)	WF
MMF is the Maintenance Multiplier Factor (Quality Factor)	QF
AMF is the Adaptation Multiplier (Legacy) Factor	AF
CFEM is the CF Multiplier Factor (Confidence Factor)	CF

Generic System Component Formulation: Project sizing is based on four parameters (B-CFs): S, T, and P

1. Project Scope (S)

		Assignment Scope (S)	***Scale Adj.***	***Component Size***	**Assignment**
		Class Production Rate(**C**)	32	1 Class/week	1 FSP
	1	Very Small Size System	2	2 Classes	1 FSP
	2	Small Size System	4	4 Classes	1 FSP
	3	Average Size System	20	20 Classes	5 FSPs
	4	Standard Size System	40	40 Classes	5 FSPs
	5	Large Size System	80	80 Classes	5 FSPs
	6	Very Large Size System	160	160 Classes	5 FSPs

Note: One Iteration is equivalent to one Timebox for the delivery of one component

2. Product Type (T)

	Model	***CFs Model***	***Component Scope (T) [8-Schema]***	***Size Mult.***	***Complexity Level***	**CMMI Level**
	UM	H-CFs	Usability and Efficiency Model	1.000	0.20	2
	OM	A-CFs	Open Architecture Model	1.500	0.30	2
	TM	**I-CFs**	**Transaction Model (JADE)**	**2.000**	**0.40**	3
	CM	**E-CFs**	**Cost Data Model (SEEM)**	**2.500**	**0.50**	3
	DM	T-CFs	Data Tracking Quality Model (PAMPA)	3.000	0.60	4

	SM	W-CFs	Solution Workflow Model	3.500	0.70	4
	RM	R-CFs	Requirements and Risks Model	4.000	0.80	5
	PM	P-CFs	Productivity Model	4.500	0.90	5
	CMM	O-CFs	Capability Maturity Model	5.000	1.00	5

Note: The Class of Service (CLOS) efficiency distribution follows a Rayleigh cumulative distribution

3. SEPA	**me work**	**Aspect Number**	**Methodology**	**Resources (FSP)**	**SA (Individual)**	**Production Rate**	**P Scale Factor**
Capabilities	CMF	*1.035736657*	IPALM	5	256	256.00	1.00
Processes	SEF	8	OO-Method	5	256	128.00	1.02
Workflows	PDF	10	Agile-XP	3	100	40.00	1.03
Best Practices	CEF	8	Agile-UP	5	100	20.00	1.05
Timeboxes	ETF	2	Agile - DSDM	12	120	12.00	1.10
Interaction Boxes	ITF	1	Agile - ASD	8	300	30.00	1.10
ServiceChargeOrder	ATF	1	Agile - FDD	10	240	12.00	1.20
GSC Factor = (C * S * T) Exponent P			Component Based	20	250	10.00	1.25
For Example:		**GSC = 12800.00** using a large ERP system **GSC = 1280.00** using a average size ERP system					

Economic Modifiers (Part 1)						
KEF Category	**Cost Driver**	**Range (1 default)**	**Stage Modifier(ES=1)**	**Total Impact**	**SL Weight**	**Weighted AVG**
PF Product -	Transformation	2.85	0	17.74752	0.24	4.2594048
Scope Control	RDBMS design	1.39				24.03%
	MDA design	4.48				
IF	Analyst capability	4.18	1	17.653394	0.096	1.694725824
Interaction -	Application Experience	1.57				9.56%
Interaction Control	Programmer capability	2.69				
	HOL Experience	1.34				
RF Project -	Methodology	2.71	1	17.415002	0.029	0.505035058
Risk Control	Automation	2.54				2.85%
	Infrastructure	2.53				
HF People -	Analyst capability	1.68	1	17.65769242	0.1332	2.35200463
Work scope	Application Experience	1.56				13.27%
Proficiency	Programmer capability	4.19				
Control	HOL Experience	1.34				

	SQL experience	1.2				
TF Pragmatics - Total Quality Control	Root-cause analysis	2.66	1	17.943296	0.0164	0.294270054
	Complexity	2.56				1.66%
	Reliability	1.7				
	Coverage	1.55				

Economic Modifiers (Part 2)

KEF Category	Cost Driver	Range (1 default)	Stage	Total Impact	SL Weight	Weighted AVG
WF Performance - Schedule Control	Sched. Compression	2.69	0	18.599736	0.195	3.62694852
	Defect reduction	2.68				20.463%
	Scope increase	2.58				
AF Artifact Sets - Production Control	Discard	1.41	1	17.69833128	0.0832	1.472501162
	Reuse	2.51				8.308%
	Functional	2.66				
	Simulation	1.88				
OF Organization -	Productivity	1.18	0	17.64884771	0.1332	2.350826515

Maturity Control	Quality	2.06				13.264%
	Stability	1.85				
	Risk mitigation	1.86				
	Confidence	2.11				
EF Practices -	Scope	1.50	0	17.70567714	0.066	1.168574691
Efficiency	Resources	1.51				6.593%
Improvement	Infrastructure	2.12				
Cost Control	Organization Policy	1.53				
	Schedule	2.41				
Team Efficiency Factor by GSC			**Weighted AVG by GSC**			**Total AVG**
640FPs	1280FPs	6400FPs	640FPs	1280FPs	6400FPs	100.001%
0.462962963	0.630119723	0.769704433	0.026120253	0.035551194	0.043426528	17.72429125

(1) TeamEff=TeamProductivity/IndividualProductivity
(2) Stage Modifiers = 1 (Applied during the Early Stage of Development)
(3) IndividualProductivity = 128 * TeamSize * TeamDuration
(4) With a GEM session of 15 min/day, a timebox of 2 weeks, the optimal team size is 5 operating at 50% capacity
(5) Team Productivity = Total Project Size / Total Project Effort Estimated

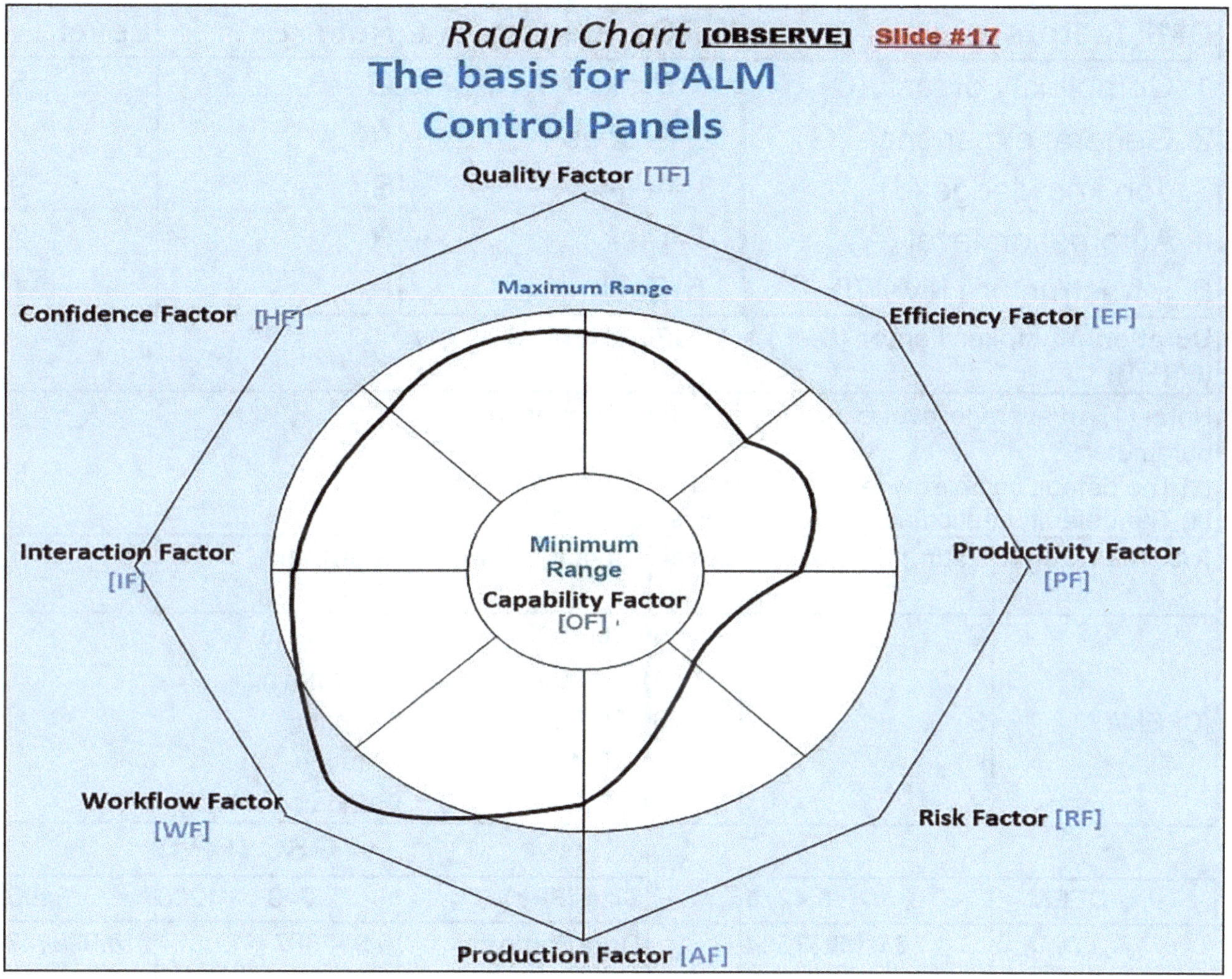
Radar Chart [OBSERVE] Slide #17
The basis for IPALM
Control Panels
Quality Factor [TF]
Maximum Range
Efficiency Factor [EF]
Confidence Factor [HF]
Interaction Factor [IF]
Minimum Range
Capability Factor [OF]
Productivity Factor [PF]
Workflow Factor [WF]
Risk Factor [RF]
Production Factor [AF]

DMF factors	WBS Category	Rating	Level
1. Complexity of task (C),	1. Project	G	5
2. General experience (G),	2. Process	A	4
3. Job knowledge (J),	3. Activity	S	3
4. Automation level (A)	4. Task	R	2
5. Infrastructure level (I)	5. Technique	P	1

Duration Multiplier Factor (DMF) = (1/CFEM)x(18/(G + J)) x (6/(I+A))

Note: (1) An average level is assumed as default for each parameter: 3
(2) The default complexity level is set to: 1
(3) The default duration adjustment factor is set to : 1

RATING Range	Rating(GRASP)	Level	Rayleigh Range	Sternberg Pattern
	G	5	900-1000	Congruent
	A	4	700-900	Anticipating
(CFEM/C)	S	3	400-700	Steering
	R	2	100-400	Routine
	P	1	0-100	Periodic

CFEM =	**0.4275**
DMF =	**6.015037594**

GSC (FPs)			
Size (FPs)	640	1200	6400
Duration(mth)	9.933587	11.007459	18.999847

Quality Goals Pursued

Estimated Adjustment Size =	**640**	**1280**	**6400**
K (Number of Defects) =	2.3	2.58883622	3.20248

MTTR (Mean-Time-To-Repair in hours) =	0.5	0.5	0.5
MTTF (Mean-Time-To-Failure in hours) =	1589	1761.193491	3039.98
System Availability (% of time) =	99.97	99.97161822	99.9836
Defects Repaired (R) per Month	10	10	10
MMF for K <= R	1	1	1
MMF for K > R	1.2	1.3	1.4

BM (business Model)	B-CFs	Size Impact	Complexity Impact (C)		
Model Type [PRODUCTS]	***CFs Model***	**FPs**	**Easy**	**Medium**	**Hard**
UM	H-CFs	15	2.20	2.23	2.00
OM	A-CFs	15	1.87	1.96	2.25
TM	**I-CFs**	20	1.87	1.91	2.50
CM	**E-CFs**	32	1.67	1.68	3.00
DM	T-CFs	60	2.47	2.58	3.25
SM	W-CFs	90	2.50	3.00	3.50
RM	R-CFs	150	3.00	4.00	3.75
PM	P-CFs	320	4.00	4.50	4.00
BM (business Model)	O-CFs	450	4.50	4.75	5.00
	Average	128	2.68	2.96	3.25
Complexity _C = [SUM (Complexity Factors) / 7] over the full code type					
CF Descriptors		**Action**	**CF Weight (Constraints)**		

CFD Description	Quality Criteria	Rating %	CF-Type	VeryLow	Low	Average	High	Very High
AA Action using HCD	Fully Responsive	18	H-CFs	1	2	3	4	5
AC Action using GSC	Verifiablity	16	A-CFs	1	2	3	4	5
AD Action using DPM	Effectiveness	14	I-CFs	1	2	3	4	5
AT Action using engineering	Applicability	12	E-CFs	1	2	3	4	5
AM Action using managemen	Understandability	12	T-CFs	1	2	3	4	5
AF Action using fast tracking	Usability	10	W-CFs	1	2	3	4	5
AS Action using CPM	Reliability	8	R-CFs	1	2	3	4	5
AP Action using PERT	Scope Limitation	6	P-CFs	1	2	3	4	5
AO Action using CMMI rating	Traceability	4	O-CFs	2	4	6	8	10
	TOTAL CFD%	100	TotalCFs	10	20	30	40	50

CFEM = (CFD_Rating X TotalCFs/1000) X Complexity_C

Note: Assignment Level

(1) For a Beginner Full-Time Staff, the complexity level is set to 1;
(2) For a Qualified Full-Time Staff, the complexity level is set to Easy;
(3) For an Advanced Full-Time Staff, the complexity level is set to Medium; and,
(4) For an Expert Full-Time Staff, the complexity level is set to Hard.

RESOURCES IMPACT

Skill(G) and Knowledge (J) Level

Skill (G)	Activity	Level
Rarely applied	1/year	1
Occasionally applied	1/month	2
Usually applied	**1/week**	**3**
Frequently applied	1/day	4
Continuously applied	1/hour	5

Knowledge (J)	Activity	Level
Understood	Test	1
Applied	Code	2
Analysed	**Model**	**3**
Synthesized	Spec's	4
Evaluated	Plan	5

Automation (A) and Infrastructure (I) Level

Automation (A)	Activity	Level
Scripting	Script	1
Standard Template	Script	2
COM/DCOM	tool	3
Design Pattern based	**tool**	**4**
Transformation based	tool	5

Infrastructure(I)	Activity	Level
Documentation	Text/Graphic	1
IDE	Code	2
Lower CASE	**Model**	**3**
Upper CASE	Requirement	4
Estimator	Plan	5

1. Workflow Team Distribution By Goals

Focus of Attention (FOA)	Element	Staff Loading Staff Weight(%	Assignment	CFs Model
Capability	Project (Mgmt & Admin)	13.320%	**PM**	**O-CFs**
Scope	System architecture	9.600%	**SA**	**I-CFs**
Process Improvement	Process and V&V (5%) Specification	13.320%	**CE**	**H-CFs**
Cost	Project Cost Control	6.640%	**SC**	**E-CFs**
Quality	Infrastructure (Pragmatics)	1.640%	**QM**	**T-CFs**
Workflow	Team Organization (People)	19.240%	**SM**	**W-CFs**
Development	Artifact Sets Production	8.320%	**SD**	**A-CFs**
Risk Management	Contingency Allocation	2.920%	**RM**	**R-CFs**
Productivity	Methodology (Practices)	25.000%	**SE**	**P-CFs**
	Total:	100.000%	**PM**	**B-CFs**

2. Technique Team Distribution by MDA Workflow (%)

MDA Team Distribution		**Scope Assignment**		
Phase	**Workflow**	**640FPs**	**1280FPs**	**6400FPs**
Inception	Object Model	11	11	11
Elaboration	Functional Model	7	7	7
	Dynamic Model	10	10	10
	Presentation Model	21	21	21
	Transformation	9	9	9
	Subtotal=	**58**	**58**	**58**
Construction	Change and V&V	30	28	28

Transition	Support & Documentation	6	7	7
	Project mgmt.	6	7	7
	Subtotal=	**42**	**42**	**42**
=		**Total 100**	**100**	**100**

3. Technique Effort distribution by MDA Workflow (%)

MDA Effort Distribution		**Scope Assignment**		
Phase	**Workflow**	**640FPs**	**1280FPs**	**6400FPs**
Inception	Object Model	11	11	11
Elaboration	Functional Model	7	7	7
	Dynamic Model	10	10	10
	Presentation Model	21	21	21
	Transformation	9	9	9
	Subtotal=	**58**	**58**	**58**
Construction	Change and V&V	30	28	28
Transition	Support & Documentation	6	7	7
	Project mgmt.	6	7	7
	Subtotal=	**42**	**42**	**42**
			Total = 100	**100 100**

4. Technique Schedule distribution by MDA Workflow (%)

MDA Schedule Distribution		**Scope Assignment**		
Phase	**Workflow**	**640FPs**	**1280FPs**	**6400FPs**
Inception	Object Model	11	11	11
Elaboration	Functional Model	7	7	7
	Dynamic Model	10	10	10
	Presentation Model	21	21	21
	Transformation	9	9	9
	Subtotal=	**58**	**58**	**58**
Construction	Change and V&V	30	28	28
Transition	Support & Documentation	6	7	7
	Project mgmt	6	7	7
	Subtotal=	**42**	**42**	**42**
	Total =	**100**	**100**	**100**

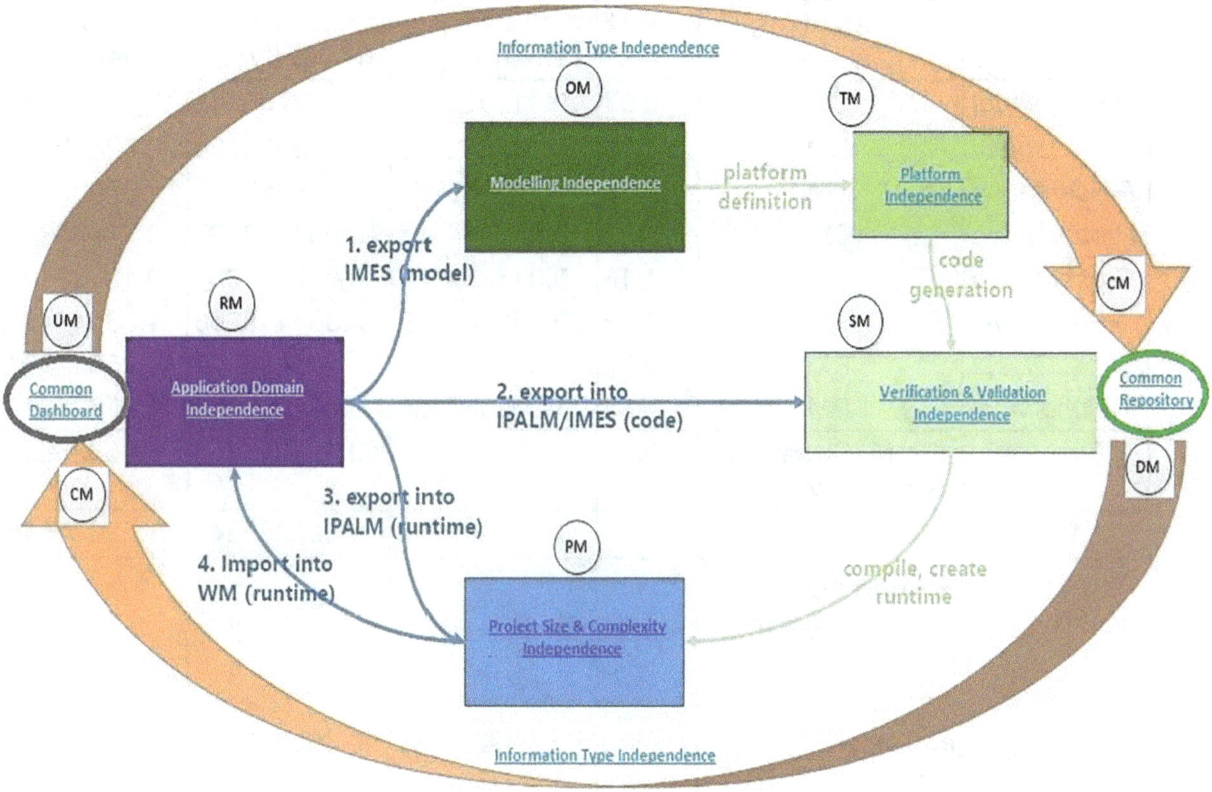

IPALM FRAMEWORK 8 SCHEMA MODEL

1. Activities Team Effort Distribution:

MDA Model Map	Iterations ROM		Scope Assignment		
	Activities	%	**640FPs (Small App.)**	**1280FPs (Avg. Sys.)**	**6400FPs (Dist. Sys.)**
Functional	UM	6.97	0.112993005	0.153790101	0.792189894
Object	OM	4.65	0.07532867	0.102526734	0.528126596
Presentation	TM	9.29	0.15065734	0.205053468	1.056253192
Presentation	CM	2.32	0.037664335	0.051263367	0.264063298
Presentation	DM	1.16	0.018832167	0.025631684	0.132031649
Functional	SM	17.42	0.282482512	0.384475253	1.980474735
Object	RM	2.24	0.036396523	0.0495378	0.255174712
Functional	PM	4.65	0.15065734	0.205053468	1.056253192
Functional	CMM (Capability Maturity Model)	9.29	0.15065734	0.205053468	1.056253192
	Sub-Total	**58.00**	**1.015669232**	**1.382385345**	**7.120820459**
	Requirements creep(per year)		17%	14.50%	10%
	Number of iterations	3	3	3	3
	Implement changes	7.00	0.340468135	0.463397083	2.387009847
	Verify changes	7.00	0.340468135	0.463397083	2.387009847
	Sub-Total	**42.00**	**0.680936269**	**0.926794166**	**4.774019694**
	Project Total	**100.00**	**1.621276832**	**2.206652777**	**11.36671356**

NOTE:

Tasks Effort Distribution	**%**	**Model Element**	**Average System**	**Distributed System**
Object Modelling Effort	16.02157	CRUD (U)	1	1
		Database (D)	1	1
Functional Modelling Effort	58.0782	Biz Algorithms (A)	4	20
Presentation Modelling Effort	22.02966	Report Control (R)	20	150
		User Menu (I)	15	50
		GUI Control (G)	25	50

: 128 FPs per month

(1) **<u>Project Sizes</u>: 640, 1280, 6400 FPs**

(2) **<u>Individual Production Rate</u>**

2. Activities Team Duration (per month) Distribution:

MDA Model Map	**Iterations ROM**		**Scope Assignment**		
	Activities	%	**640FPs (Small App.)**	**1280FPs (Avg. Sys.)**	**6400FPs (Dist. Sys.)**
Functional	UM	6.97	0.692309814	0.767152087	1.324172229
Object	OM	4.65	0.461539876	0.511434725	0.882781486
Presentation	TM	9.29	0.923079753	1.022869449	1.765562972
Presentation	CM	2.32	0.230769938	0.255717362	0.441390743
Presentation	DM	1.16	0.115384969	0.127858681	0.220695372
Functional	SM	17.42	1.730774536	1.917880218	3.310430573
Object	RM	2.24	0.223002034	0.247109708	0.426533171

Functional	PM	4.65	0.923079753	1.022869449	1.765562972
Functional	CMM (Capability Maturity Model)	9.29	0.923079753	1.022869449	1.765562972
	Sub-Total	**58.00**	**6.223020426**	**6.895761129**	**11.90269249**
	Requirements creep (per year)				
	Number of iterations	3			
	Implement changes (**IC**)	7.00	2.086053303	2.311566457	3.989967778
	Verify changes (**VC**)	7.00	2.086053303	2.311566457	3.989967778
	Sub-Total	**42.00**	**4.172106605**	**4.623132914**	**7.979935556**
	Project Total	**100.00**	**9.933587155**	**11.00745932**	**18.99984656**
	Tasks Hour Distribution	**%**	**Model Element**	**Average System**	**Distributed System**
	Object Modelling Effort	16.02157	CRUD (U)	1	1
			Database (D)	1	1
	Functional Modelling Effort	58.0782	Biz Algorithms (A)	4	20

NOTE:

Presentation Modelling Effort	22.02966

Report Control (R)	20	150
User Menu (I)	15	50
GUI Control (G)	25	50

(1) The number of hours per month is 160 hours

(2) The FSP multiplied by 160 resulted in the hour distribution table

3. Activities Team Size Estimation

MDA Model Map	**Iterations ROM**	**Scope Assignment**			
	Activities	**Distribution (**	**%640FPs Small App.)**	**1280FPs (Avg.Sys.)**	**6400FPs (Large Sys)**
Functional	UM	6.97	0.011374844	0.013971444	0.041694542
Object	OM	4.65	0.007583229	0.009314296	0.027796361
Presentation	TM	9.29	0.015166459	0.018628592	0.055592722
Presentation	CM	2.32	0.003791615	0.004657148	0.013898181
Presentation	DM	1.16	0.001895807	0.002328574	0.00694909
Functional	SM	17.42	0.02843711	0.03492861	0.104236354
Object	RM	2.24	0.003663986	0.004500385	0.013430356
Functional	PM	4.65	0.015166459	0.018628592	0.055592722

Functional	CMM (Capability Maturity Model)	9.29	0.015166459	0.018628592	0.055592722
	Sub-Total	**58.00**	**0.102245968**	**0.125586232**	**0.374783051**
	Requirements creep/year		17%	14.50%	10%
	Number of iterations	3	3	3	3
	Implement changes (**IC**)	7.00	0.03427444	0.04209846	0.125633112
	Verify changes (**VC**)	7.00	0.03427444	0.04209846	0.125633112
	Sub-Total	**42.00**	**0.06854888**	**0.08419692**	**0.251266224**
	Project Total	**100.00**	0.163211618	0.200468856	0.598252913
	Tasks FSP Distribution	**%**	**Model Element**	**Average/System**	**LargeSystem**
	Object Modelling Effort	16.02157197	CRUD (U)	1	1
			Database (D)	1	1
	Functional Modelling Effort	58.07819838	Biz Algorithms (A)	4	20
	Presentation Modelling Effort	22.02966145	Report	20	150
			Control (R)	15	50

Large Size:	Log10	10^
1. Log (Effort) =	1.055635	11.36671
2. Log (Duration) =	1.27875	18.99985
3. Log (TeamSize) =	-0.22312	0.598253
4. Log (Prod.) =	2.750545	563.0475

1	-0.30103
2	0
3	0.30103
4	0.477121
5	0.60206
6	0.69897

	User Menu (I)		
	GUI Control (G)	25	5 0

1	1.491362
2	1.491362
3	1.792392
4	2.792392
5	3.093422
6	3.394452
7	3.871573

Medium Size:	Log10	10^
1. Log (Effort) =	0.343734	2.206653
2. Log (Duration) =	1.041687	11.00746

		3. Log (TeamSize) =	-0.69795	0.200469
1.44915	-1.36224	4. Log (Prod.) =	2.462446	290.032

Project Size Calculation

Scope Assignment (SA)

EMF = -1.58302 -

DMF = 0.779238

Interm Size:	Log10	10^
1. Log (Effort) =	0.209857	1.621277
2. Log (Duration) =	0.997106	9.933587
3. Log (TeamSize) =	-0.78725	0.163212
4. Log (Prod.) =	2.596323	394.7506

SA	Size Multiplier (PT)					
Log10	-0.30103	0	0.30103	0.477121	0.60206	0.69897
1.50515	1.20412	1.50515	1.80618	1.982271	2.10721	2.20412
1.50515	1.20412	1.50515	1.80618	1.982271	2.10721	2.20412
1.80618	1.50515	1.80618	2.10721	2.283301	2.40824	2.50515
2.80618	2.50515	**2.80618**	2.80618	2.982271	3.10721	3.20412
3.10721	2.80618	**2.80618**	3.40824	3.584331	3.70927	**3.80618**
3.40824	3.10721	3.40824	3.70927	3.885361	4.0103	4.10721
3.885361	3.584331	3.885361	4.186391	4.362482	4.487421	4.584331

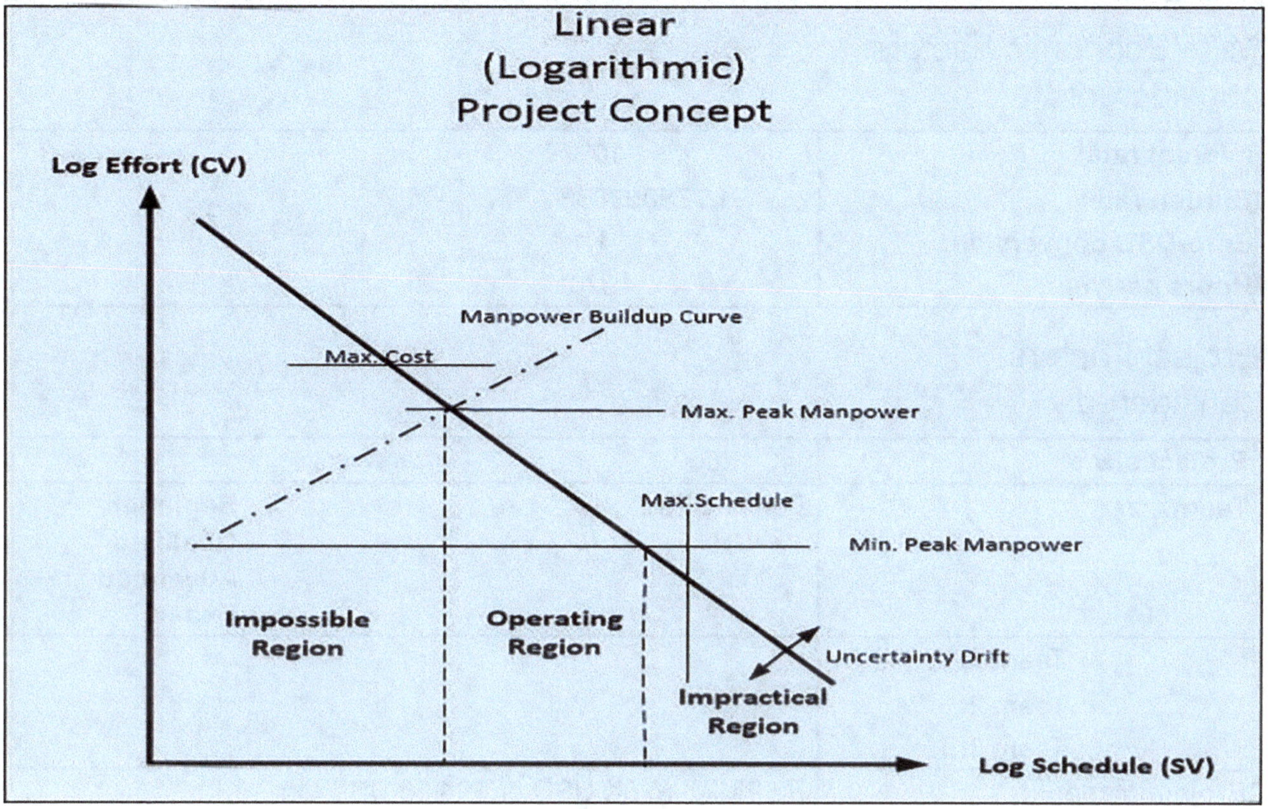
Linear
(Logarithmic)
Project Concept
Log Effort (CV)
Manpower Buildup Curve
Max. Cost
Max. Peak Manpower
Max.Schedule
Min. Peak Manpower
Impossible
Region
Operating
Region
Uncertainty Drift
Impractical
Region
Log Schedule (SV)

MDA Economic Factors considered:

Interest rate:	10%
Burden rate:	1.778093883
Euro-USD conversion:	1.1
Hours per year:	1920

Project Factors considered:

Project sizes:	640-12800					
Team size:	2 to 4 FSPs				**Beginner Qualified Advanced Expert**	
Team 1:		1	1			
Team 2:			1	1		
Team 3:		1	1	1		1
Project Manager:	1/2 PM @ $70K USD or $94.33 USD per hour (loaded)					
Project duration (months)	**by Project size 00**	**640**	**1280 64**		**12800**	
Team 1:	2.66					
Team 2:		1.6	3.2			
Team 3:			12			24
Loaded hourly salary:						
Beginner FSP:	$89.84					
Qualified FSP:	$107.82					

Advanced FSP:	$125.78
Expert FSP or PM:	$157.76
License cost (per month) **Seat** **License:** **Modeller:**	 $1,875 $3250 USD (5 year plan) $87.24 per month @ 10%

Average Project Size Calculations Factors:

Effort = Capability1 X EMF X (GSC X (SMF X MMF X AMF)) Exponent (Process1)		
	Capability1 =	2.5 (depends on reliability, complexity, root-cause, coverage)
	Process1 =	0.73 (depends on process improvement)
Example:	SMF =	6400
	EMF =	(default value) 1
	Effort =	1432.156
	EMF =	(IMES value) 30
	Effort =	47.73854
Duration = Capability2 X DMF X (Effort) Exponent (Process2)		
	Capability2 =	2.5 (depends on scope, time, cost, risk and quality)
	Process2 =	0.366 (depends on capability maturity improvement)
Example:	SMF =	6400
	DMF =	(default value) 1
	Duration =	2.5 X (1440) Exp (0.366) = 36
	DMF =	(MDA value) 3
	Duration =	12

NOTE: 1. Qualified Staff: Can handle one Key Process Area (Role) at a time competently
2. Advanced Staff: Can handle three to four Key Process Area (Role) at a time competently
3. Expert Staff: Can hand 4 to six Key Process Area (Role) at a time competently
4. Management Roles: PM, QM, RM, SM, CM
5. Technical Roles: CE, SE, SA, SD, SI, PC, QC, SC
6. Beginner Staff: Trained personnel assigned on a first project

Team 1 and 640 FPs		
OpsPro Scenario #1:	***Total cost:*** $127,670	
	Seat License cost:	$9,975.00
	Beginner FSP cost:	$38,236
	Qualified FSP cost:	$45,888
	PM at 1/2 time:	$33,571.33
Team 2 and 640 FPs		
OpsPro Scenario #2:	***Total cost:*** $85,995	
	Seat License cost:	$6,000
	Qualified FSP cost:	$27,602
	Advanced FSP cost:	$32,200
	PM at 1/2 time:	$20,193.28
Team 2 and 1280 FPs		
OpsPro Scenario #3:	***Total cost:*** $171,990	
	Seat License cost:	$12,000
	Qualified FSP cost:	$55,204
	Advanced FSP cost:	$64,399
	PM at 1/2 time:	$40,386.56

Average cost per function point:

Scope Assignment	640	1280	6400	12800
Scenario #1	$199.49			
Scenario #2	$134.37			
Scenario #3		$134.37		
Scenario #4			$182.41	
Scenario #5				$206.08

	Team 2 and 6400 FPs		
OpsPro Scenario #4:	***Total cost:***	$1,167,447	
		Seat License cost:	$90,000
		Modeler cost:	$2,094
		Beginner FSP cost:	$172,493
		Qualified FSP cost:	$207,014
		Advanced FSP cost:	$241,498
		Expert FSP cost:	$302,899
		PM at 1/2 time:	$151,449.60
	Team 2 and 12800 FPs		
OpsPro Scenario #5:	***Total cost:***	$2,637,794	
		Seat License cost:	$180,000
		Modeler cost:	$4,188
		Beginner FSP cost:	$344,986
		Qualified FSP cost:	$414,029
		Advanced FSP cost:	$482,995
		Expert FSP cost:	$605,798
		PM at Full time:	$605,798.40

Large Project Scenario:

(Project size: 6200 FPs approximately)

Average cost per function point: $220.34

Team Size = Effort/Duration		
Example:	Competitor	39.78211978
	MDA Provider	3.978211978

Productivity =	**Size/Duration/FSP**	
Example:	Competitor	4.468785946
	MDA Provider	134.0635784

WBS Level	WBS Aspects	WBS Estimates	Factors
Business Model (Baldrige Framework)	WBS Elements PM Estimator Performance Factor Scope Assignment Factor	Management Proposal Technical Proposal Financial Proposal Project Charter	5 Levels EVS BPF GSC
Project Model (Level 5) Project Scope Assignment	Cosysmo based Economics Project Sizes based on GSC Project Effort based on HCD Project Schedule based on DPM	Effort Estimation Time Estimation Size Estimation Team Estimation	EEF EPML CFEM OPA
Process Model (Level 4) (Processes - Metrics) Process Scope Assignment	PMBOK Process Model	Integration Management Quality Management Risk Management Cost Management Scope Management Schedule Management Production Management Resource Management Comm Management	OSL TSL RSL ESL PSL WSL ASL HSL ISL

		Integ_CMF_Control	
Activity Model (Level 3)	Open Process Framework Model	Quality_QF_Control	EMF
(Activities - Calibration Factors)	Five Level WBS	Risk_RF_Control	SMF
	Process Differentiator	Cost_EF_Control	MMF
Activity Scope Assignment		Scope_PF_Control	AMF
		Schedule_WF_Control Production_AF_Control Resource_CF_Control Comm_IF_Control	DMF
	Organization Impact	OSL_OF	OF
Task Model (Level 2)	Quality Impact	TSL_TF	TF
(Tasks Measures)	Risk Impact	RSL_RF	RF
	Efficiency Impact	ESL_EF	EF
Task Scope Assignment	Productivity Impact	PSL_PF	PF
	Workload Impact	WSL_WF	WF
	Production Impact	ASL_AF	AF
	Human-Centered Design Impact	HSL_HF	HF
	Interaction Impact	ISL_IF	IF
	Measurement		EFP
Product Level (Level 1)	Workflow	ModelSchedule	P
(Techniques - Scaling Factors)	Inception Plan	ModellingEffort	P1
	Elaboration Plan	ModellingTeam	P2
Technique Scope Assignment	Construction Plan		C1
	Transition Plan Service Level Agreement		C2

Risks Constraints (EPML) Project GSC Sizing(SMF)Task Specification (PRODUCTS)

PFV Productivity Factor Variance F Forms
OFV Capability Factor Variance Reports
WFV Workflow Factor Variance Algorithms
EFV Efficiency Factor Variance Classes
RFV Risk Factor Variance T Tables
HFV HCD PI Factor Variance Agents
AFV Artifact Factor Variance L Links
BFV Baldrige Factor Variance Services
IFV Interaction Factor Variance
TFV Total Quality Factor Variance

PM Productivity Model
RRM Requirements and Risk Model
AOM Open Architecture Model
CDM Data Tracking Model
UM Usability Model
ACM Cost Data Model
TM Transaction Model
SSM Solution Workflow Model

Knowledge Analysis (CFEM)

SE Software Engineer
RM Risk Management
SD System Developer
QM Quality Management
CE Cognitive Engineer
SC System Cost Control
SA System Architect
SM System Manager

Skills Analysis (OPA)

ANTLR Another Tool for Language Recognition

DI Decision Intelligence

DPM Dynamic Progress Method

Workflow Analysis (DMF)

PSL= Productivity Control Staff loading
OSL= Organization Control Staff Loading
WSL= Workload Control Staff Loading
ESL= Efficiency Control Staff Loading
RSL= Risk Control Staff Loading
HSL= HCD Control Staff Loading

Scope Assignment (EMF)

PCF Productivity CF
OCF Organization CF
WCF Workflow CF
ECF Efficiency CF
RCF Risk CF
HCF Human-Centered Design CF

	ASL= Artifact Production Staff Loading	**ACF** Artifact Production CF
HCD Human Centered Design	**BSL=** Project Scope Assignment	**BCF** Business Modeling CF
	ISL= Interaction Control Staff Loading	**ICF** Interaction CF
JADE Joint Active Design Elicitation	**TSL=** Total Quality Control Staff Loading	**TCF** Total Quality CF
	Action Specification (DPM)	**Quality Considerations (MTBF))**
MDA Model Driven Architecture	**AA** Action using automation with MDE	**CPLX** Complexity
	AC Action using CPM	**IF** interface Mismatch
SEEM Systems Engineering Economics Model	**AD** Action using DPM	**FEA** Feature Missing
	AT Action using technical assignment	**COV** Coverage
TM Tree Methodology	**AM** Action using management assignment	**REL** Reliability
	AF Action using fast tracking assignment	**RC** Root-Cause
YAWL Yet Another Workflow Language	**AS** Action using sequential assignment	**PI** Process Improvement
	AP Action using PERT	**OH** Overhead assignment
PAMPA Project Attribute Monitoring and Predicting Agent	**AO** Action using CMMI rating	**DC** Direct Cost assignment
PICK Pairwise Independent Combinational KPU		

Pessimistic Scenario

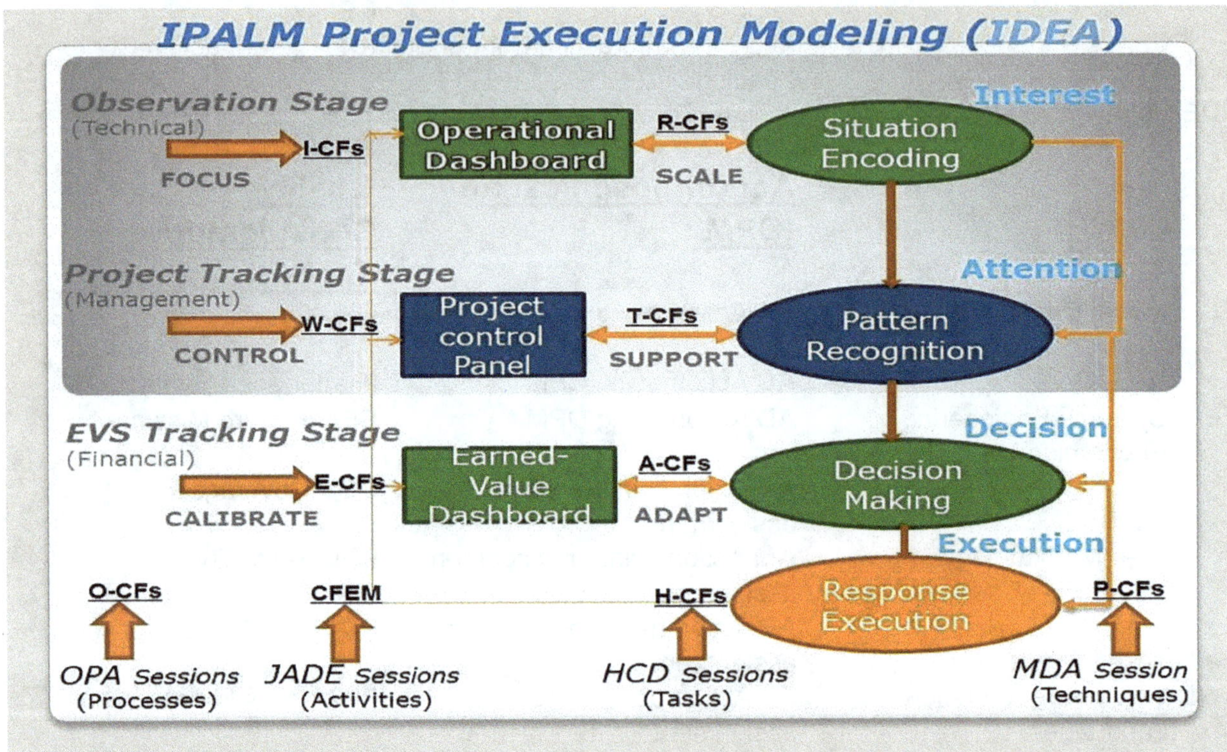

Software Engineering Economic Model (SEEM) Process

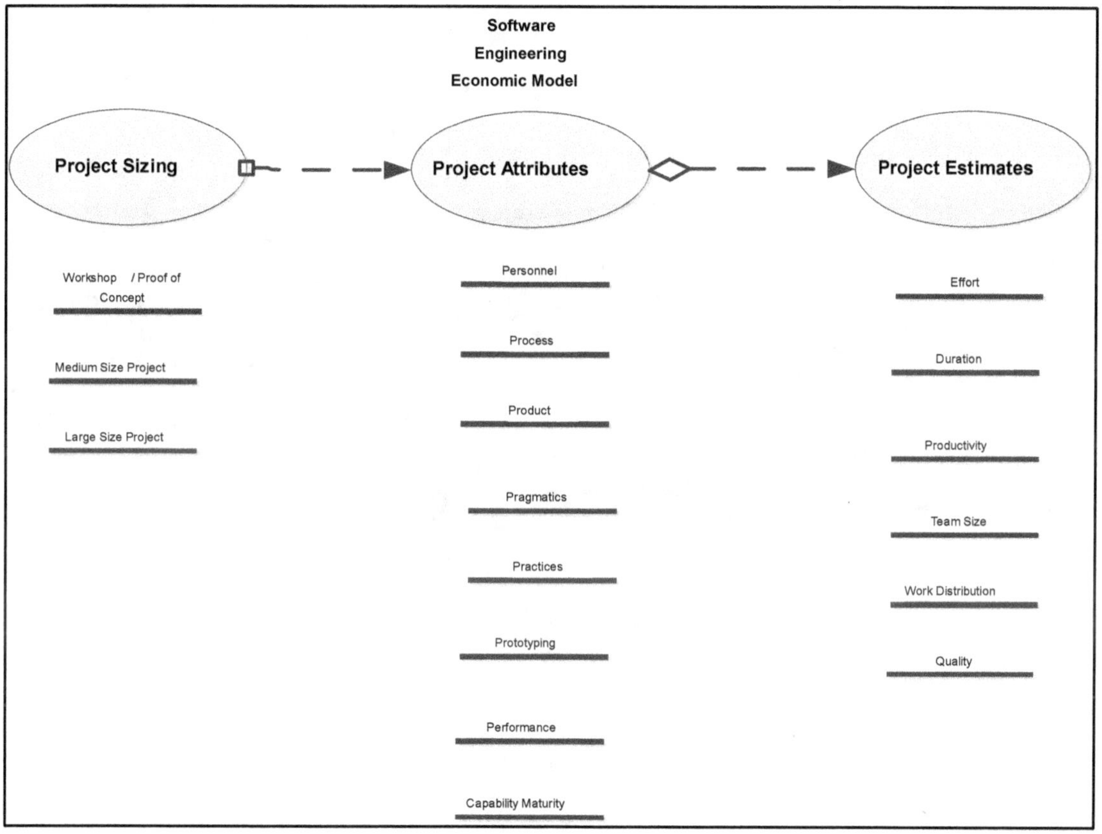

Linear Project Concept

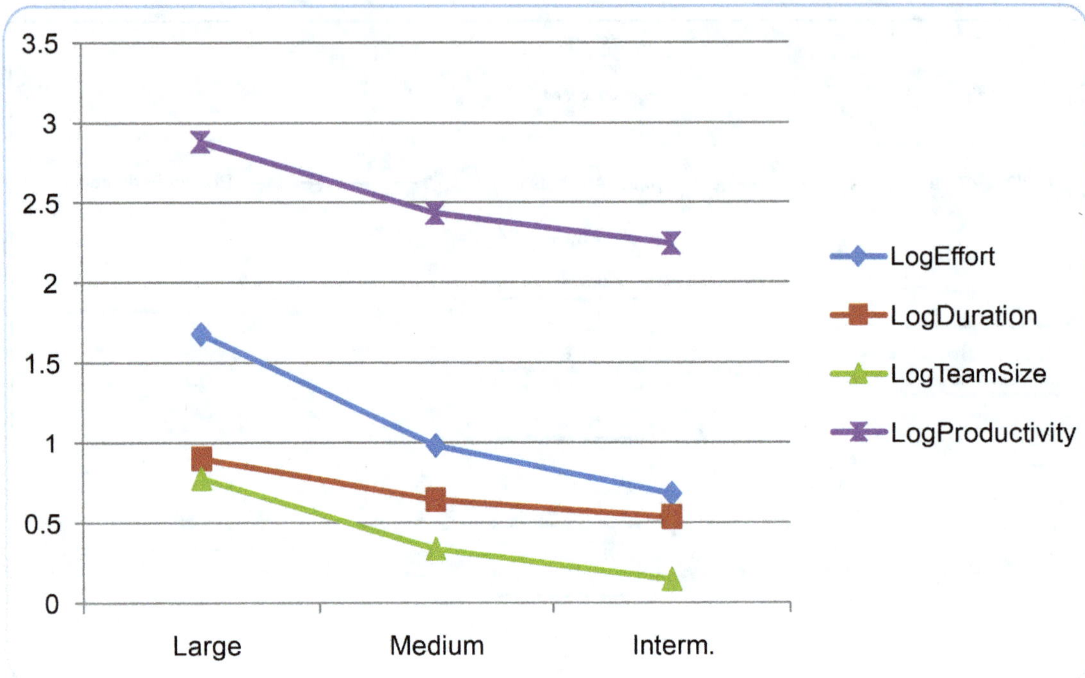

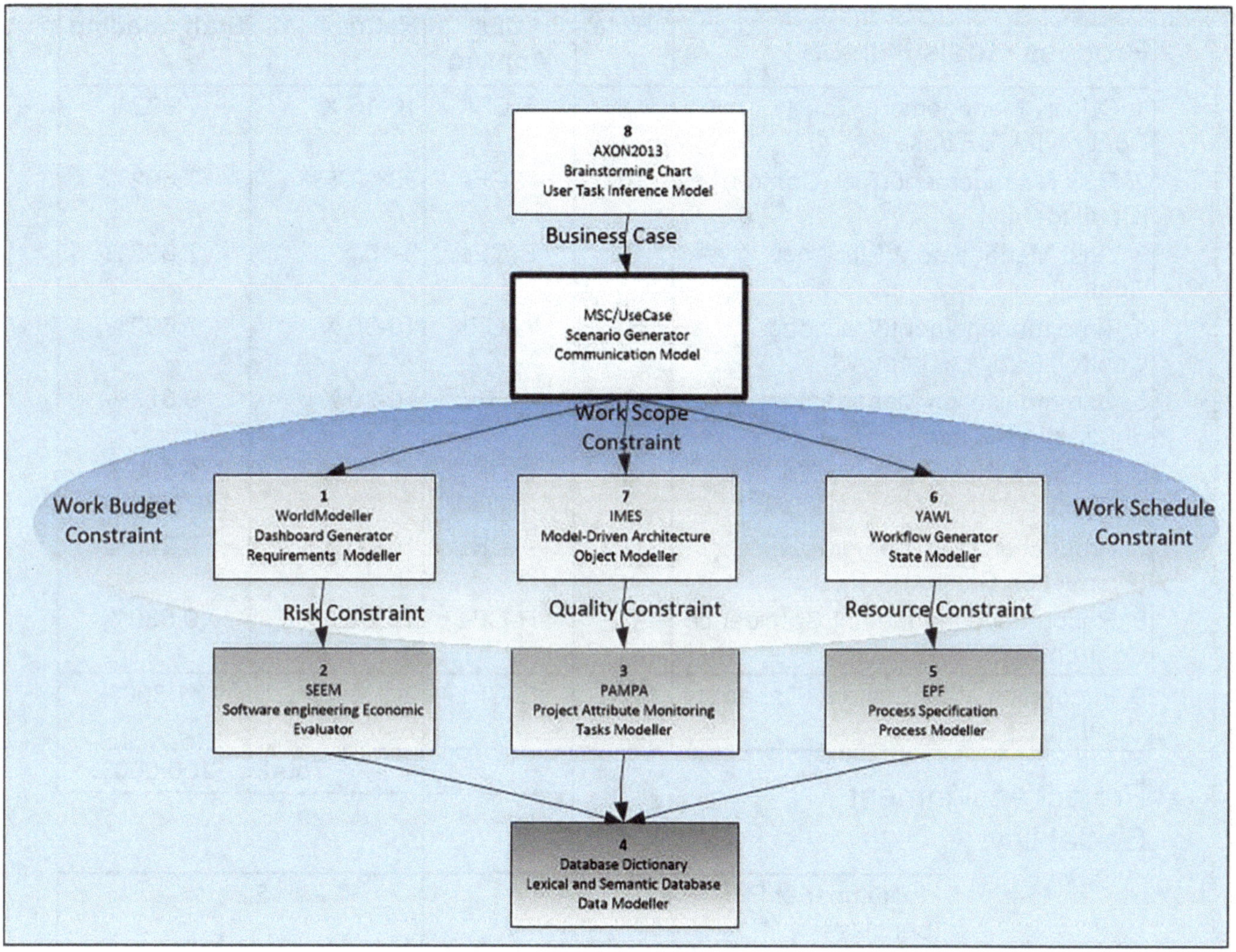
8
AXON2013
Brainstorming Chart
User Task Inference Model
Business Case
MSC/UseCase
Scenario Generator
Communication Model
Work Scope
Constraint
Work Budget
Constraint
1
WorldModeller
Dashboard Generator
Requirements Modeller
7
IMES
Model-Driven Architecture
Object Modeller
6
YAWL
Workflow Generator
State Modeller
Work Schedule
Constraint
Risk Constraint
Quality Constraint
Resource Constraint
2
SEEM
Software engineering Economic
Evaluator
3
PAMPA
Project Attribute Monitoring
Tasks Modeller
5
EPF
Process Specification
Process Modeller
4
Database Dictionary
Lexical and Semantic Database
Data Modeller

Process Goals Pursued	Role	CFs Applied	Range	Staff Loading
1. Quality Management(Quality Control) [MTBF based]	QM	T-CFs	10-15 X	7.692%
2. Risk Management (Risk Control) [Contingency]	RM	R-CFs	90%-95%	7.692%
3. Cost Management(Efficiency Control)	SC	E-CFs	5-10 X	7.692%
4. Time management(Workload Control) [Process Improv.]	SM	W-CFs	10-30 X	7.692%
5. Communication Management (Interaction Control)	SA	I-CFs	10-20 X	9.672%
6. Scope Management (Productivity Control)	SE	P-CFs	10-30 X	9.200%
7. Production Management (Production Control)	SD	A-CFs	10-30 X	9.200%
8. Resource Management(Confidence Control)	CE	H-CFs	10%-25%	9.560%
9. Integration Management (Capability Control)	PM	O-CFs	2-3 X	31.600%
			Total:	100.000%

Project Assignment Scalability:	B-CFs
1. Number of FPs per class	32
2. FSP Throughput per month	128
3. Number of timeboxes (TB) per month	2

	Type	Size (FPs)	Staff(Max)	AvgDuration	MaxCost ($US)
	4. Component size assigment in FPs(1 TB)			64	
	5. Project Scope Assignment (in FPs)			640, 1280, 6400, 12800	
Applicable Projects	**Type**	**Size (FPs)**	**Staff(Max)**	**AvgDuration**	**MaxCost ($US)**
1. Workshop	Demo	32-64	1 FSPs	1-2 weeks	$14,080.00
2. Small Application	Small	320-640	2 FSPs	5-10 weeks	$140,800.00
3. Average business App.	Medium	1280-2560	5 FSPs	2-4 months	$563,200.00
4. Distr. Enterprise App.	Large	3840-7680	5 FSPs	6-12 months	$1,689,600.00

Note: (1) A **Timebox** represents a two-week effort or 64 FPs at $220/FP

(2) By applying a **Group Elicitation Method**, 5 **Timeboxes** can be assigned independently (320 FPs)

Overhead Ratio Goals Pursued:

1. Development %: SA + SE + CE + SD = 37.74%
2. Overhead %: PM + QM + SM + RM + SC = 62.37%
3. Overhead Ratio: Overhead/Development 1.652395
4. Charging Rate: Development+Overhead 2.652395

PMBOK ID	Class	Description	Focus	Method	Dashboard	
1	CostMgmt	Cost Management	Cost Control	EarnedValueMethod	IterationDashboard	[2]
2	OrgMgmt	Resource Management	Resource Control	CognitiveFunctionMethod	CFAdashboard	[5]
3	CommMgmt	Communication Control	Interaction Control	AgileDesignMethod	GEMdashboard	[3]
4	QualityMgmt	Quality Management	Quality Control	CombinationalMethod	SLAdashboard	[4]
5	ScopeMgmt	Scope Management	Productivity Control	ModelDrivenMethod	ModelDashboard	[7]
6	IntegrationMgmt	Integration Management	Integration Control	DecisionEngMethod	CMMIdashboard	[1]
7	TimeMgmt	Time Management	Schedule Control	DynamicProgressMethod	PIdashboard	[6]
8	RiskMgmt	Risk Management	Risk Control	GenericTreeMethod	RiskDashboard	[8]

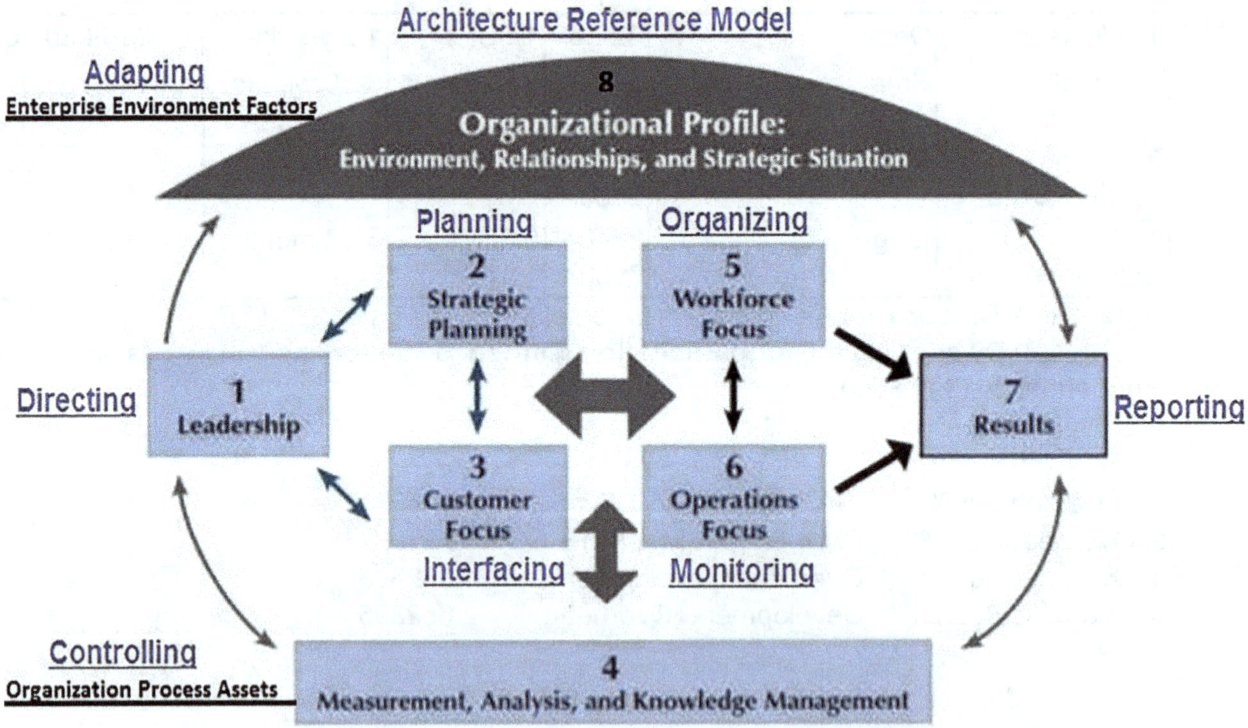

Best Practices embedded with project attributes

Attributes (Focus of Attention)	***Key Practices Description***	***8 Schema Model used*** **[PRODUCTS]**	***Staff Loading***
Confidence Control	Human-Centered Design Control	Usability and EfficiencyModel [UM]	HSL/HF
Total Quality Control	Data Tracking control	Data Tracking Quality Model [DM]	TSL/TF
Efficiency Control	Cost tracking and control	Cost Data Model [CM]	ESL/EF
Workload Control	Workload tracking and control	Solution Workflow Model [SM]	WSL/WF
Interaction Control	Communication interaction control	Open Architecture Model [OM]	ISL/IF
Risk Control	Risk control	Risks Model [RM]	RSL/RF
Productivity Control	Productivity estimation and control	Productivity Model [PM]	PSL/PF
Production Control	Production estimation and control	Transaction Model [TM]	ASL/AF
Organization Control	Capability maturity assessment	Capability Maturity Model [CMM]	OSL/OF
Performance Control	Baldrige Performance assessment	Badrige Performance Model [BM]	BSL/BF

Model	**Actor**	**Goals**	**Focus of Attention**	**Staff Loading**
UM	CE [DC]	Resource Control	Scalability and diversity impact analysis with process reuse	HCD SL
DM	QM [OH]	Quality Control	Issues and Actions tracking and analysis	Total Quality SL
CM	SC [OH]	cost Control	Artifact Set Cost tracking and analysis	Efficiency SL
SM	SM [OH]	Schedule Control	Goal-driven workflow analysis for effort control	Workflow SL
OM	SA [DC]	Comm. Control	Correct or change the economic model using SMF/DMF/EMF	Interaction SL

RM	RM [OH]	Risk Control	Risk Mitigation Analysis	Risk SL
PM	SE [DC]	Scope Control	Team/Individual productivity analysis using SCRUM and PI	Productivity SL
TM	SD [DC]	Production Control	Artifact Set Generation	Artifact SL
CMM	PM [OH]	Performance Control	Project goals tracking and analysis	Organization SL

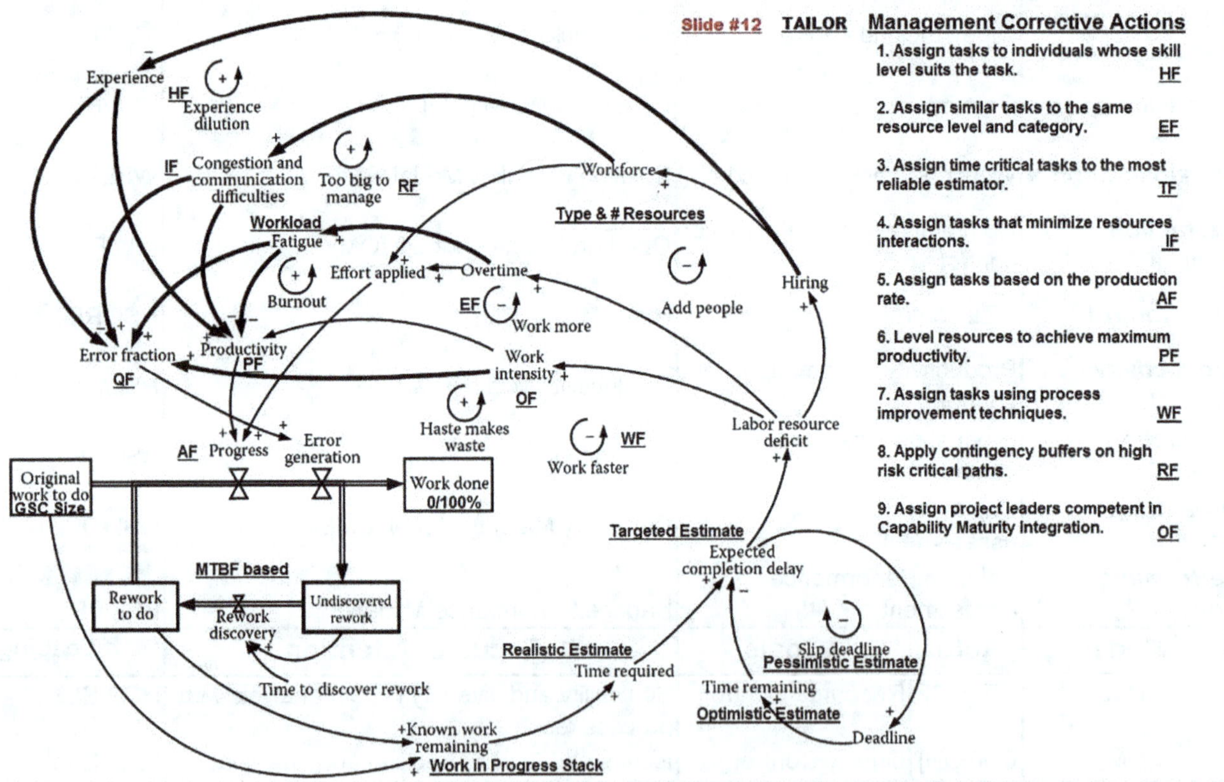

SEEM Task Loading Scenarios

Activity Type	**Tasks Staff Loading Formula**											**Total**
ArtifactSet Factor (Production Control) Production Mgmt	**ASL =**	**Forms +** 18%	**Reports +** 15%	**Algor. +** 20%	**Classes +** 6%	**Tables +** 23%	**Agents +** 7%	**Links +** 6%	**Services** 5%			100 %
Productivity Factor (Productivity Control) Productivity Mgmt	**PSL =**	**PM +** 6%	**RM +** 15%	**OM +** 20%	**DM +** 6%	**UM +** 28%	**CM +** 7%	**TM +** 6%	**SM +** 6%	**BM** 6%		100 %
Workflow Factor (Schedule Control) Time Mgmt	**WSL =**	**PM +** 10%	**SM +** 10%	**SC +** 5%	**SA +** 25%	**SE +** 10%	**RM +** 5%	**CE +** 10%	**QM +** 10%	**SD** 15 %		100 %
Interaction Factor (Project Control) Integration Mgmt	**ISL=**	**P_CF +** 7%	**O_CF +** 13%	**W_CF +** 12%	**E_CF +** 26%	**R_CF +** 27%	**H_CF +** 10%	**A_CF** 5%	**B_CF** 5%	**I_CF** 5%	**T_CF** 5%	100 %
Org. Capability Factor	**OSL =**	**PF +**	**OMF +**	**WF +**	**EF +**	**RF +**	**HF +**	**AF +**	**BF**	**IF**	**TQF**	

Capability Control) Project Mgmt		12%	7%	13%	26%	14%	10%	8%	10%	10 %	10%	100 %
Risk Variance Factor (Risk Control) Risk Mgmt	**RSL =**	**PF_V +** 12%	**OF_V +** 7%	**WF_V +** 13%	**EF_V +** 26%	**RF_V +** 14%	**HF_V +** 10%	**AF_V +** 8%	**BF_V** 10%	**IF_V** 10 %	**TF_V** 10%	100 %
Total Quality Factor (Quality Control) Quality Mgmt	**TSL =**	**CPLX +** 11%	**IF +** 25%	**FEA +** 15%	**COV +** 7%	**REL +** 12%	**Root-Cause** 10%	**PI** 10%	**OH** 5%	**DC** 5%		100 %
Cost Factor (Cost Control) Cost Mgmt	**ESL =**	**AA +** 5%	**AC +** 10%	**AD +** 15%	**AT +** 20%	**AM +** 15%	**AF +** 10%	**AS +** 10%	**AP +** 10%	**AO** 5%		100 %
HCD Proficiency Factor (Confidence Control) Resource Mgmt	**HSL =**	**PAMPA +** 10%	**JADE +** 10%	**PICK +** 10%	**MDA +** 10%	**HCD +** 10%	**ANTLR +** 10%	**SEEM +** 10%	**YACC +** 10%	**DPM +** 10 %	**DI** 10%	100 %
Baldrige Perf. Factor	**BSL =**	**Lever +**	**External +**	**Interm +**	**Outcome**							

(BPF Control) Decision Intelligenc e		12%	26%	30%	32%							100 %

<u>NOTE:</u> Ratio of time spent on an activity related to a goal associated with a performance factor

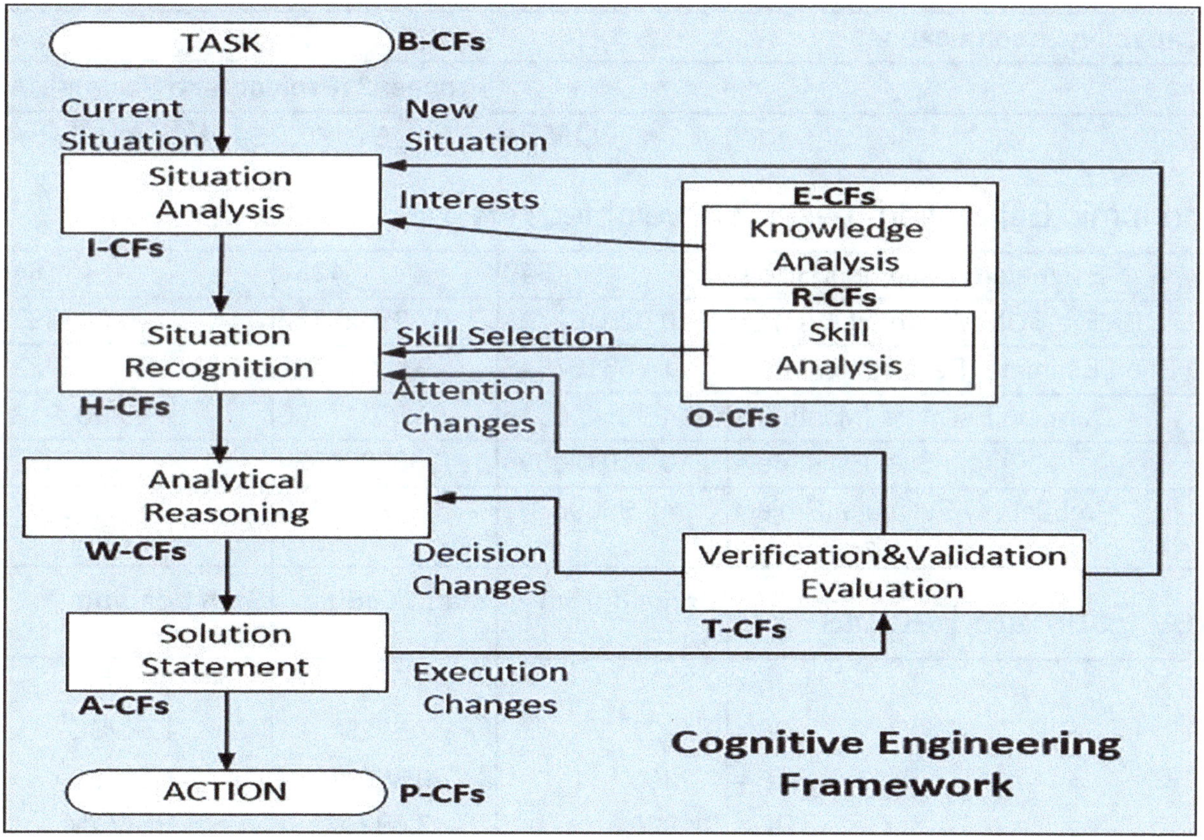

Cognitive Engineering Framework

SEEM Economic Analysis Formula

Effort = C1 X EMF X (GSC X (SMF +MMF +AMF+IMF)) Exponent (P1)	
Capability1 (management) =	1.559
Process1(Team Productivity) =	0.91
Duration = C2 X DMF X (Effort) Exponent (P2)	
Capability2(technical) =	0.941
Process2 (Project Size Scale)=	0.79

DMF= 6.015037594 **WF =** DMF/10

Economic Estimation (based on weighted AVG)

Estimated Adjustment Size =	**640**	**1280**	**6400**
EMF = SUM(Weighted AVG) =	0.026102721	0.035527332	0.04339738
Effort Estimate (Person-Month) =	14.56167648	19.81929502	35.0132289
Duration Estimate (Months) =	46.95400516	59.90117406	93.90291269
Team Size Estimate =	0.310126398	0.330866554	0.372866271
Productivity Estimate (Project Size/Effort) =	43.95098332	32.29176413	182.7880547
Key Estimate Factors	**Derived from SL**	**Staff Loading %**	**Staff Loading Formula**
IF =	0.2418	9.672%	ISL/SA
EF =	0.1923	7.692%	ESL/SC
HF =	0.2390	9.560%	HSL/CE
RF =	0.1923	7.692%	RSL/RM
TF =	0.1923	7.692%	TSL/QM

PF =	0.2300	9.200%	PSL/SE
WF=	0.1923	7.692%	WSL/SM
AF =	0.2300	9.200%	ASL/SD
OF =	0.7900	31.600%	OSL/PM
Total	2.5000	100.000%	

Software Engineering Economic Model (SEEMformula 2016)

$$GSC = (ProductType * \text{Class Size} * Project\ Scope)^{P}$$

$$Effort = C_1 * EMF * (GSC * (SMF * AMF * MMF))^{P_1}$$

$$Duration = C_2 * DMF * (Effort)^{P_2}$$

$$Productivity = Size / Effort$$

$$OPA = SMF * AMF * MMF$$

$$EEF = EMF / DMF$$

Where:	**Economic Factors**
GSC is the Generic System Components	GSC
C_2 is the Engineering Capability (Direct Charging Factor)	DC
C_1 is the Management Capability (Overhead Factor)	OH
SMF is the System Multiplier Factor (Interaction Factor)	IF
P is the Lifecycle Model Factor (Efficiency Factor)	EF
P_2 is the Management Capability (Capability Maturity Factor)	CMF
P_1 is the Process Improvement Factor (Productivity Factor)	PF
EMF is the Effort Multiplier Factor (Risk Factor)	RF
DMF is the Duration Multiplier Factor (Workflow Factor)	WF
MMF is the Maintenance Multiplier Factor (Quality Factor)	QF
AMF is the Adaptation Multiplier (Legacy) Factor	AF
CFEM is the CF Multiplier Factor (Confidence Factor)	CF

Generic System Component Formulation: Project sizing is based on four parameters (B-CFs): S, T, and P

1. Project Scope (S)

		Assignment Scope (S)	***Scale Adj.***	***Component Size***	**Assignment**
		Class Production Rate(**C**)	32	1 Class/week	1 FSP
	1	Very Small Size System	2	2 Classes	1 FSP
	2	Small Size System	4	4 Classes	1 FSP
	3	Average Size System	20	20 Classes	5 FSPs
	4	Standard Size System	40	40 Classes	10 FSPs
	5	Large Size System	80	80 Classes	20 FSPs
	6	Very Large Size System	160	160 Classes	40 FSPs

Note: One Iteration is equivalent to one Timebox for the delivery of one component and 128 FPs/Month/FSP

2. Product Type (T)

	Model	***CFs Model***	***Component Scope (T) [8-Schema]***	***Size Mult.***	***Complexity Level***	**CMMI Level**
	UM	H-CFs	Usability and Efficiency Model	1.000	0.20	2
	OM	A-CFs	Open Architecture Model	1.500	0.30	2
	TM	**I-CFs**	**Transaction Model (JADE)**	**2.000**	**0.40**	3
	CM	**E-CFs**	**Cost Data Model (SEEM)**	**2.500**	**0.50**	3
	DM	T-CFs	Data Tracking Quality Model (PAMPA)	3.000	0.60	4

	SM	W-CFs	Solution Workflow Model	3.500	0.70	4
	RM	R-CFs	Requirements and Risks Model	4.000	0.80	5
	PM	P-CFs	Productivity Model	4.500	0.90	5
	CMM	O-CFs	Capability Maturity Model	5.000	1.00	5

Note: The Class of Service (CLOS) efficiency distribution follows a Rayleigh cumulative distribution

3. SEPA	**newor k**	**Aspect Number**	**Methodology**	**Resources (FSP)**	**SA (Individual)**	**Production Rate**	**P Scale Factor**
Capabilities	CMF	*1.035736657*	IPALM	5	256	256.00	1.00
Processes	SEF	8	OO-Method	5	256	128.00	1.02
Workflows	PDF	10	Agile-XP	3	100	40.00	1.03
Best Practices	CEF	8	Agile-UP	5	100	20.00	1.05
Timeboxes	ETF	2	Agile - DSDM	12	120	12.00	1.10
Interaction Boxes	ITF	1	Agile - ASD	8	300	30.00	1.10
ServiceChargeOrder	ATF	1	Agile - FDD	10	240	12.00	1.20
GSC Factor = (C * S * T) Exponent P Based			Component	20	250	10.00	1.25

For Example:

GSC = 12800.00 using a large ERP system

GSC = 1280.00 using a average size ERP system

Economic Modifiers (Part 1)						
KEF Category	**Cost Driver**	**Range (1 default)**	**Stage Modifier(ES=1)**	**Total Impact**	**SL Weight**	**Weighted AVG**
PF Product - Scope Control	Transformation	2.894	0	16.50313629	0.092	1.518288539
	RDBMS design	2.391				8.56%
	MDA design	2.385				
IF Interaction - Interaction Control	Analyst capability	4.120	1	16.582176	0.09672	1.603828063
	Application Experience	1.560				9.04%
	Programmer capability	2.580				
	HOL Experience	1.380				
RF Project - Risk Control	Methodology	2.572	1	16.55273357	0.07692	1.273236266
	Automation	2.562				7.18%
	Infrastructure	2.512				
HF People - Work scope Proficiency	Analyst capability	1.623	1	16.54786393	0.0956	1.581975792
	Application Experience	1.530				8.92%
	Programmer capability	4.110				

Control	HOL Experience SQL experience	1.340 1.210				
TF Pragmatics - Total Quality Control	Root-cause analysis Complexity Reliability Coverage	2.450 2.420 1.785 1.565	1	16.56280973	0.07692	1.274011324 7.18%

Economic Modifiers (Part 2)

KEF Category	Cost Driver	Range (1 default)	Stage	Total Impact	SL Weight	Weighted AVG
WF Performance - Schedule Control	Sched. Compression Defect reduction Scope increase	2.692 2.482 2.471	0	16.51009522	0.07692	1.269956525 7.16%
AF Artifact Sets - Production Control	Discard Reuse Functional Simulation	1.420 2.680 2.400 1.810	1	16.5315264	0.092	1.520900429 8.58%

OF Organization - Maturity Control	Productivity	1.18	0	20.31431036	0.316	6.419322072
	Quality	2.07				36.22%
	Stability	1.85				
	Risk mitigation	1.85				
	Confidence	2.43				
EF Practices - Efficiency Improvement Cost Control	Scope	1.752	0	16.57146049	0.07692	1.274676741
	Resources	2.110				7.19%
	Infrastructure	1.660				
	Organization Policy	1.530				
	Schedule	1.765				
Team Efficiency Factor by GSC			**Weighted AVG by GSC**			**Total AVG**
640FPs	1280FPs	6400FPs	640FPs	1280FPs	6400FPs	100.026%
0.462962963	0.630119723	0.769704433	0.026102721	0.035527332	0.04339738	17.73619575

(1) TeamEff=TeamProductivity/IndividualProductivity
(2) Stage Modifiers = 1 (Applied during the Early Stage of Development)
(3) IndividualProductivity = 128 * TeamSize * TeamDuration
(4) With a GEM session of 15 min/day, a timebox of 2 weeks, the optimal team size is 5 operating at 50% capacity
(5) Team Productivity = Total Project Size / Total Project Effort Estimated

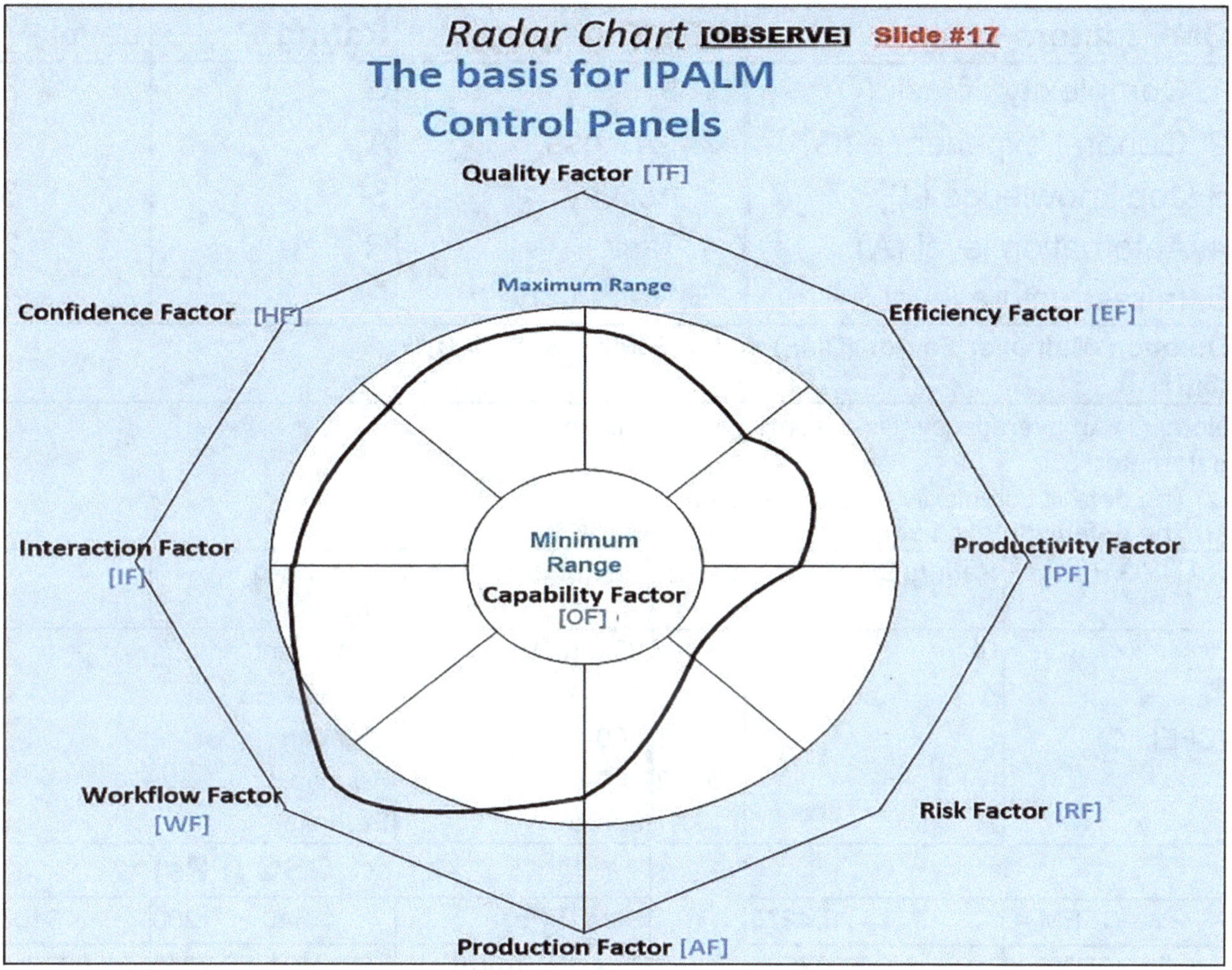
Radar Chart [OBSERVE] Slide #17
The basis for IPALM
Control Panels
Quality Factor [TF]
Maximum Range
Confidence Factor [HF]
Efficiency Factor [EF]
Interaction Factor
[IF]
Minimum
Range
Capability Factor
[OF]
Productivity Factor
[PF]
Workflow Factor
[WF]
Risk Factor [RF]
Production Factor [AF]

DMF factors	WBS Category	Rating	Level
1. Complexity of task (C),	1. Project	G	5
2. General experience (G),	2. Process	A	4
3. Job knowledge (J),	3. Activity	S	3
4. Automation level (A)	4. Task	R	2
5. Infrastructure level (I)	5. Technique	P	1
Duration Multiplier Factor (DMF) = (1/CFEM)x(18/(G + J)) x (6/(I+A))			
Note: (1) An average level is assumed as default for each parameter: 3 (2) The default complexity level is set to: 1 (3) The default duration adjustment factor is set to : 1			

RATING Range	Rating(GRASP)	Level	Rayleigh Range	Sternberg Pattern	
(CFEM/C)	G	5	900-1000	Congruent	
	A	4	700-900	Anticipating	
	S	3	400-700	Steering	
	R	2	100-400	Routine	
	P	1	0-100	Periodic	

CFEM =	**0.4275**
DMF =	**6.015037594**

GSC (FPs)			
Size (FPs)	640	1200	6400
Duration(mth)	46.9540174	59.9011	93.902913

Quality Goals Pursued

Estimated Adjustment Size =	**640**	**1280**	**6400**
K (Number of Defects) =	1.686	1.844823945	2.32648
MTTR (Mean-Time-To-Repair in hours) =	0.5	0.5	0.5
MTTF (Mean-Time-To-Failure in hours) =	7513	9584.187849	15024.5
System Availability (% of time) =	99.99	99.99478335	99.9967
Defects Repaired (R) per Month	10	10	10
MMF for K <= R	1	1	1
MMF for K > R	1.2	1.3	1.4

BM (business Model)	B-CFs	**Size Impact**	**Complexity Impact (C)**		
Model Type [PRODUCTS]	***CFs Model***	**FPs**	**Easy**	**Medium**	**Hard**
UM	H-CFs	15	2.20	2.23	2.00
OM	A-CFs	15	1.87	1.96	2.25
TM	**I-CFs**	20	1.87	1.91	2.50
CM	**E-CFs**	32	1.67	1.68	3.00
DM	T-CFs	60	2.47	2.58	3.25
SM	W-CFs	90	2.50	3.00	3.50
RM	R-CFs	150	3.00	4.00	3.75
PM	P-CFs	320	4.00	4.50	4.00
BM (business Model)	O-CFs	450	4.50	4.75	5.00
	Average	128	2.68	2.96	3.25

Complexity _C = [SUM (Complexity Factors) / 7] over the full code type								
CF Descriptors		**Action**	**CF Weight (Constraints)**					
CFD Description	**Quality Criteria**	**Rating %**	**CF-Type**	**VeryLow**	**Low**	**Average**	**High**	**Very High**
AA Action using HCD	Fully Responsive	18	H-CFs	1	2	3	4	5
AC Action using GSC	Verifiablity	16	A-CFs	1	2	3	4	5
AD Action using DPM	Effectiveness	14	I-CFs	1	2	3	4	5
AT Action using engineering	Applicability	12	E-CFs	1	2	3	4	5
AM Action using management	Understandability	12	T-CFs	1	2	3	4	5
AF Action using fast tracking	Usability	10	W-CFs	1	2	3	4	5
AS Action using CPM	Reliability	8	R-CFs	1	2	3	4	5
AP Action using PERT	Scope Limitation	6	P-CFs	1	2	3	4	5
AO Action using CMMI rating	Traceability	4	O-CFs	2	4	6	8	10
	TOTAL CFD%	100	TotalCFs	10	20	30	40	50

CFEM = (CFD_Rating X TotalCFs/1000) X Complexity_C

Note: Assignment Level

(1) For a Beginner Full-Time Staff, the complexity level is set to 1;
(2) For a Qualified Full-Time Staff, the complexity level is set to Easy;
(3) For an Advanced Full-Time Staff, the complexity level is set to Medium; and,
(4) For an Expert Full-Time Staff, the complexity level is set to Hard.

RESOURCES IMPACT

Skill(G) and Knowledge (J) Level

Skill (G)	Activity	Level
Rarely applied	1/year	1
Occasionally applied	1/month	2
Usually applied	**1/week**	**3**
Frequently applied	1/day	4
Continuously applied	1/hour	5

Knowledge (J)	Activity	Level
Understood	Test	1
Applied	Code	2
Analysed	**Model**	**3**
Synthesized	Spec's	4
Evaluated	Plan	5

Automation (A) and Infrastructure (I) Level

Automation (A)	Activity	Level
Scripting	Script	1
Standard Template	Script	2

Infrastructure(I)	Activity	Level
Documentation	Text/Graphic	1
IDE	Code	2

COM/DCOM	tool	3	**Lower CASE**	**Model**	**3**
Design Pattern based	**tool**	**4**	Upper CASE	Requirement	4
Transformation based	tool	5	Estimator	Plan	5

1. Workflow Team Distribution By Goals				
Focus of Attention (FOA)	**Element**	**Staff Loading Weight(%**	**Assignment**	**CFs Model**
Capability	Project (Mgmt & Admin)	31.600%	**PM**	**O-CFs**
Scope	System architecture	9.672%	**SA**	**I-CFs**
Process Improvement	Process and V&V (5%) Specification	9.672%	**CE**	**H-CFs**
Cost	Project Cost Control	7.692%	**SC**	**E-CFs**
Quality	Infrastructure (Pragmatics)	7.692%	**QM**	**T-CFs**
Workflow	Team Organization (People)	7.692%	**SM**	**W-CFs**
Development	Artifact Sets Production	9.200%	**SD**	**A-CFs**
Risk Management	Contingency Allocation	7.692%	**RM**	**R-CFs**
Productivity	Methodology (Practices)	9.200%	**SE**	**P-CFs**
	Total:	100.112%	**PM**	**B-CFs**

2. Technique Team Distribution by MDA Workflow (%)

MDA Team Distribution		Scope Assignment		
Phase	**Workflow**	**640FPs**	**1280FPs**	**6400FPs**
Inception	Object Model	11	11	11
Elaboration	Functional Model	7	7	7
	Dynamic Model	10	10	10
	Presentation Model	21	21	21
	Transformation	9	9	9
	Subtotal=	**58**	**58**	**58**
Construction	Change and V&V	30	28	28
Transition	Support & Documentation	6	7	7
	Project mgmt.	6	7	7
	Subtotal=	**42**	**42**	**42**
=		**Total 100**	**100**	**100**

3. Technique Effort distribution by MDA Workflow (%)

MDA Effort Distribution		Scope Assignment		
Phase	**Workflow**	**640FPs**	**1280FPs**	**6400FPs**
Inception	Object Model	11	11	11
Elaboration	Functional Model	7	7	7
	Dynamic Model	10	10	10
	Presentation Model	21	21	21
	Transformation	9	9	9
Construction	**Subtotal=**	**58**	**58**	**58**

Transition	Change and V&V	30	28	28
	Support & Documentation	6	7	7
	Project mgmt.	6	7	7
	Subtotal=	**42**	**42**	**42**
		Total = 100		**100 100**

4. Technique Schedule distribution by MDA Workflow (%)

MDA Schedule Distribution		**Scope Assignment**		
Phase	**Workflow**	**640FPs**	**1280FPs**	**6400FPs**
Inception	Object Model	11	11	11
Elaboration	Functional Model	7	7	7
	Dynamic Model	10	10	10
	Presentation Model	21	21	21
	Transformation	9	9	9
	Subtotal=	**58**	**58**	**58**
Construction	Change and V&V	30	28	28
Transition	Support & Documentation	6	7	7
	Project mgmt	6	7	7
	Subtotal=	**42**	**42**	**42**
		Total = 100		**100 100**

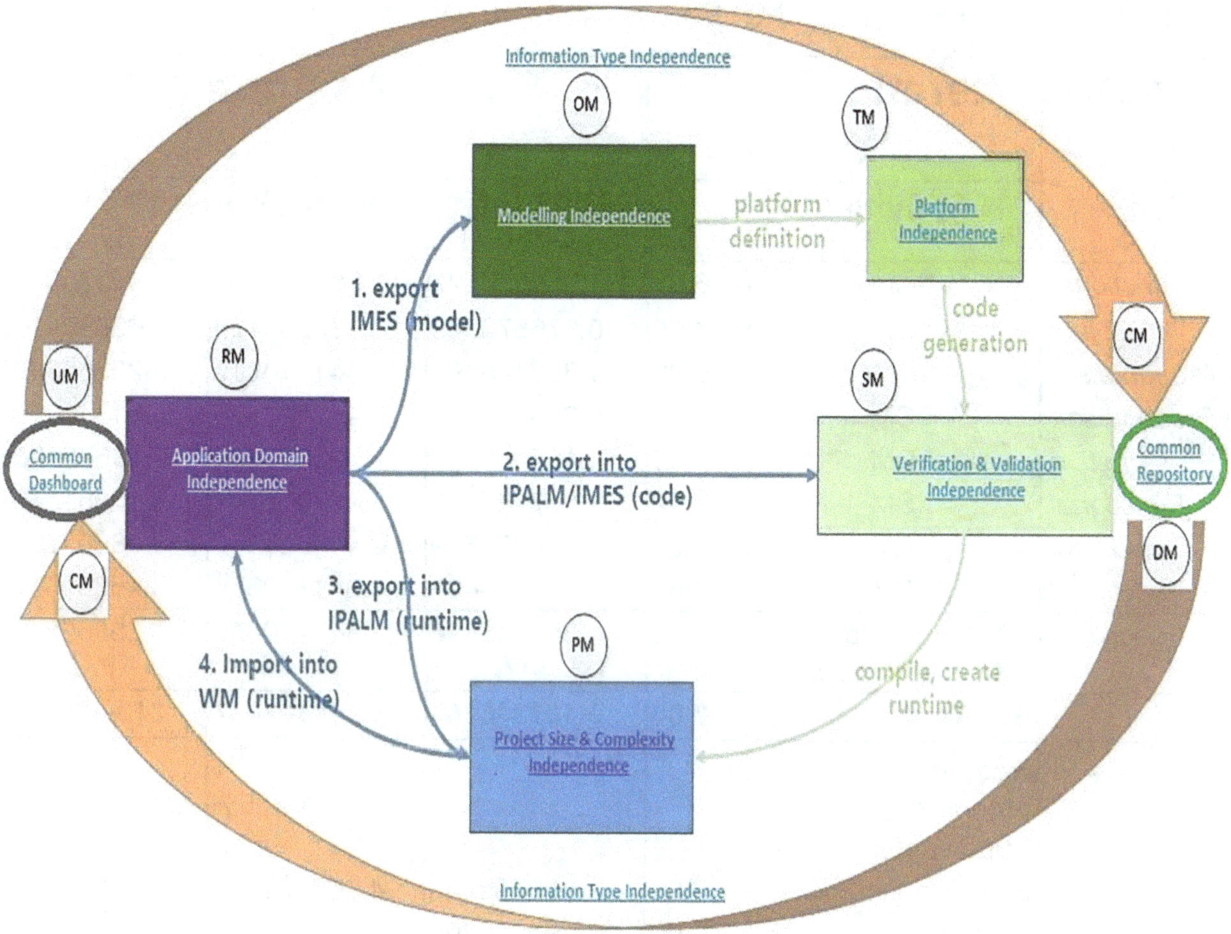

IPALM FRAMEWORK 8 SCHEMA MODEL

1. Activities Team Effort Distribution:

MDA Model Map	**Iterations ROM**		**Scope Assignment**		
	Activities	%	**640FPs (Small App.)**	**1280FPs (Avg. Sys.)**	**6400FPs (Dist. Sys.)**
Functional	UM	6.97	1.014859122	1.381282737	2.440206304
Object	OM	4.65	0.676572748	0.920855158	1.626804203
Presentation	TM	9.29	1.353145496	1.841710316	3.253608406
Presentation	CM	2.32	0.338286374	0.460427579	0.813402101
Presentation	DM	1.16	0.169143187	0.23021379	0.406701051
Functional	SM	17.42	2.537147806	3.453206843	6.100515761
Object	RM	2.24	0.326899379	0.444929212	0.786022324
Functional	PM	4.65	1.353145496	1.841710316	3.253608406
Functional	CMM (Capability Maturity Model)	9.29	1.353145496	1.841710316	3.253608406
	Sub-Total	**58.00**	**9.122345106**	**12.41604627**	**21.93447696**
	Requirements creep(per year)		17%	14.50%	10%
	Number of iterations	3	3	3	3
	Implement changes	7.00	3.05795206	4.162051954	7.352778068
	Verify changes	7.00	3.05795206	4.162051954	7.352778068
	Sub-Total	**42.00**	**6.115904121**	**8.324103907**	**14.70555614**
	Project Total	**100.00**	**14.56167648**	**19.81929502**	**35.0132289**

NOTE:

Tasks Effort Distribution	**%**	**Model Element**	**Average System**	**Distributed System**
Object Modelling Effort	16.02157	CRUD (U)	1	1
		Database (D)	1	1
Functional Modelling Effort	58.0782	Biz Algorithms (A)	4	20
Presentation Modelling Effort	22.02966	Report Control (R)	20	150
		User Menu (I)	15	50
		GUI Control (G)	25	50

: 128 FPs per month

(1) **<u>Project Sizes</u>: 640, 1280, 6400 FPs**
(2) **<u>Individual Production Rate</u>**

2. Activities Team Duration (per month) Distribution:

MDA Model Map	Iterations ROM		Scope Assignment		
	Activities	%	640FPs (Small App.)	1280FPs (Avg. Sys.)	6400FPs (Dist. Sys.)
Functional	UM	6.97	3.272404832	4.174742724	6.54445439
Object	OM	4.65	2.181603221	2.783161816	4.362969593
Presentation	TM	9.29	4.363206442	5.566323632	8.725939187
Presentation	CM	2.32	1.090801611	1.391580908	2.181484797
Presentation	DM	1.16	0.545400805	0.695790454	1.090742398
Functional	SM	17.42	8.181012079	10.43685681	16.36113598
Object	RM	2.24	1.054084339	1.344739161	2.108054241
Functional	PM	4.65	4.363206442	5.566323632	8.725939187
Functional	CMM (Capability Maturity Model)	9.29	4.363206442	5.566323632	8.725939187
	Sub-Total	**58.00**	**29.41492621**	**37.52584277**	**58.82665896**
	Requirements creep(per year)				
	Number of iterations	3			
	Implement changes (**IC**)	7.00	9.860341083	12.57924655	19.71961167
	Verify changes (**VC**)	7.00	9.860341083	12.57924655	19.71961167
	Sub-Total	**42.00**	**19.72068217**	**25.1584931**	**39.43922333**
	Project Total	**100.00**	**46.95400516**	**59.90117406**	**93.90291269**

NOTE:

Tasks Hour Distribution	%
Object Modelling Effort	16.02157
Functional Modelling Effort	58.0782
Presentation Modelling Effort	22.02966

Model Element	Average System	Distributed System
CRUD (U)	1	1
Database (D)	1	1
Biz Algorithms (A)	4	20
Report Control (R)		
User Menu	20	150
(I)	15	50
GUI Control (G)	25	50

(1) The number of hours per month is 160 hours

(2) The FSP multiplied by 160 resulted in the hour distribution table

3. Activities Team Size Estimation

MDA Model Map	Iterations ROM	Scope Assignment			
	Activities	Distribution (%	640FPs (Small App.)	1280FPs (Avg.Sys.)	6400FPs (Large Sys)
Functional	UM	6.97	0.021613899	0.02305936	0.025986482
Object	OM	4.65	0.014409266	0.015372907	0.017324321
Presentation	TM	9.29	0.028818532	0.030745813	0.034648642
Presentation	CM	2.32	0.007204633	0.007686453	0.008662161
Presentation	DM	1.16	0.003602316	0.003843227	0.00433108
Functional	SM	17.42	0.054034747	0.0576484	0.064966204
Object	RM	2.24	0.006962119	0.007427721	0.008370585
Functional	PM	4.65	0.028818532	0.030745813	0.034648642
Functional	CMM (Capability Maturity Model)	9.29	0.028818532	0.030745813	0.034648642
	Sub-Total	58.00	0.194282577	0.207275508	0.233586758
	Requirements creep/year		17%	14.50%	10%
	Number of iterations	3	3	3	3
	Implement changes (IC)	7.00	0.065126544	0.069481976	0.078301917
	Verify changes (VC)	7.00	0.065126544	0.069481976	0.078301917
	Sub-Total	42.00	0.130253087	0.138963953	0.156603834
	Project Total	100.00	0.310126398	0.330866554	0.372866271
	Tasks FSP Distribution	%	Model Element	Average/System	LargeSystem
	Object Modelling Effort	16.02157197	CRUD (U)	1	1
			Database (D)	1	1
	Functional Modelling Effort	58.07819838	Biz Algorithms (A)	4	20
	Presentation Modelling Effort	22.02966145	Report Control (R)	20	150
			User Menu (I)	15	50
			GUI Control (G)	25	50

Large Size:	Log10	10^
1. Log (Effort) =	1.544232	35.01323
2. Log (Duration) =	1.972679	93.90291
3. Log (TeamSize) =	- 0.42845	0.372866
4. Log (Prod.) =	2.261948	182.7881
Medium Size:	**Log10**	**10^**
1. Log (Effort) =	1.297088	19.8193
2. Log (Duration) =	1.777435	59.90117
3. Log (TeamSize) =	- 0.48035	0.330867
4. Log (Prod.) =	1.509092	32.29176
Interm Size:	**Log10**	**10^**
1. Log (Effort) =	1.163211	14.56168
2. Log (Duration) =	1.671673	46.95401
3. Log (TeamSize) =	- 0.50846	0.310126
4. Log (Prod.) =	1.642969	43.95098

1	- 0.30103
2	0
3	0.30103
4	0.477121
5	0.60206
6	0.69897

1	1.491362
2	1.491362
3	1.792392
4	2.792392
5	3.093422
6	3.394452
7	3.871573

Scope Assignment (SA)

EMF = -1.58331

-1.44944 -1.36254

DMF = 0.779238

Project Size Calculation

SA	Size Multiplier (PT)					
Log10	- 0.30103	0	0.30103	0.477121	0.60206	0.69897
1.50515	1.20412	1.50515	1.80618	1.982271	2.10721	2.20412
1.50515	1.20412	1.50515	1.80618	1.982271	2.10721	2.20412
1.80618	1.50515	1.80618	2.10721	2.283301	2.40824	2.50515
2.80618	2.50515	2.80618	2.80618	2.982271	3.10721	3.20412
3.10721	2.80618	2.80618	3.40824	3.584331	3.70927	3.80618
3.40824	3.10721	3.40824	3.70927	3.885361	4.0103	4.10721
3.885361	3.584331	3.885361	4.186391	4.362482	4.487421	4.584331

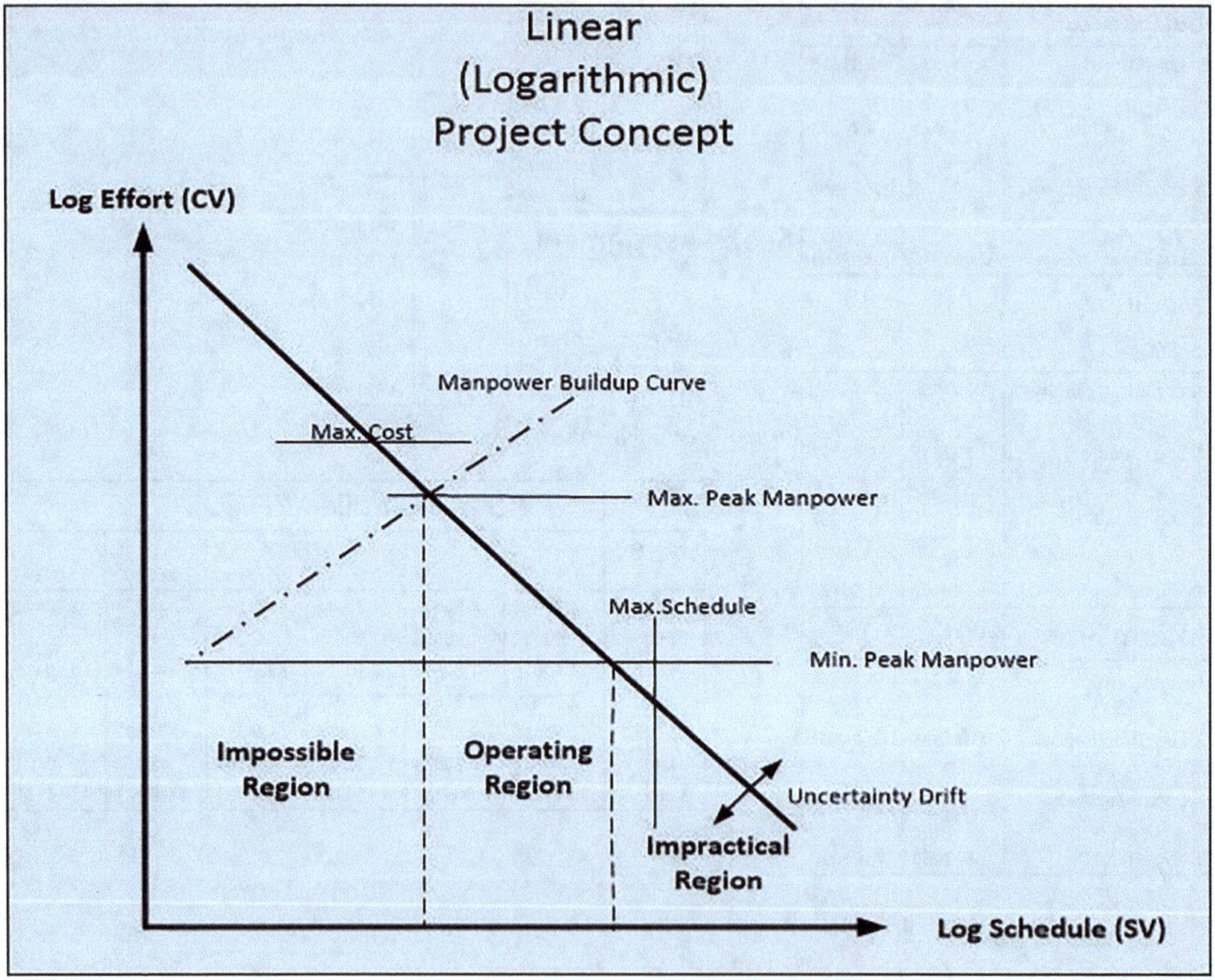
Linear
(Logarithmic)
Project Concept
Log Effort (CV)
Manpower Buildup Curve
Max. Cost
Max. Peak Manpower
Max.Schedule
Min. Peak Manpower
Impossible Region
Operating Region
Uncertainty Drift
Impractical Region
Log Schedule (SV)

MDA Economic Factors considered:

Interest rate:	10%
Burden rate:	2.652395083
Euro-USD conversion:	1.1
Hours per year:	1920

Project Factors considered:

Project sizes:	640-12800				
Team size:	2 to 4 FSPs			**Beginner Qualified Advanced Expert**	
Team 1:		1	1		
Team 2:			1	1	
Team 3:		1	1	1	1
Project Manager:	1/2 PM @ $70K USD or $94.33 USD per hour (loaded)				
Project duration (months)	**by Project size 00**	**640**	**1280 64**	**12800**	
Team 1:	2.66				
Team 2:		1.6	3.2		
Team 3:			12		24
Loaded hourly salary:					
Beginner FSP:	$89.84				
Qualified FSP:	$107.82				

Advanced FSP:	$125.78
Expert FSP or PM:	$157.76
License cost (per month) **Seat** **License:** **Modeller:**	 $1,875 $3250 USD (5 year plan) $87.24 per month @ 10%

Average Project Size Calculations Factors:

Effort = Capability1 X EMF X (GSC X (SMF X MMF X AMF)) Exponent (Process1)			
	Capability1 =	2.5 (depends on reliability, complexity, root-cause, coverage)	
	Process1 =	0.73 (depends on process improvement)	
Example:	SMF =		6400
	EMF =	(default value)	1
	Effort =		1432.156
	EMF =	(IMES value)	30
	Effort =		47.73854
Duration = Capability2 X DMF X (Effort) Exponent (Process2)			
	Capability2 =	2.5 (depends on scope, time, cost, risk and quality)	
	Process2 =	0.366 (depends on capability maturity improvement)	
Example:	SMF =		6400
	DMF =	(default value)	1
	Duration =	2.5 X (1440) Exp (0.366) =	36
	DMF =	(MDA value)	3
	Duration =		12

NOTE: 1. Qualified Staff: Can handle one Key Process Area (Role) at a time competently

2. Advanced Staff: Can handle three to four Key Process Area (Role) at a time competentlly

3. Expert Staff: Can hand 4 to six Key Process Area (Role) at a time competently

4. Management Roles: PM, QM, RM, SM, CM

5. Technical Roles: CE, SE, SA, SD, SI, PC, QC, SC

6. Beginner Staff: Trained personnel assigned on a first project

Team 1 and 640 FPs		
OpsPro Scenario #1:	***Total cost:*** $127,670	
	Seat License cost:	$9,975.00
	Beginner FSP cost:	$38,236
	Qualified FSP cost:	$45,888
	PM at 1/2 time:	$33,571.33
Team 2 and 640 FPs		
OpsPro Scenario #2:	***Total cost:*** $85,995	
	Seat License cost:	$6,000
	Qualified FSP cost:	$27,602
	Advanced FSP cost:	$32,200
	PM at 1/2 time:	$20,193.28
Team 2 and 1280 FPs		
OpsPro Scenario #3:	***Total cost:*** $171,990	
	Seat License cost:	$12,000
	Qualified FSP cost:	$55,204
	Advanced FSP cost:	$64,399
	PM at 1/2 time:	$40,386.56

Average cost per function point:

Scope Assignment	640	1280	6400	12800
Scenario #1	$199.49			
Scenario #2	$134.37			
Scenario #3		$134.37		
Scenario #4			$182.41	
Scenario #5				$206.08

	Team 2 and 6400 FPs		
OpsPro Scenario #4:	***Total cost:*** $1,167,447		
		Seat License cost:	$90,000
		Modeler cost:	$2,094
		Beginner FSP cost:	$172,493
		Qualified FSP cost:	$207,014
		Advanced FSP cost:	$241,498
		Expert FSP cost:	$302,899
		PM at 1/2 time:	$151,449.60
	Team 2 and 12800 FPs		
OpsPro Scenario #5:	***Total cost:*** $2,637,794		
		Seat License cost:	$180,000
		Modeler cost:	$4,188
		Beginner FSP cost:	$344,986
		Qualified FSP cost:	$414,029
		Advanced FSP cost:	$482,995
		Expert FSP cost:	$605,798
		PM at Full time:	$605,798.40

Large Project Scenario:

(Project size: 6200 FPs approximately)

Average cost per function point: $220.34

Team Size = Effort/Duration		
Example:	Competitor	39.78211978
	MDA Provider	3.978211978

Productivity = Size/Duration/FSP		
Example:	Competitor	4.468785946
	MDA Provider	134.0635784

WBS Level	WBS Aspects	WBS Estimates	Factors
	WBS Elements	Management Proposal	5 Levels
Business Model	PM Estimator	Technical Proposal	EVS
(Baldrige Framework)	Performance Factor	Financial Proposal	BPF
	Scope Assignment Factor	Project Charter	GSC
	Cosysmo based Economics	Effort Estimation	EEF
Project Model (Level 5)	Project Sizes based on GSC	Time Estimation	EPML
Project Scope Assignment	Project Effort based on HCD	Size Estimation	CFEM
	Project Schedule based on DPM	Team Estimation	OPA
		Integration Management	OSL
Process Model (Level 4)	PMBOK Process Model	Quality Management	TSL
(Processes - Metrics)		Risk Management	RSL
		Cost Management	ESL
Process Scope Assignment		Scope Management	PSL
		Schedule Management	WSL
		Production Management	ASL
		Resource Management	HSL
		Comm Management	ISL
		Integ_CMF_Control	
Activity Model (Level 3)	Open Process Framework Model	Quality_QF_Control	EMF
(Activities - Calibration Factors)	Five Level WBS	Risk_RF_Control	SMF

Activity Scope Assignment	Process Differentiator	Cost_EF_Control Scope_PF_Control Schedule_WF_Control Production_AF_Control Resource_CF_Control Comm_IF_Control	MMF AMF DMF
Task Model (Level 2) (Tasks Measures) Task Scope Assignment	Organization Impact Quality Impact Risk Impact Efficiency Impact Productivity Impact Workload Impact Production Impact Human-Centered Design Impact Interaction Impact	OSL_OF TSL_TF RSL_RF ESL_EF PSL_PF WSL_WF ASL_AF HSL_HF ISL_IF	OF TF RF EF PF WF AF HF IF
Product Level (Level 1) (Techniques - Scaling Factors) Technique Scope Assignment	Measurement Workflow Inception Plan Elaboration Plan Construction Plan Transition Plan Service Level Agreement	ModelSchedule ModellingEffort ModellingTeam	EFP P P1 P2 C1 C2

Risks Constraints (EPML) **Task Specification** **Knowledge Analysis**
Project GSC Sizing(SMF)(PRODUCTS) **(CFEM)**

PFV Productivity Factor Variance **F** Forms **PM** Productivity Model **SE** Software Engineer
OFV Capability Factor Variance **R** Reports **RM** Requirements and Risk Model **RM** Risk Management
WFV Workflow Factor Variance **A** Algorithms **OM** Open Architecture Model **SD** System Developer
EFV Efficiency Factor Variance **C** Classes **DM** Data Tracking Model **QM** Quality Management
RFV Risk Factor Variance **T** Tables **UM** Usability Model **CE** Cognitive Engineer
HFV HCD PI Factor Variance **A** Agents **CM** Cost Data Model **SC** System Cost Control
AFV Artifact Factor Variance **L** Links **TM** Transaction Model **SA** System Architect

BFV Baldrige Factor Variance **S** Services **SM** Solution Workflow Model **SM** System Manager
IFV Interaction Factor Variance
TFV Total Quality Factor Variance

Skills Analysis (OPA)

ANTLR Another Tool for Language Recognition

DI Decision Intelligence

DPM Dynamic Progress Method

HCD Human Centered Design

JADE Joint Active Design Elicitation

MDA Model Driven Architecture

SEEM Systems Engineering Economics Model

TM Tree Methodology

YAWL Yet Another Workflow Language

Workflow Analysis (DMF)

PSL= Productivity Control Staff loading
OSL= Organization Control Staff Loading
WSL= Workload Control Staff Loading
ESL= Efficiency Control Staff Loading
RSL= Risk Control Staff Loading
HSL= HCD Control Staff Loading
ASL= Artifact Production Staff Loading
BSL= Project Scope Assignment
ISL= Interaction Control Staff Loading
TSL= Total Quality Control Staff Loading

Scope Assignment (EMF)

PCF Productivity CF
OCF Organization CF
WCF Workflow CF
ECF Efficiency CF
RCF Risk CF
HCF Human-Centered Design CF
ACF Artifact Production CF
BCF Business Modeling CF
ICF Interaction CF
TCF Total Quality CF

Action Specification (DPM)

AA Action using automation with MDE
AC Action using CPM
AD Action using DPM
AT Action using technical assignment
AM Action using management assignment
AF Action using fast tracking assignment
AS Action using sequential assignment

Quality Considerations (MTBF))

CPLX Complexity
IF interface Mismatch
FEA Feature Missing
COV Coverage
REL Reliability
RC Root-Cause
PI Process Improvement

PAMPA Project Attribute Monitoring and Predicting Agent

PICK Pairwise Independent Combinational Test

AP Action using PERT

AO Action using CMMI rating

OH Overhead assignment

DC Direct Cost assignment

Appendix F LearnEdge Application Generation in Action Check list

LearnEdge Application Generation in Action Check list (5 Key Performance Units each): JAPIGO Factors

1. What is AGIA about? Chapter 9 **J**ob Knowledge Factor.
2. What are the key features of AGIA? Overview **A**rchitecture Knowledge Factor.
3. Who is AGIA for? Chapter 2 **I**nfrastructure knowledge Factor.
4. What is exciting about AGIA? Para 1.1 **J**ob Knowledge Factor
5. Is AGIA a methodology or an environment? Para 1.3 **P**erformance knowledge Factor.
6. Why should I learn about AGIA? Chapter 3 **G**eneral Knowledge Factor.
7. What methodology does AGIA support? Chapter 4, 7, 8,10, 11 **O**perational Knowledge Factor
8. Does AGIA cover my development processes? Chapter 12 **O**perational Knowledge Factor.
9. Does AGIA integrate MDA development? Chapter 6 **A**rchitecture Knowledge Factor.
10. Does AGIA integrate Model Driven Engineering? Chapter 5 **G**eneral Knowledge Factors.
11. Does AGIA integrate Project Management? Chapter 5 **P**erformance Knowledge Factor
12. What languages does AGIA support? Chapter 6 **I**nfrastructure Knowledge Factor

The Effective Progress Management Level achieved is formulated as follows:

$$EPML = [(J/G) + (A/I) + (O/P)]/3$$

where each factor has a range of 1..5 for a total of 60 KPUs.

There are 12 qualification questions corresponding to 6 qualification factors. The formula favors the technical knowledge over the management one.

For example, if G, I and P were assessed as 1 while J, A and I were assessed as 5, the EPML reached would be 5, indicating a 20% management level. In essence, the Technical Staff delivers the products or services required under a contract.

LearnEdge Training is based on 56 KPUs, the remaining 4 KPUs are considered electives (See Appendix J)

Appendix G Methodology Comparison

Criteria	**Methodology**						
	Agile	**CBD**	**DSDM**	**XP**	**OO**	**PBSD**	**IMES**
Average Size of Project	500	5000	1500	300	2500	2000	1500
Time box applied	2 Weeks		2 Weeks	2 Weeks			2 Weeks
Schedule Exponent Factor	0.33	0.36	0.33	0.33	0.25	0.35	<0.25
Team Size Average	5			10	3		2
Assignment Scope per Staff	100		125	100	200	300	128
Production Rate per SM	36		12	40	18	34	>128
Defect Potential (%)	3.5		4	3	4.5	3	0.03
Removal Efficiency (%)	92		90	95	92	90	>95
Maint. Assignment Scope	1500		1500	1500	2500	2000	2500
Reusable Component Size		200					1000
Component Reuse Ratio		60%				60-75%	100%

Note:

(1) CBD : Component Based Development

(2) DSDM: Dynamic System Development Method
(3) XP: Extreme Programming
(4) OOD: Object-Oriented Development
(5) PBSD: Pattern-Based Software Development
(6) The project size average is in Function Points, as defined by IFPUG.

(7) The Schedule Exponent Factor is applied against the project size to estimate a project duration in months.

(8) The table is consistent with the information presented in
Estimating Software Costs Chapter 7 (Second Edition) by Capers Jones.

(9) IMES column is a rough estimate based on the information discussed with Capers Jones

Table 8 Methodology Comparison

Appendix H Concept of Operations Overview

Concept of Operations Overview

At any phases or stages of a project, the work assignment offers a key opportunity for process improvement. Such process improvement calls for cultural change driven by the following four layers of process modeling considerations, based on Bloom's taxonomy top four layers, see Appendix P and Q:

- Meta Process Layer to tackle the management considerations ("Plan the work");
- Macro Process Layer to tackle the LCM considerations ("Work the plan");
- Micro Process Layer to tackle the MDA considerations ("Plan the measure"); and,
- Atomic Process Layer to tackle the Market considerations ("Work the measure").

The independence of operations of each project team member and the protocol for the peer's group communication expresses as status reports represent the cornerstone for a successful project execution. For a fixed price contract, the project team size will be fixed also. For a cost-plus contract, the project team size will vary depending on the productivity of the team. In either case, team productivity is the key factor.

Responsibility Assignments Considerations

Another key factor is time boxing. The lowest WBS element is assigned a fixed production cycle schedule. Given the known proficiency level of the team members, what is a reasonable workload that must be applied to deliver a work product in the time allotted? To achieve maximum efficiency, a cognitive function evaluation matrix is applied for each work assignment:

- Who is responsible for the product?
- What requirements are embedded within each work product?
- When is the work product due?
- Where does the work product fit within the architecture and the schedule?
- Why is the work product done – what goals must be met?
- How is the work conducted (activities, tasks and techniques)?
- How many resources must be assigned?
- How well must the product perform and to what degree?
- How soon must the iterations be paced to deliver results to the stakeholders?

In essence, a work assignment is considered concurrent if accomplished in the required time box or sequential if spread over multiple time boxes. A work assignment refers to one producer. Given the scalability of a product, for example the system level versus the component level, concurrency occurs when a specific number of artifacts are delivered under a specific time box. There is an upper limit to team size to achieve optimal efficiency and confidence while minimizing complexity of interactions.

Appendix I Knowledge Progression Rules of Thumb

This is based on university programs offered by surveyed universities from Canada, USA, Europe and Australia. The Bloom's Taxonomy in North America or the SOLO Taxonomy in Europe serves as basis for knowledge progression (going from 1 to 5 in Europe to 6 in NA).

"Skills Institutes" such as Knowledge Tree was surveyed for programs offered matching such university programs, including the cost differential as well as diploma recognition. In short, you can price the cost paid by individuals to achieve their knowledge. From that angle, you then extrapolate the ROI from their investment to decide to work with a specific firm, a bit like a loan payment.

So here goes the estimation process based on the assessment introduced in Appendix G:

Qualification Estimation Table

Factor	Modeler	Architect	Leader
	360	480	680
2	8	8	8
3	5	5	5
4	3	3	3
5			

6	12	12	12
7	9	9	9
8	-	-	-
9	12	12	12
	12	12	12
10	-	-	-
11	24	27	30
	- 4	- 4	- 4
12	-	-	-
	22	22	22
	-	-	-

Table 9 ***Qualification Estimation Table***

Criteria Listed

1. There are 3 categories of programs considered: **M**odeler, **A**rchitect and **T**eam Lead.

2. The program duration is 4 years at 2 semesters per year.

3. The number of courses per semester is 3 core, 2 electives.

4. The number of topics per week and per course is set to 3.

5. The number of weeks per semester is set at 12.

6. The number of credits per course is set to 9 (3 for attendance and 6 for preparation or 1/3 student time on course).

7. The number of hours per credit is set to 12.

8. The number of hours per project per semester is set to 144 [35% of the marks].

9. The number of exercises per semester is set at 48 to 60 of ½ hour each [30% of the marks].

10. The number of exams per semester is set at 2 of 2 hours each [35% of the marks].

11. The cost per credit is set at $370 for a foreign student, $80 for a Canadian student, $325 for Learning Tree student and $22 for a LearnEdge™ student.

12. The formula calculates the workload per week in hours and the topics qualification per semester.

That is the basis of LearnEdge™ cognitive engineering approach: The LearnEdge™ way!

The Formulation for the Hourly Workload:

M_WWL = (8. / 5.) + (9. / 5.) + (10. / 5.) + (3. x 6. x 7. / 5.) Example of a weekly workload (WWL):

M_WWL = (144/12) + (24/12) + (4/12) +(5x9x12/12) = 59.3 hours The Formulation for the Program Size in Credits and Completion Rate per Week:

M_PS = 3. x 2. X 6.

Example of Program Completion:

M_PS = 5 x 8 x 9 = 360

M_CRW = (2. x 3. x 6.)/ (5. x 2.)

Appendix J LearnEdge™ Sizing Formulations

Overhead Ratio Calculation

1. Development %: SM + SE + CE + SC = 55.00%
2. Overhead %: PM + QC + PC + RC = 30.00%
3. Overhead Ratio: Overhead/Development 0.545454545
4. Charging Rate: Development+Overhead 1.545454545

Where:

A. **SM** stands for System Management ratio
B. **SE** stands for Software Engineering ratio
C. **CE** stands for Cognitive Engineering ratio
D. **SC** stands for System Control ratio (Configuration Management)
E. **PM** stands for Project Management ratio
F. **QC** stands for Quality Control/Management ratio
G. **PC** stands for Project Control ratio;
H. **RC** stands for Risk Control ratio

Workflow Distribution by Goals			
Focus of Attention (FOA)	**Element**	**Risk Weight(%)**	**Assignment**
Business Management	G&A	15.00%	**BM**
Capability	Project (Mgmt & Admin)	10.00%	**PM**
Process Improvement	Process and V&V (5%) Specification	5.00%	**PC**
Scope	Product Specification	15.00%	**SC**
Quality	Infrastructure (Pragmatics)	10.00%	**QC**

Work	Team Organization (People)	12.00%	**CE**
System	System Management	12.00%	**SM**
Financial Value (Risk)	Performance	5.00%	**RC**
Productivity	Methodology (Practices)	16.00%	**SE**

Total: 100.00%

Table 10 ***Methodology Distribution***

Appendix K LearnEdge™ Monad Scope Formulations

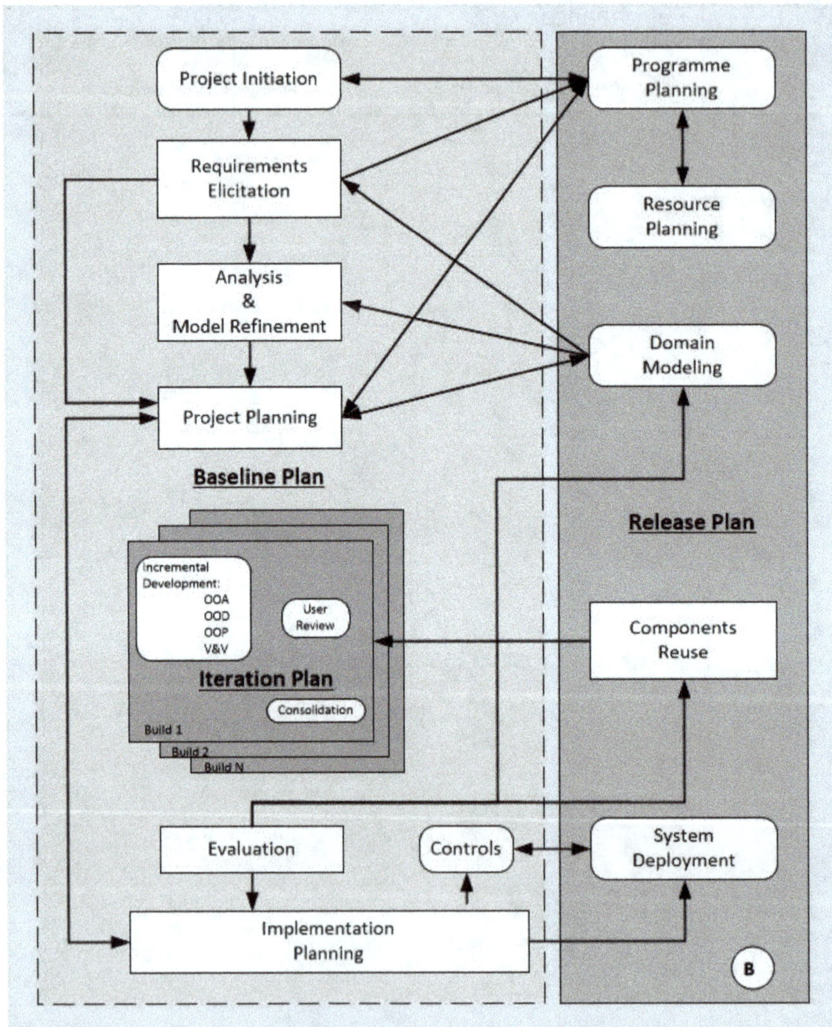

Figure 40 IPALM Release Plan

Based on the Joint Active Development Environment Method impact and the Tree Methodology, the Lowest WBS element will be characterized as follows:

1. Assigned to 1 Full-Time Staff Personnel (FSP).

2. Time box of 2 weeks.

3. Deliverable of 1 component comprised of 2 classes up to 10 classes.

4. Measured at an average of 64 Function Points.

5. Based on a GEM session of 15 minutes per day.

6. Generating on average 2 Use Cases at 16 Story Points per Use Case and up to 10 Use Cases.

7. Generating on average 32 Story Points at 2 Function Points per Story Point up to 160 Story Points.

8. Documentation of 32 pages of design.

9. Verification and Validation of 8 to 40 times.

10. Defects not exceeding 0.003 per Function Point or 1 defect per 3 months.

11. Changes not exceeding 0.02 per Function Point or 1 change per month; and,

12. Number of Features incorporated not exceeding 5 to 9 per Use Case

Appendix L Software Engineering Tree-Methodology

Hierarchical Structure

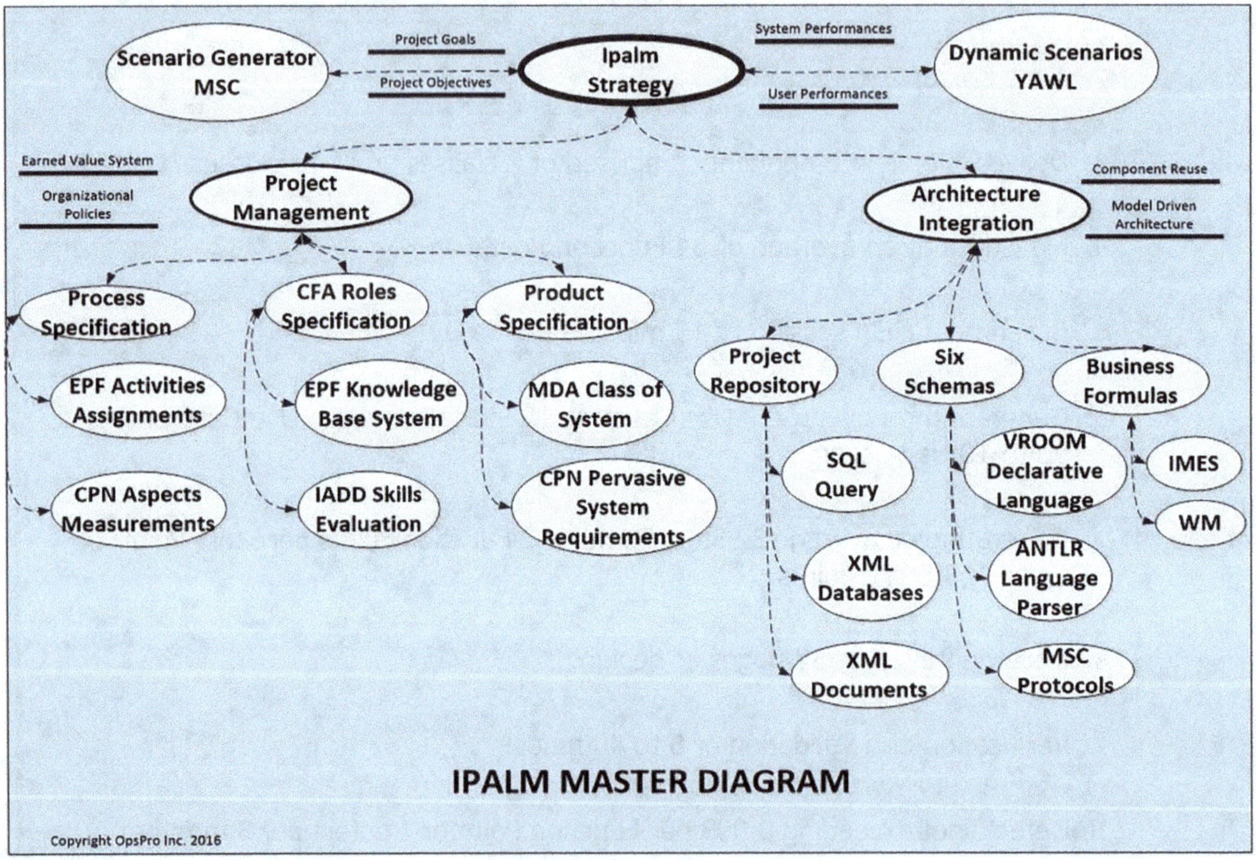

Figure 41 IPALM Master Diagram

The following is based on the work of Dr. Lem O. Ejogu called Software Engineering with Formal Metrics.

Let the given software problem be denoted by the symbol Δ. For the purpose of analysis, this is coined a complex, a unit of thought or uniform composition of function.

As of the object of refinement, this complex is further decomposed into simple complexes; the process may be continued up to irreducible complexes or monadic functions, called monads.

Each refined complex, by analogy, will be made to correspond uniquely to a node of a tree. In software engineering, the tree is inverted, so that the root sits at the highest point of the tree.

In terms of levels, the root exists at L = 0. Each subsequent order of refinement of a node complex will occupy level L = L + 1, where its parent node currently sits at level L.

In order to show explicit origination, and therefore uniqueness, of complexes, each complex is associated with a superscript <*>, to denote a sequence of integers corresponding to its orders of child refinements, e.g. $\Delta^{<0>}$ for the root complex, note that the superscript can be ignored at L = 0.

At that level, the initial refinement becomes Δ_1, Δ_2, etc. Δ_n. Similarly, at the next level, L = 1, the parent refinement becomes $\Delta^{<0,1>}$, and so on till you reach the monadic functions, at L = m, e.g. $\Delta^{<0,1,\ldots m>}$.

Formal Notation of a node

An arbitrary node of a tree may be denoted as $\Delta_i^{<u>}$. The superscript <u> traces the path of every leg of nesting. A complete combination of these nesting paths, or legs of nesting, forms the ground space for software measurement. The superscript <u> is called the Trace of Hierarchy (TOH).

Twin Number

A node is an executable software complex having the potential of independent compilation. The node can be described by its function, its logic or its context. The i under script is the target explosion node of the parent node located in the preceding level. The maximum i under script is called the Twin Number of the parent node. It is the total number of explosion numbers of a node. The Twin Number of the root node is R_t.

Height of a tree

The height of an arbitrary node of a tree is given by h= |<u>| - 1. The height of the Root Node is h = |<0>| = 1.

The height of a tree is given by

$H = \max (h_1, h_2, \ldots, hm\}$.

Monadicity

The monadicity of a tree is the total number of monadic functions {=monads/leaves} of the tree

$\mathbf{M = {}^t\sum_{I=1} M_i}$ **or** $\mathbf{M(T_i)}$ where t = twin number of the root node; T_i = leg of nesting.

For a one node tree, set H = R_t (root twin number) = M = 1.

Structural and Psychological Complexity

The structural complexity of a software module is then defined as

$$\mathbf{S_c = H * R_t * M.}$$

The psychological complexity is

$P_c = 1/S_c$.

Entropy

The entropy e of a node N is given by $e = (I * k)^{-1}$ (single-entry, single-exit).

Size of Software

The size of a software module is the total number of nodes of its software structure less the root node.

$S_z = \ _{Rt}\sum_{i=1} \ _{Lk}\sum_{j=1} \ _{Mi}\sum_{k=1} t_{ijk}$.

Where $^{L}{}_{k}$ = Number of nesting per root's explosion number;

$^{M}{}_{i}$ = Number of nodes per leg; $^{R}{}_{t}$

= Root's twin number; and, t_{ijk} = An explosion

number of the root node.

Definitions

Scientific Methodology: To engineer effective control of software productivity by creating SMART metrics for carrying out *processes* required to produce a software product.

Software Engineering: To apply objective knowledge to the creation of plans, and the conduct *activities* for analyses and designs, and means for achieving desired technical objectives.

Software Technology: To apply systematic knowledge and *tasks* to any recurrent activity dealing with *techniques* required for carrying out plans and designs.

Techniques: any systematic way of obtaining measurement information about a scientific nature or to obtain a desired product using manual or automated tools.

IPALM TREE Demonstration

Note:

1. Root Twin Number = 8
2. Height of Tree = 7
3. Monadicity = Sum(M1 to M8) = 137
4. Structural Complexity = 7 * 8 * 137 = 7672
5. Psychological Complexity = 1/Structural Complexity = 0.0001303

6. Size of Software = 227-16 = 211

Table 11 SAFE Recording

CLASS NAME	WBScode	Explosion #	Nesting Level	Monads
BudgetModel 1				M1 = 15
AMF	1233.2		3	1233.2
BudgetModelFacade	1	1	1	
CostIndicators	121345.1		4	121345.1
CosKPA	12434.1		4	12434.1
CostMgmt	1243		3	
CostTracking	1213		3	
CPIestimation	12134		4	
DurationRange	125324.1		4	125324.1
EarnedValueSys	121345.2		5	121345.2
EffortEstimation	12531		3	
EffortRange	125314.1		4	125314.1
GSC	1233.4		3	1233.4
IPALMestimation	125		2	
MethodologyPattern	123354.5		4	123354.5
MMF	1233.3		3	1233.3
OverheadFactor	124		2	
ProcessPattern_P	123354.4		4	123354.4
ProductScale	123		2	
ProductScope_S	123354.2		4	123354.2
ProductType_T	123354.1		4	123354.1
ProjectSizeRange	1233.1		3	1233.1
SMF	12335		3	
SystemSize	1233.6		3	1233.6
Throughput_C	123354.3		4	123354.3

TimeEstimation	12532		3	
TrackingPERT	121		2	
Variance	12.2		2	
ScheduleModel2				M2 = 18
ActivityUsage	227		2	
Baseline	22834.2		4	22834.2
ConstraintDates	226324256.2		6	226324256.2
DMF	22834.1		4	22834.1
DynamicProcessModel	2	2	1	
MDAspec	2243.1		3	2243.1
OPENspec	2243.2		3	2243.2
PERT_Node	2263.1		3	2263.1
PMBOKspec	2243.3		3	2243.3
ProcComplexity	2293.1		3	2293.1
ProdComplexity	2293.2		3	2293.2
ProjectBuffer	229		2	
ProjectFinish	22.2		2	22.2
ProjectSpec	224		2	
ProjectStart	22.1		2	22.1
SchedIndicators	72834.3		4	22834.3
ScheduleKPA	22.3		2	22.3
ScheduleTracking	228		2	
SPIestimation	2283		3	
TaskDependency	22632		3	
TaskLink	226324256.1		6	226324256.1
TaskSelection	2263242		4	2263242
TaskUsage	2273.1		3	2273.1
TimeKPA	2253.1		3	2253.1
Timeline	226324.1		4	226324.1
TimeMgmt	225		2	

WorkStagesMgmt	226		2	
WUduration	22632425		5	
CommModel3				M3 = 13
ArtifactsSets	324		2	
AssessmentSet	3243.7		3	3243.7
CommFacade	3	3	1	
CommKPA	3213		3	
CommMgmt	321		2	
Curriculum	322324.1		4	322324.1
DeploymentSet	3243.6		3	3243.6
DesignSet	3243.4		3	3243.4
DevelopmentSet	3243.2		3	3243.2
GuidelinesMgmt	323		2	
ManagementSet	3243.1		3	3243.1
MDLtraining	322324.2		4	322324.2
MetricGathering	3234.1		4	3234.1
ProducersImpact	322		2	
ProductionSet	3243.5		3	3243.5
ReqRiskSet	3243.3		3	3243.3
SAtraining	322324.4		4	322324.4
SCRUMefficiency	322314.1		4	322314.1
SCRUMsession	32231		3	
TLtraining	322324.3		4	322324.3
Workshops	32232		3	
QualityModel4				M4 = 12
Complexity	4253.1		3	4253.1
Coverage	4263.2		3	4263.2
DefectCorrection	425		2	
DPMscaling	424		2	

OptimisticDev	4223.1		3	4223.1
PessimisticDev	4223.3		3	4223.3
ProcessApplied	4253.1		3	4253.1
ProcessScale	4243.1		3	4243.1
ProdBuild	42334.1		4	42334.1
ProdRelease	42334.2		4	42334.2
ProductivityScale	4243.2		3	4243.2
QualityDashboard	426		2	
QualityKPA	4213		3	
QualityMgmt	421		2	
QualityModelFacade	4	4	1	
RealisticDev	4223.2		3	4223.2
Reliability	4263.3		3	4263.3
RootCause	4263.4		3	4263.4
SWArchitecture	4233		3	
SystArchitecture	423		2	
TechComplexity	422		2	

ScopeModel5				M5 = 15
ActivityAssignment	5223.3		3	5223.3
AdaptationFactor	52134.9		4	52134.9
CapabilityMaturityFactor	52134.8		4	52134.8
ConfidenceFactor	52134.1		4	52134.1
DecisionIntelligence	523		2	
DifferentiatorMatrix	5213		3	
EfficiencyFactor	52134.3		4	52134.3
EffortMultiplierFactor	521		2	
InteractionFactor	52134.7		4	52134.7
ProcessAssignment	5223.2		3	5223.2
ProductionKPA	523324.1		4	523324.1
ProductionMgmt	52332		3	

ProductivityFactor	52134.4		4	52134.4
ProjectAssignment	5223.1		3	5223.1
QualityFactor	52134.2		4	52134.2
RiskFactor	52134.6		4	52134.6
ScopeKPA	523314.1		4	523314.1
ScopeMgmt	52331		3	
ScopeModelFacade	5	5	1	
Task_Allocation	522		2	
TaskAssignment	52234		3	
TechniqueAssignment	522345.1		5	522345.1
WorkflowFactor	52134.5		4	52134.5
IntegModel6				M6 = 14
CFAdashboard	62.2		2	62.2
CFD	6223.1		3	6223.1
Checkpoints	621324.1		4	621324.1
IntegrationFacade	6	6	1	
IntegrationKPA	6233.1		3	6233.1
IntegrationMgmt	623		2	
Iterations	62132		3	
LCMactivities	6213425		5	6213425
LCMselection	62134		3	
LCMtasks	62134256		6	
LCMtechniques	621342567.1		7	621342567.1
Maintenance	62134415.1		5	62134415.1
MDAmodels	621334.1		4	621334.1
MDAplan	621		2	
MDAsupport	6213441		4	
MDAtraining	62134415.4		5	62134415.4
MDAtransform	621334.3		4	621334.3
MDAuserDoc	62134415.2		5	62134415.2

MDAwebDemos	62134415.3	5	62134415.3
ModelViews	621334.2	4	621334.2
ReqAnalysis	6213.1	3	6213.1
StoryPoints	62132425	5	
TechEstimation	62133	3	
Usecases	6213242	4	
ResourceModel 7			M7 = 29
ASL_AF	7243.2	3	7243.2
Automation_A	722334.3	4	722334.3
BSL_BF	7213.1	3	7213.1
ConfidenceLevel	722334.5	4	722334.5
ESL_EF	7243.1	3	7243.1
HSL_HF	7213.2	3	7213.2
Infrastructure_I	722334.1	4	722334.1
ISL_IF	7223.6	3	7223.6
IterationPlan	72331	3	
Knowledge_J	722334.2	4	722334.2
MgmtComplexity	721	2	
MgmtTeam	7223.2	3	7223.2
ModellingEffort	723314.1	4	723314.1
ModellingTeam	723314.2	4	723314.2
ModelTime	723314.3	4	723314.3
OSL_OMF	7223.7	3	7223.7
PATeam	7223.5	3	7223.5
Personnel	7273.3	3	7273.3
PITeam	7223.4	3	7223.4
Proficiency_Level	72233	3	
PSL_PF	7263.2	3	7263.2
QualificationLevel	7273.5	3	7273.5
ResourceKPA	7253.1	3	7253.1

ResourceMgmt	725		2	
ResourceModelFacade	7	7	1	
ResourceSheet	7273.2		3	7273.2
ResourceUsage	7273.6		3	7273.6
RSL_RF	7263.3		3	7263.3
SalaryLevel	7273.4		3	7273.4
Skill_G	722334.4		4	722334.4
Technical Team	7223.1		3	7223.1
TSL_TF	7263.1		3	7263.1
WorkCapabilityMgmt	726		2	
Workload	7273.1		3	7273.1
WorkPackageMgmt	727		2	
WorkProducersMgmt	722		2	
WorkproductsMgmt	724		2	
WorkunitsMgmt	723		2	
WSL_WF	7233.2		3	7233.2

RiskModel8				M8 = 19
Adaptability	828		2	
AFV	8233425.3		5	8233425.3
Average_TC	8243.3		3	8243.3
CalibrationFactor	8283		3	
DecisionIntelligenceFactor	82.5		2	82.5
EFV	8283452.1		5	8283452.1
HFV	8283415.3		5	8283415.3
High_TC	8243.4		3	8243.4
IcFV	82.6		2	82.6
Low_TC	8243.2		3	8243.2
MgmtCapability	828341		4	
OFV	82.7		2	82.7

PFV	82.6		2	82.6
RFV	8283415.1		5	8283415.1
RiskKPA	8213.1		3	8213.1
RiskMgmt	82.1		2	82.1
RiskModelFacade	8	8	1	
TeamEfficiency	823		2	
TeamEstimation	822		2	
TeamProductivity	8233.1		3	8233.1
TeamRange	8223.1		3	8223.1
TechCapability	828342		4	
TFV	8283415.2		5	8283415.2
TripleConstraints	824		2	
VeryHigh_TC	8243.5		3	8243.5
VeryLow_TC	8243.1		3	8243.1
WFV	8283452.2		5	8283452.2

Note:

1. Root Twin Number = 8
2. Height of Tree = 7
3. Monadicity = Sum(M1 to M8) = 137
4. Structural Complexity = 7 * 8 * 137 = 7672
5. Psychological Complexity = 1/Structural Complexity = 0.0001303
6. Size of Software = 227-16 = 211

Top Ten Risks and Monitored Parameters

1. Managers are "Techies" EPML
2. New Programming Language JAVA, C#, PYTHON
3. New Processes CFEM, EPML

4. Lack of Credible Estimates — EMF, SMF, DMF
5. New Size Metrics — EFP
6. Size Growth — Type, Scope, Pattern, Class
7. Personnel Turnover — Communication Pattern
8. New Methods and Tools — PMMI, PMBOK, SWEBOK
9. Volatile Requirements — SAFE algorithm, DEVCOMPLX
10. Aggressive Schedule — SCED, PI, CFEM, EPML, DEVCOMPLX

Priority Setting

1. Probability of occurrence: 3 defects per month at 1000 FPs per month production or .3%
2. Defects Removal Potential: 10 per month at 1000 FP per month production or 100%

3. Priority = Probability of occurrence x Percent Impact or 30%

Appendix M AGIA Requirements Engineering

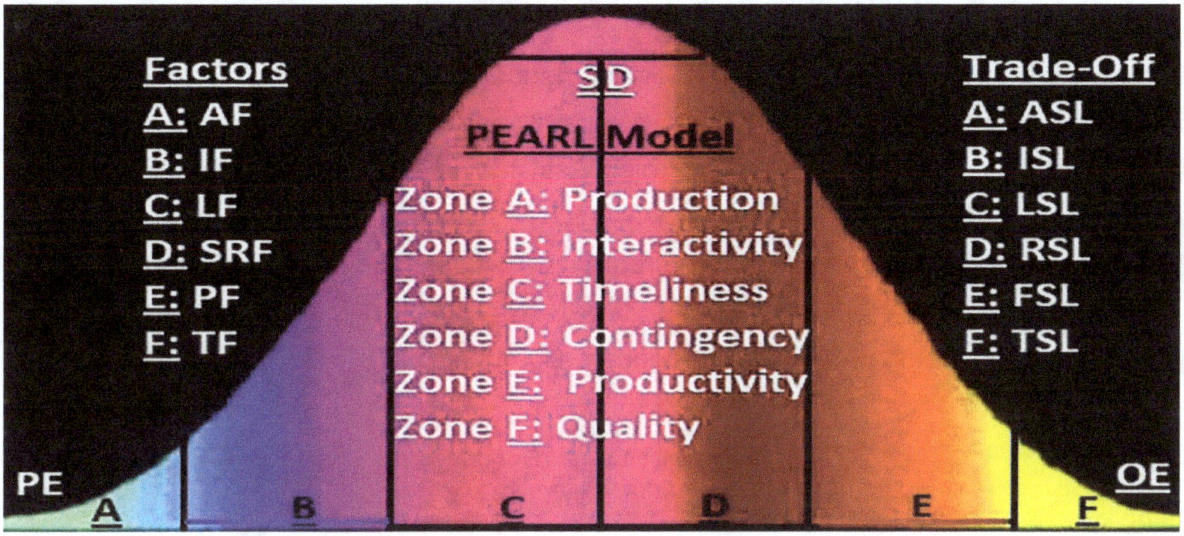

Figure 42 Optimistic to Pessimistic Scenarios Evaluation

LearnEdge™ integrates 9 performance factors is establishing the Systems Engineering economics for each scenarios explored.

The operational approach presented in this manual supports the following best practices:

1.LearnEdge™ introduces a multidisciplinary Joint Active Development Environment (**JADE**): CF factor

2 LearnEdge™ maps the development process a single Systems Engineering Economics Model (**SEEM**): SF factor.

3. LearnEdge™ presents a System Architectural Feature Evaluation methodology (**SAFE**): SRF factor.

4. LearnEdge™ a performance-based Project Evaluation, Analysis and Review over the full LCM (**PEARL**): LF factor.

5. LearnEdge™ establishes a Project Attribute Monitoring and Predicting Agent (**PAMPA**) capability: PF factor.

6. LearnEdge™ maps the system under development against PMBOK and Baldrige Excellence Framework (**FRACTAL**): CMF factor

7. LearnEdge™ introduces an Intelligent Project Assistant in LCM Management (**IPALM**): IF factor

8. LearnEdge™ supports a Verifiable Requirements in OO Methodology (**VROOM**) capability: AF factor.

9. LearnEdge™ supports a Pairwise-Independent-Combinational-KPU (PICK) test capability: TF factor.

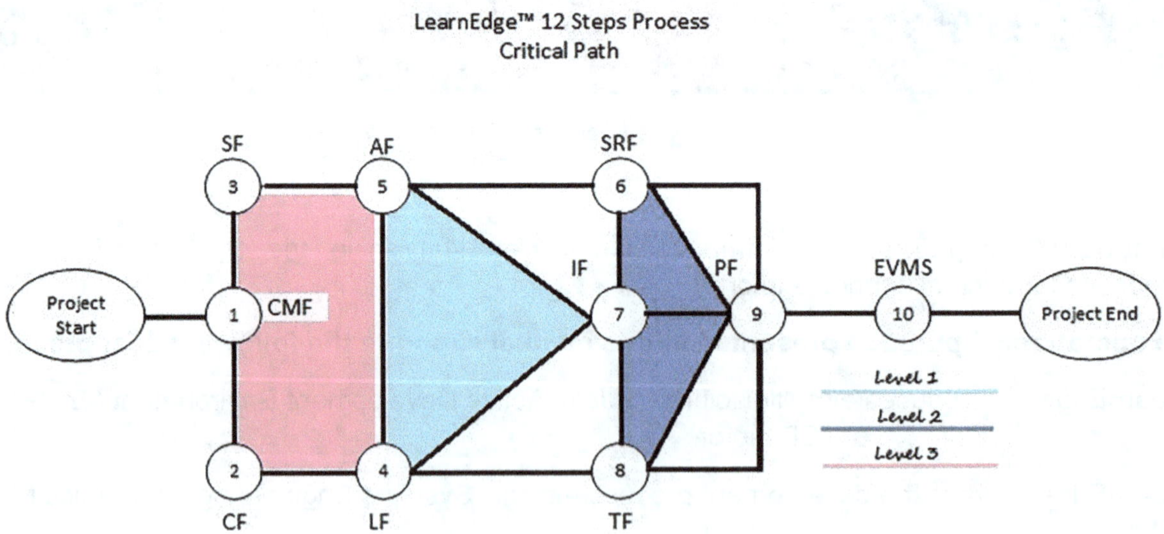

Figure 43 LearnEdge Worflow

1. Capability Maturity Factor (CMF).

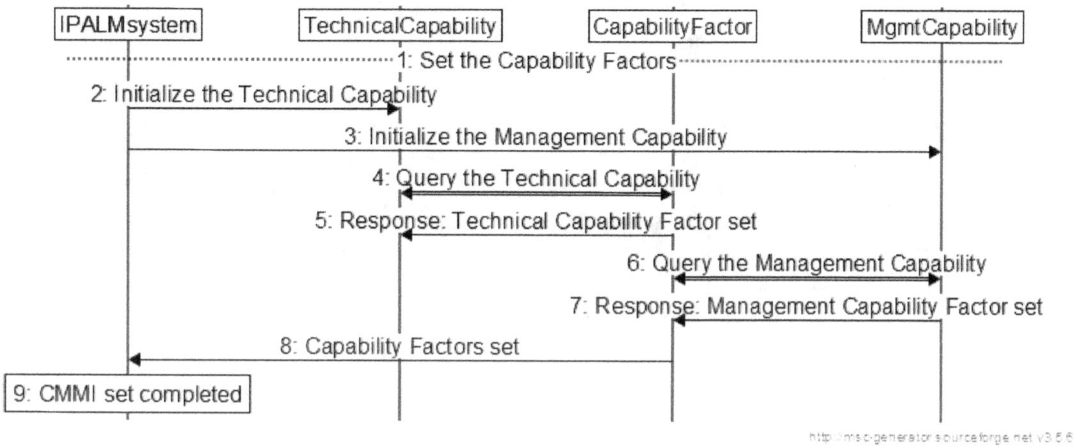

Figure 44 LearnEdge CMF

2. Efficiency Factor. (SF/EF)

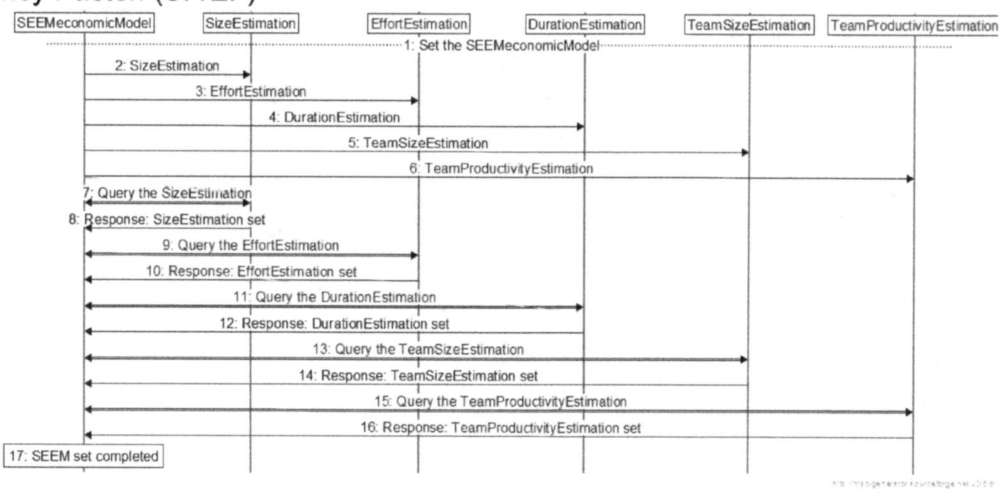

Figure 45 LearnEdge SF

3. Confidence Factor. (CF)

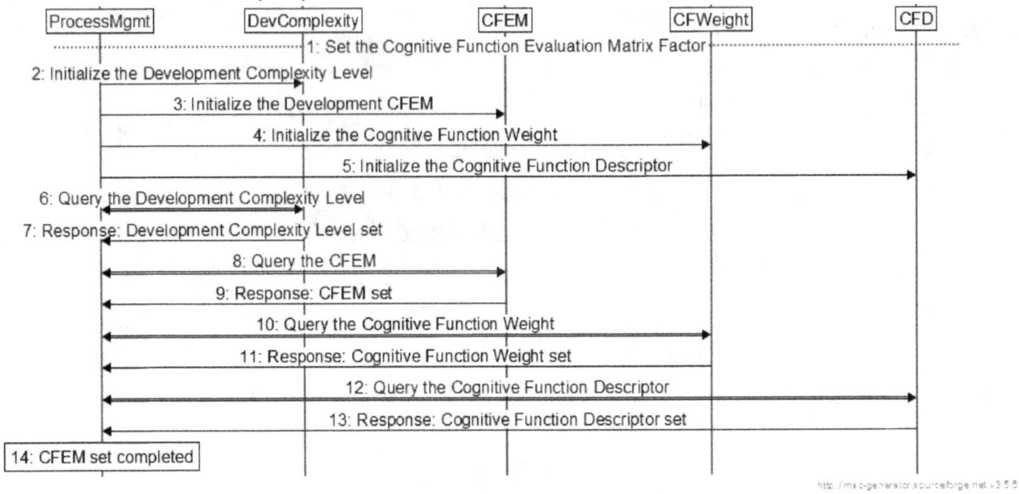

Figure 46 LearnEdge CF

4. Total Quality Factor. (TF/QF)

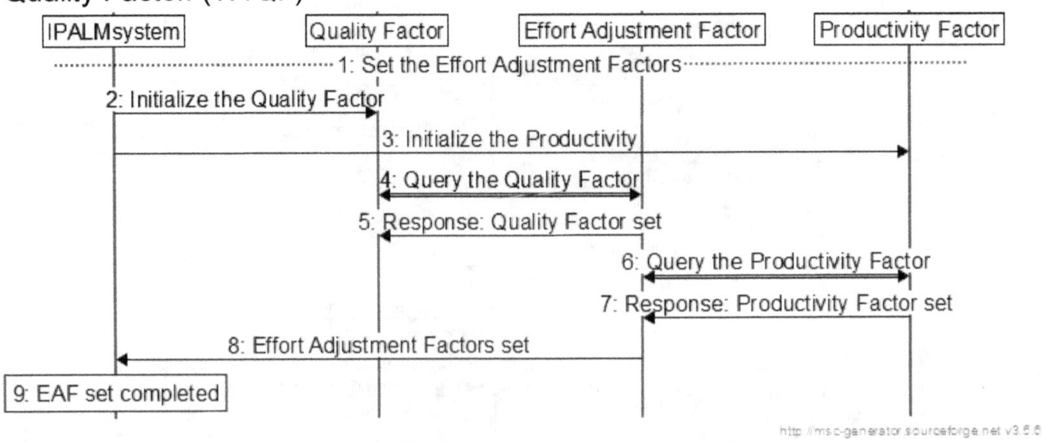

Figure 47 LearnEdge TF

5. Risk Mitigation Factor. (SRF/RF)

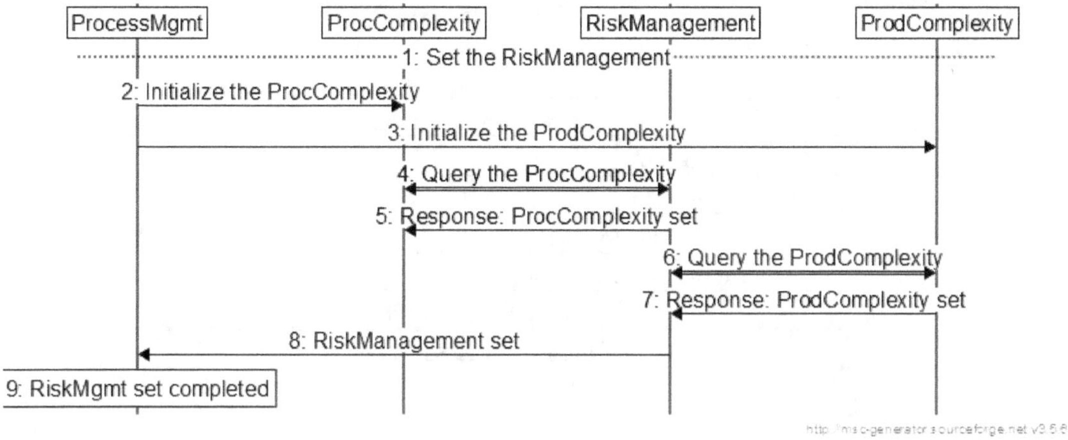

Figure 48 LearnEdge SRF

6. Productivity Factor. (PF)

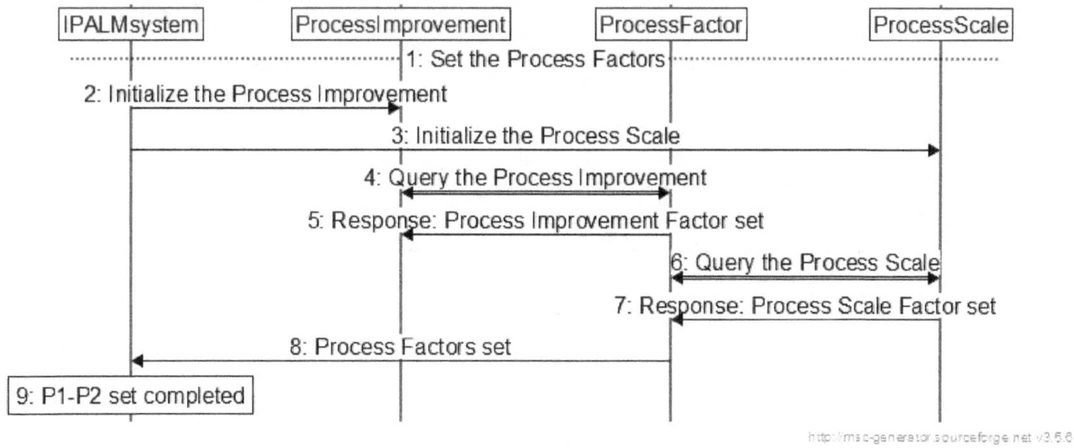

Figure 49 LearnEdge PF

7. Dependency Factor. (LF/WF)

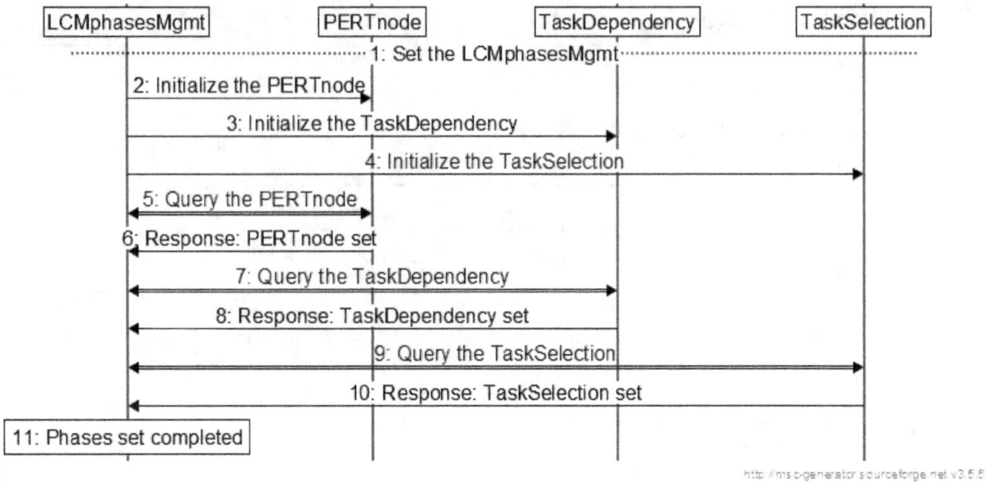

Figure 50 LearnEdge LF

8. Interactivity Facto (IF)

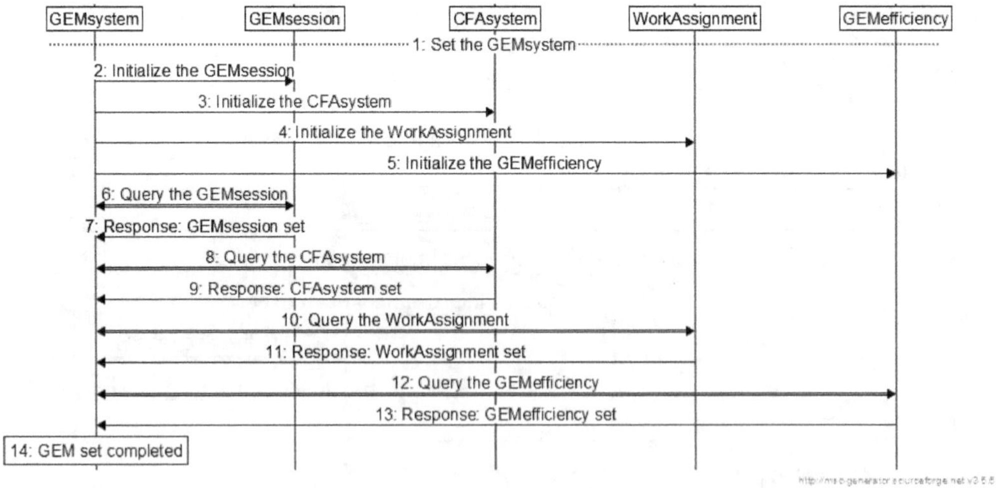

Figure 51 LearnEdge IF

9. Adaptability Factor. (AF)

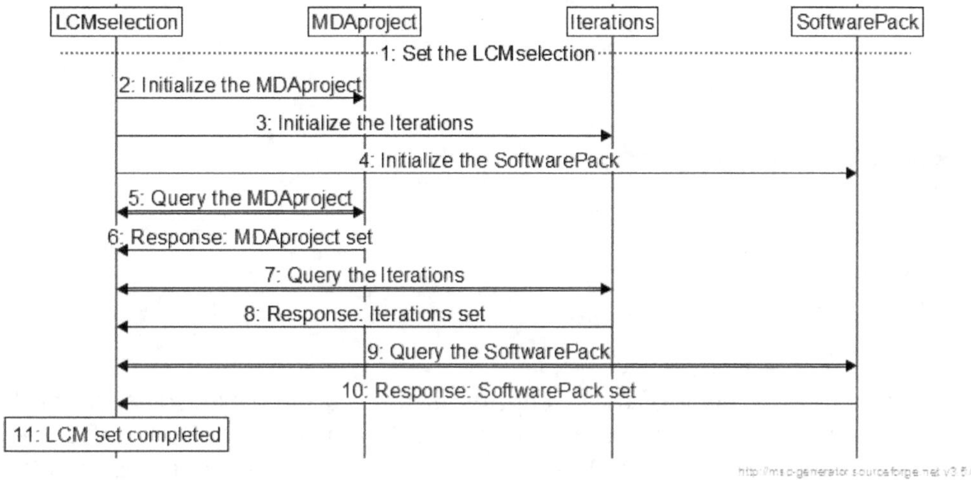

Figure 52 LearnEdge AF

Appendix N MDA in Practice -RentalCar Demo (Small Project)

Example: Rental Car System

1. Requirements

The major business activity of the company is renting cars without a driver. Since the company is located in the main tourist area, most cars are acquired at the beginning of the high season (summer months) and are sold once they are over, although car sales can occur at any time if a price and delivery date are agreed upon with the buyer.

The company works with two kinds of customers: agencies and direct clients. Agencies are other companies (or divisions of the same company) that usually rent cars to re- rent them (keeping a certain margin), whereas direct clients are individuals who directly rent cars. Direct clients can benefit from certain discounts.

Renting a car implies the creation of a contract between company and customer, which captures the rental details (car plate number, tariff, date, rental duration in days, place of return, etc.). The contract stays open until the car is returned, when the final computation of charges is performed and when the bond is returned, if appropriate, and the amount due, if any, is paid. While the contract is open, some details such as the date or place of return can be altered, and extras (such as car phones or baby seats) can be added or removed.

2. Goal

The Rent-a-Car business management system will be used to familiarize the reader with the problem domains that will be solved in the Model -Driven Architecture in Practice book.

Figure 53 Car Rental Demo Application

Specifically, we will structure the development of a Conceptual Schema around the following models:

- Object Model, which defines the structure and static relationships between the classes that have been identified in the problem domain, as well as the services activators objects.
- Dynamic Model, which defines the possible sequences of services for the objects of a given class (possible valid lives) and the aspects related to the interactions amongst them.
- Functional Model, which captures the semantics associated to object state changes, triggered by the occurrence of events.
- Presentation Model, which extends conventional conceptual modeling by incorporating a view responsible for capturing the information that defines the characteristics of the user interface and the way in which users will interact with the system.

The first version of this document will only focus on the Object Model.

3. Object Model

Starting up Integranova Modeler

When *Integranova* **Modeler** is opened, the Class Diagram is shown by default with an empty work area.

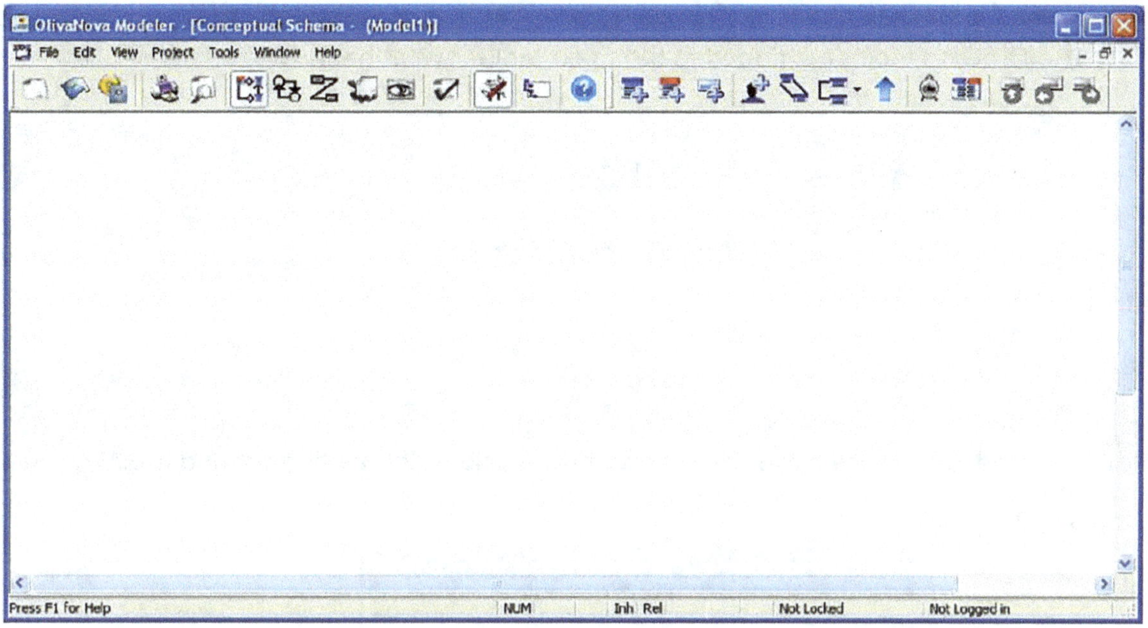

Figure 54 Object Model

By default, the toolbar does not display the Drawing toolbar. Click on the *Drawing toolbar*

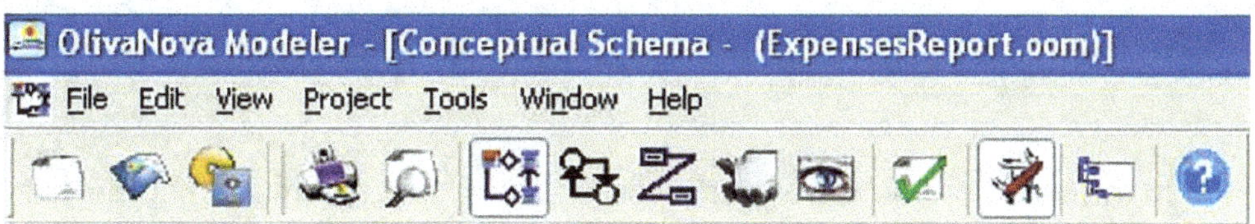

Figure 55 ***Integranova Modeler toolbar***

The Drawing toolbar is added to the main toolbar with these elements.

Figure 56 ***Drawing toolbar elements***

Creating a Class

Select the class icon From the Drawing toolbar. Click on the work area and the *New Class* dialog is shown:

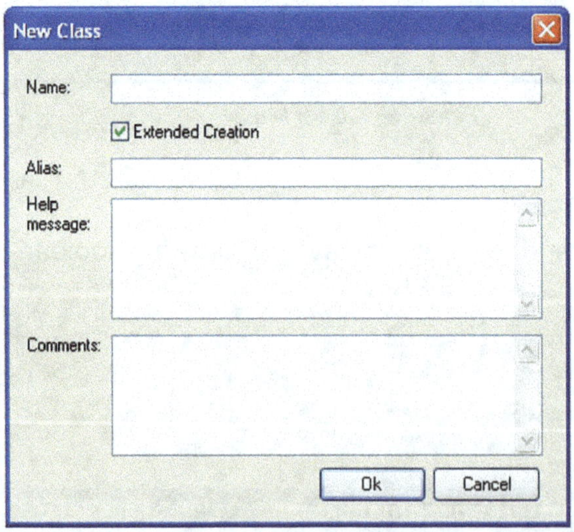

Figure 57 New Class Dialog

Fill in the fields on the lower part of the tab with the information summarized in the table below and click OK when finished.

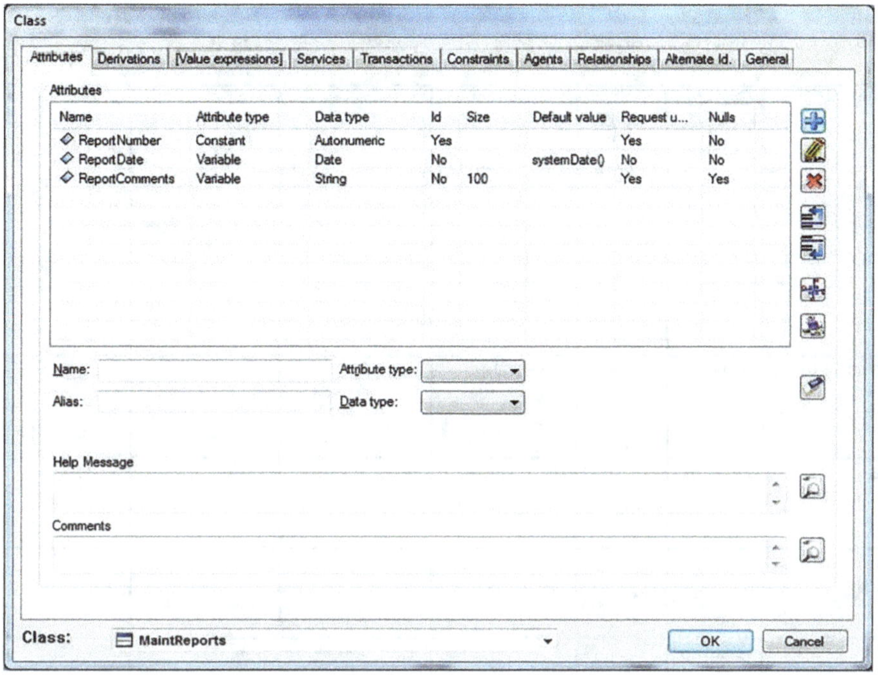

Figure 58 ***Defining Class Attributes***

Fill in the fields on the lower part of the tab with the information summarized in the tables below, click the "+" button to record them and then click OK when finished.

Attribute Name	Alias	Attribute Type	Data Type	Size	Default Value	Required On Creation	Nulls Allowed	Comment	Help message
AttrName	*Name*	*Constan Variable Derived*	*String Real Date Integer*	*Optional* *systemDate()*		*V*	*X*	*Analyst usage*	*End-User usage*
PlateNumber	Plate Number	Constant	Auto numeric			V	X		
CreationDate	Creation Date	Constant	Date	systemDate()		V	X		
Make	Make	Variable	String	10		V	X		
Model	Model	Variable	String	20		V	X		
Fuel	Fuel	Variable	Real			V	X		
Kilometres	Kilometres	Variable	Real			V	X		
Status	Status	Variable	String	1	"A"	V	X		
Notes	Notes	Variable	String	100		V	V		
RentalCount	Rental Count	Derived	Integer	2					
SalePrice	Sale Price	Variable	Real			V	X		

Table 12 **Attributes of Class Vehicle**

Attribute Name	Alias	Attribute Type	Data Type	Size	Default Value	Required On Creation	Nulls Allow ed	Comment	Help message
AttrName	*Name*	*Constant Variable Derived*	*String Real Date Integer*	*Optional systemDate()*		*V*	*X*	*Analyst usage*	*End- User usage*
ClientId	Client ID	Constant	Auto numeric			V	X		
CreationDate	Creation Date	Constant	Date	systemDate()		V	X		
GivenName	Given Name	Variable	String			V	X		
FamilyName	Family Name	Variable	String			V	X		
Address	Address	Variable	String			V	X		
RentalCount	Rental Count	Derived	Integer	2					
RentalBalance	Rental Balance	Variable	Real			V	X		
PendingBalance	Pending Balance	Derived	Real						

Table 13 **Attributes of Class Client**

Attribute Name	Alias	Attribute Type	Data Type	Size	Default Value	Required On Creation	Nulls Allow ed	Comment	Help message
AttrName	*Name*	*Constant Variable Derived*	*String Real Date Integer*	*Optional systemDate()*		*V*	*X*	*Analyst usage*	*End- User usage*
TariffId	Client ID	Constant	Auto numeric			V	X		
Description	Description	Variable	String	30		V	X		
RentalRate	Rental Rate	Variable	Real			V	X		
InsuranceRate	Insurance Rate	Variable	String			V	X		
VehicleClass	Vehicle Class	Constant	String	1		V	X		
VehicleLevel	Vehicle Level	Constant	Integer	1		V	X		

Table 14 **Attributes of Class Tariff**

AttrName	*Name*	*Constant Variable Derived*	*String Real Date Integer*	*Optional systemDate()*		*V*	*X*	*Analyst usage*	*End-User usage*
VehicleTypeId	Vehicle Type ID	Constant	Auto Numeric			V	X		
VehicleTypeDescription	Vehicle Type Description	Variable	String	20		V	X		
VehicleClass	Vehicle Class	Variable	String	1		V	X		
VehicleLevel	Vehicle Level	Variable	String	1					

Table 15 **Attributes of Class VehicleType**

Attribute Name	**Alias**	**Attribute Type**	**Data Type**	**Size**	**Default Value**	**Required On Creation**	**Nulls Allowed**	**Comment**	**Help message**
AttrName	*Name*	*Constant Variable Derived*	*String Real Date Integer*	*Optional systemDate()*		*V*	*X*	*Analyst usage*	*End-User usage*
RetiredVehicleId	Client ID	Constant	Auto numeric			V	X		
RetirementReason	Retirement Reason	Variable	String	30		V	X		

Table 16 **Attributes of Class RetiredVehicle**

AttrName	*Name*	*Constant Variable Derived*	*String Real Date Integer*	*Optional systemDate()*		*V*	*X*	*Analyst usage*	*End-User usage*
BuyerId	Vehicle Type ID	Constant	Auto Numeric			V	X		
BuyerName	Buyer Name	Variable	String	20		V	X		

Table 17 **Attributes of Class Buyer**

AttrName	*Name*	*Constant Variable Derived*	*String Real Date Integer*	*Optional systemDate()*		*V*	*X*	*Analyst usage*	*End-User usage*
RentalId	Rental ID	Constant	Auto Numeric			V	X		
Status	Status	Variable	String	1	"E"	V	X		
Bookings	Bookings	Variable	Integer			V	X		
RentalDate	Rental Date	Variable	Date	systemDate()		V	X		
Amount	Amount	Variable	Real			V	X		

Table 18 **Attributes of Class Rental**

Attribute Name	Alias	Attribute Type	Data Type	Size	Default Value	Required On Creation	Nulls Allow ed	Comment	Help message
AttrName	*Name*	*Constant Variable Derived*	*String Real Date Integer*	*Optional systemDate()*		*V*	*X*	*Analyst usage*	*End- User usage*
ExtraId	Extra ID	Constant	Auto numeric			V	X		
ExtraDescription	Extra Description	Variable	String	30		V	X		

Table 19 **Attributes of Class Extra**

AttrName	*Name*	*Constant Variable Derived*	*String Real Date Integer*	*Optional systemDate()*		*V*	*X*	*Analyst usage*	*End- User usage*
ReportNumber	Report Number	Constant	Auto Numeric			V	X		
ReportDate	Report Date	Variable	Date	systemDate()		V	X		
ReportComments	Report Comments	Variable	String			V	X		

Table 20 **Attributes of Class MaintReports**

AttrName	*Name*	*Constant Variable Derived*	*String Real Date Integer*	*Optional systemDate()*		*V*	*X*	*Analyst usage*	*End-User usage*
DNI	DNI	Constant	Auto Numeric			V	X		
DriverLicense	Driver License	Variable	String		“E”	V	X		
CreditCardNumber	Credit Card Number	Variable	String			V	X		
CreditCardType	Credit Card Type	Variable	String			V	X		

Table 21 **Attributes of Class DirectClient**

Attribute Name	**Alias**	**Attribute Type**	**Data Type**	**Size**	**Default Value**	**Required On Creation**	**Nulls Allowed**	**Comment**	**Help message**
AttrName	*Name*	*Constant Variable Derived*	*String Real Date Integer*	*Optional systemDate()*		*V*	*X*	*Analyst usage*	*End-User usage*
CIF	CIF	Constant	Auto numeric			V	X		
BusinessName	Business Name	Variable	String	30		V	X		
ContactPerson	Contact Person	Variable	String	30		V	X		
MarginRate	Margin Rate	Variable	Real			V	X		

Table 22 **Attributes of Class AgencyClient**

AttrName	*Name*	*Constant Variable Derived*	*String Real Date Integer*	*Optional* *systemDate()*		*V*	*X*	*Analyst usage*	*End-User usage*
IssuedInvoiceID	Issued Invoice ID	Constant	Auto Numeric			V	X		
IssueDate	Issue Date	Variable	Date	systemDate()		V	X		
TaxRate	Tax Rate	Variable	Real			V	X		

Table 23 **Attributes of Class IssuedInvoice**

AttrName	*Name*	*Constant Variable Derived*	*String Real Date Integer*	*Optional* *systemDate()*		*V*	*X*	*Analyst usage*	*End-User usage*
InvoiceID	Invoice ID	Constant	Auto Numeric			V	X		
InvoiceDate	Invoice Date	Variable	Date	systemDate()		V	X		
InvoiceAmoun t	Invoice Amount	Variable	Real			V	X		
Payed	Payed	Variable	Boolean			V	X		

Table 24 **Attributes of Class Invoice**

Attribute Name	Alias	Attribute Type	Data Type	Size	Default Value	Required On Creation	Nulls Allowed	Comment	Help message
AttrName	*Name*	*Constant Variable Derived*	*String Real Date Integer*	*Optional* *systemDate()*		*V*	*X*	*Analyst usage*	*End- User usage*
InvoiceLineID	Invoice Line ID	Constant	Auto numeric			V	X		
LineItem	Line Item	Variable	String			V	X		
ItemDuration	ItemDuration	Variable	Real			V	X		
DailyCost	Item Cost	Variable	Real			V	X		
LineItemCost	Line Item Cost	Variable	Real			V	X		

Table 25 **Attributes of Class InvoiceLine**

The new class will be placed in the work area where you have clicked on.

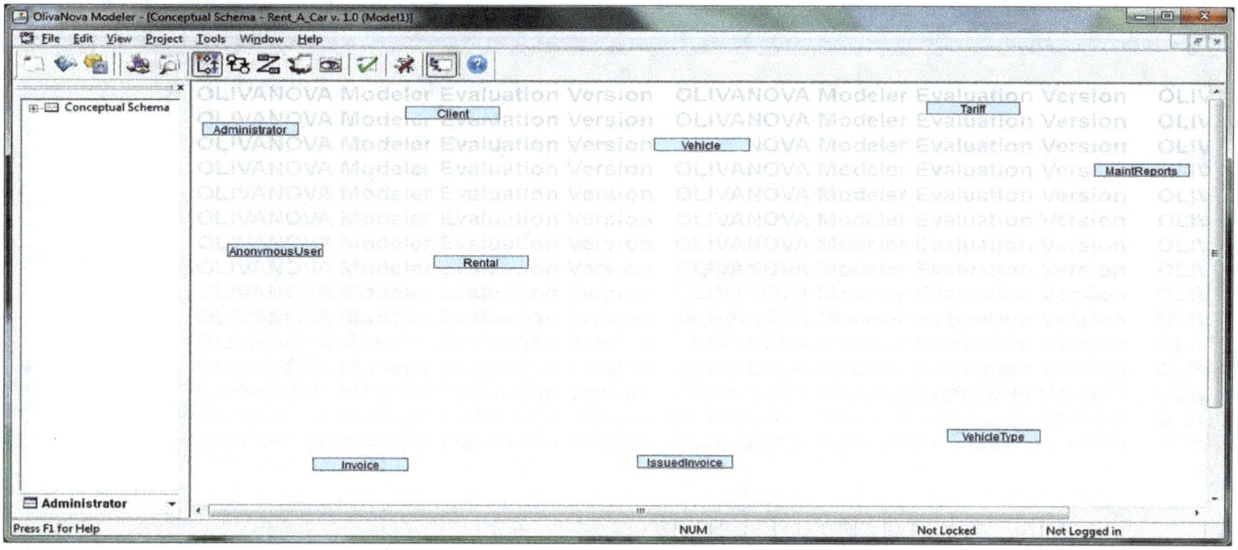

Figure 59 ***Rent-a-Car Classes***

The following figures will illustrate the actual entries of the attributes cited above in the tables.

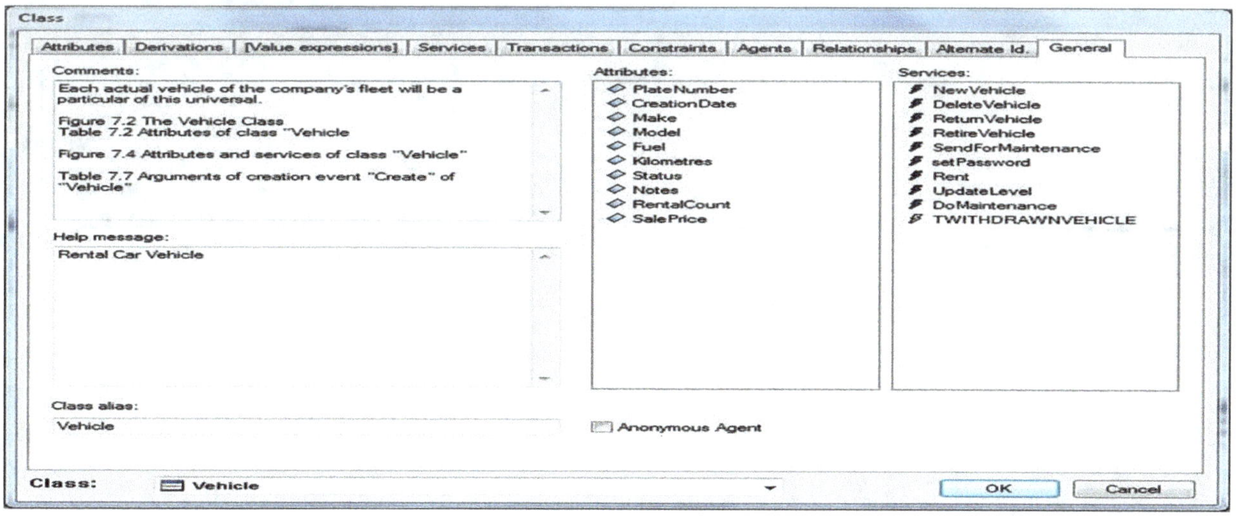

Figure 60 ***Rent-a-Car Vehicle Class***

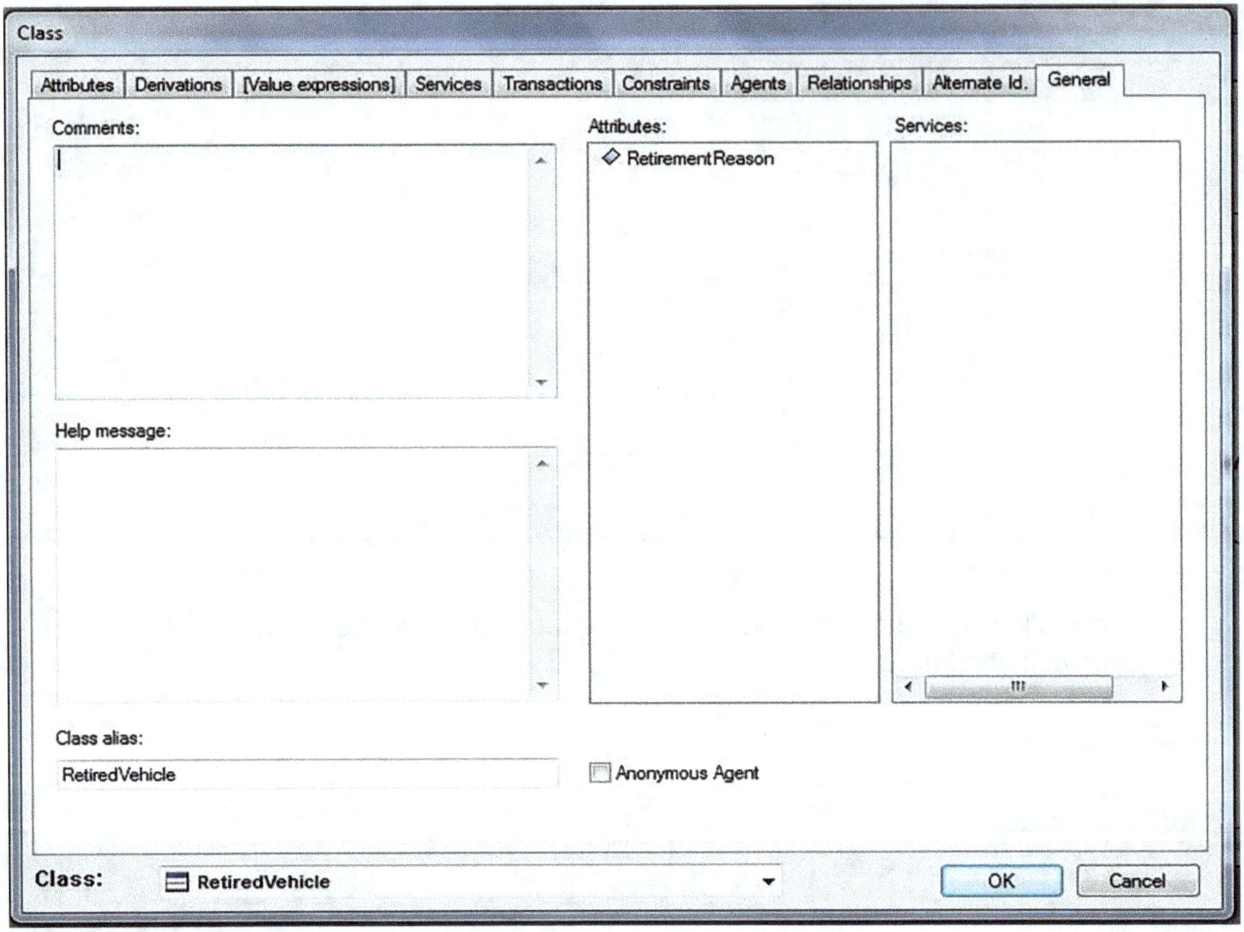

Figure 61 ***Rent-a-Car RetiredVehicle Class***

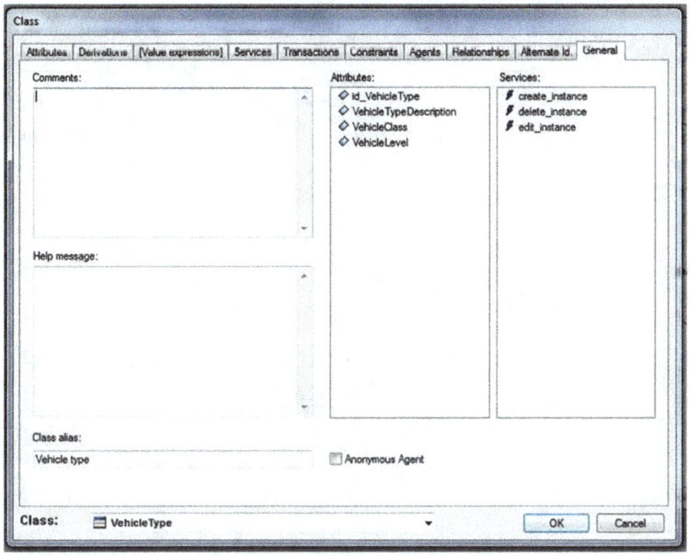

Figure 62 ***Rent-a-Car VehicleType Class***

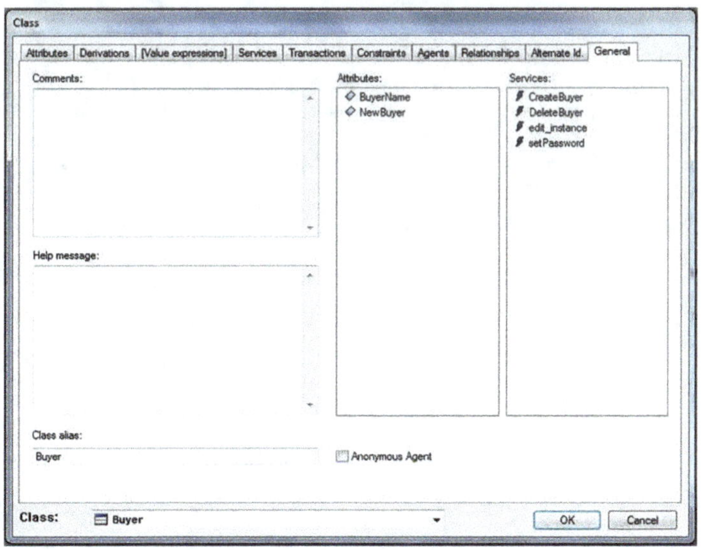

Figure 63Rent a car Buyer Class

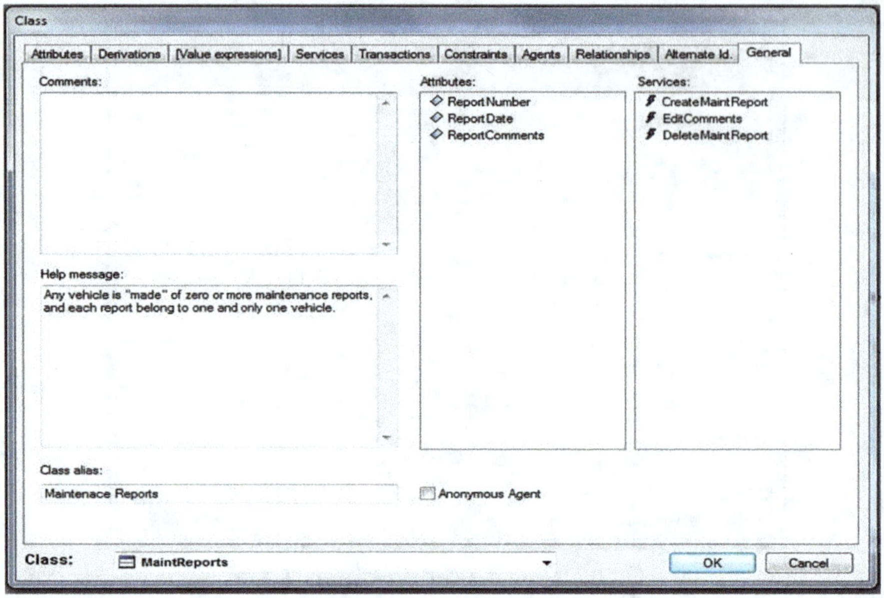

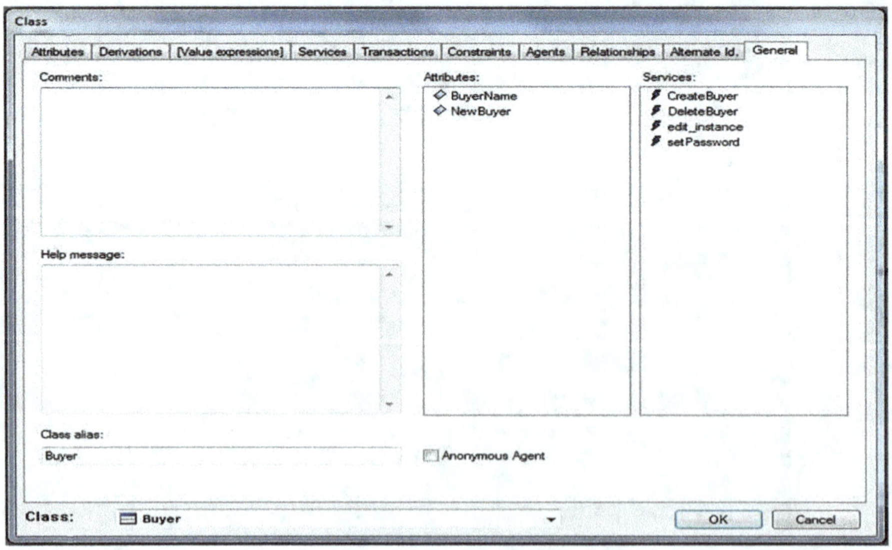

Figure 64 ***Buyer Class***

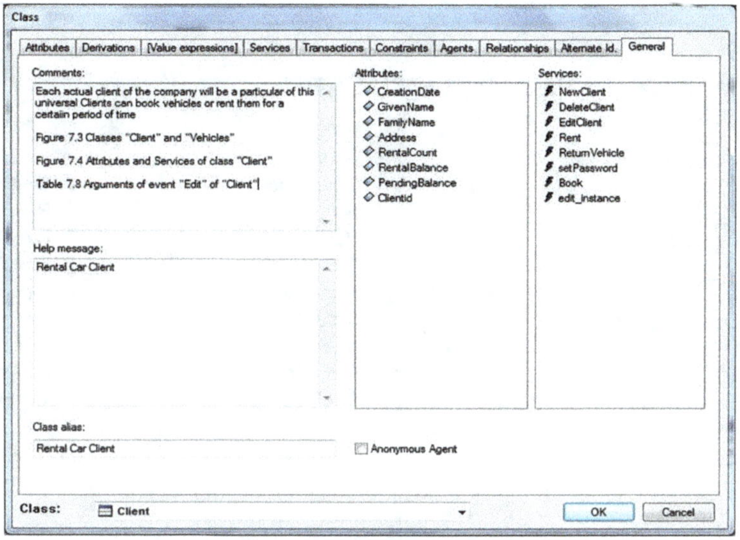

Figure 13 Rent-a-Car Client Class

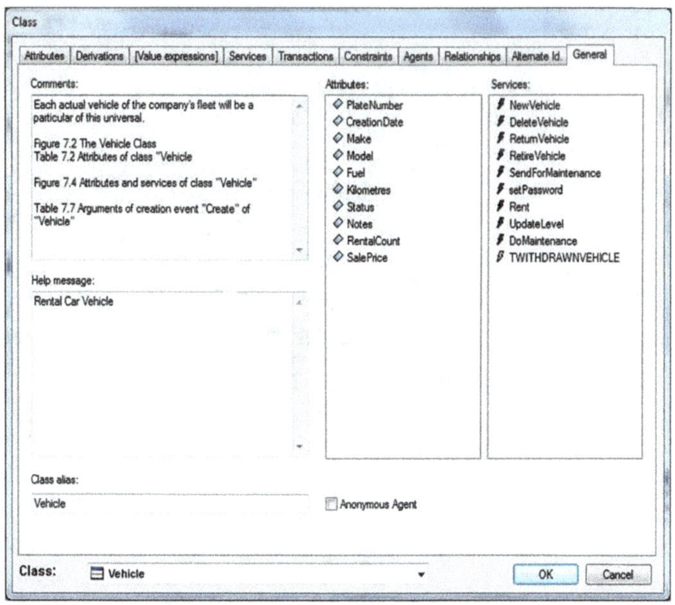

Figure 65 ***14 Rent-a-Car Vehicle Class***

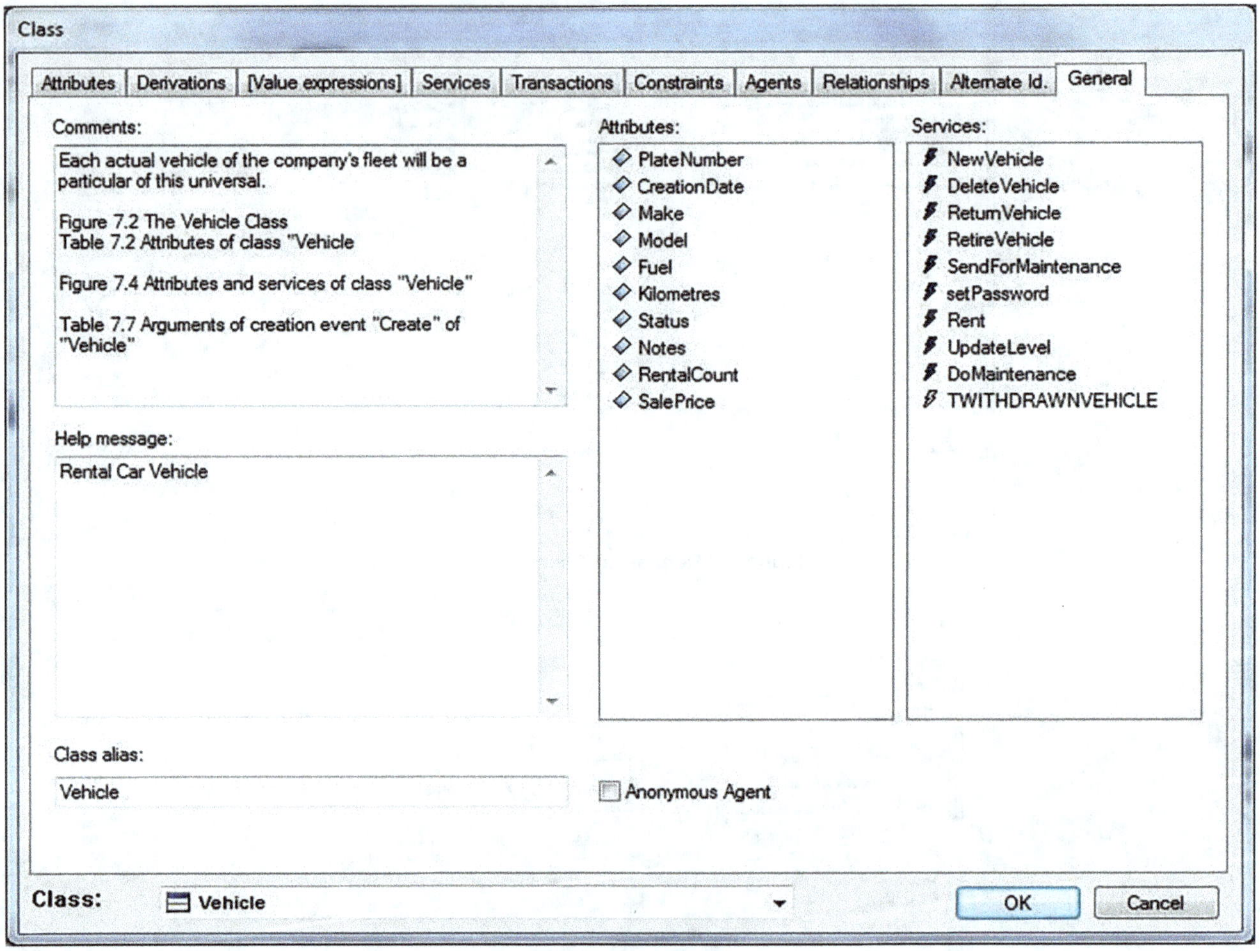

Figure 66 Rent a car Vehicle Class Attributes

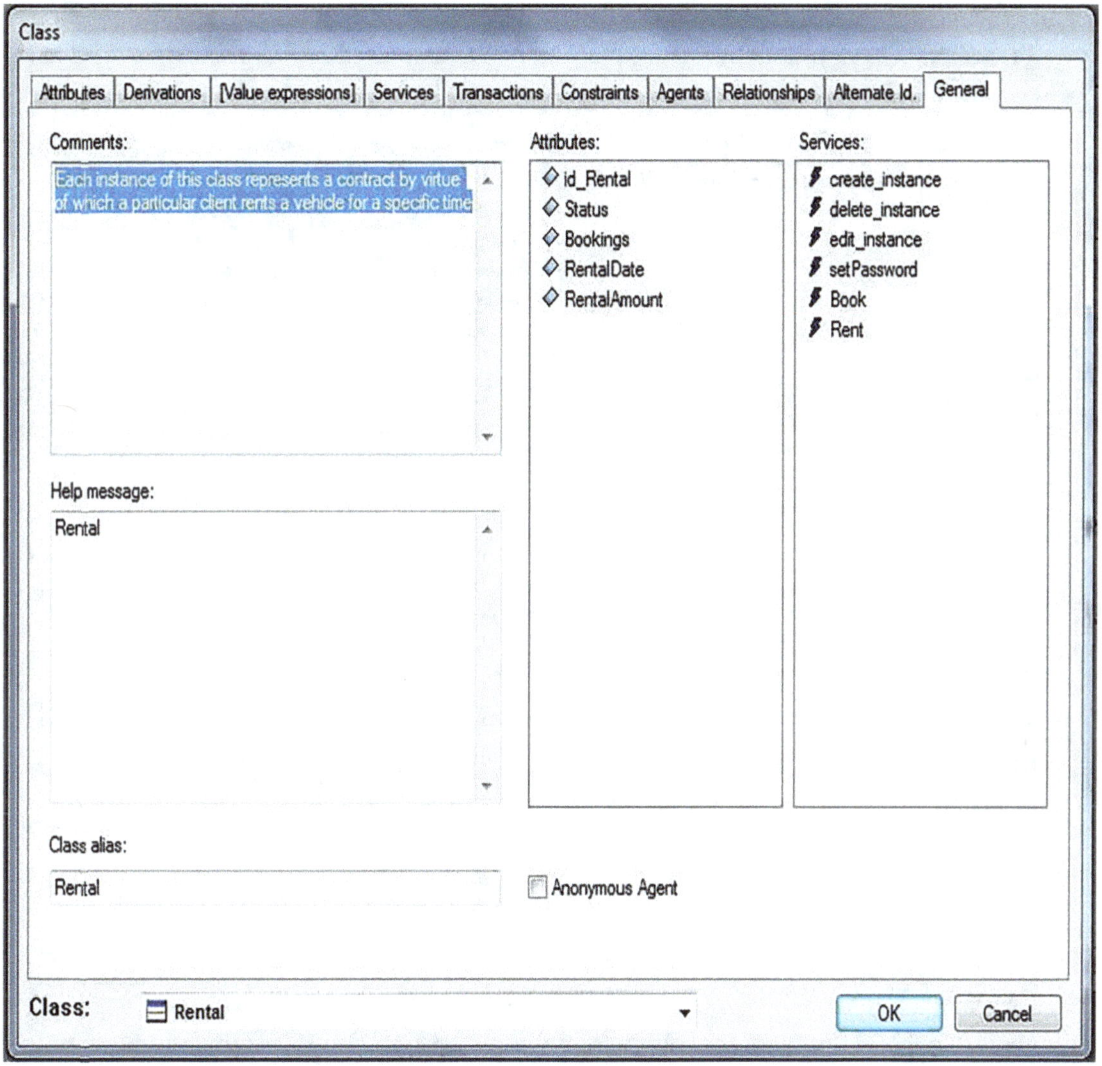

Figure 67 Rent a car Rental Class

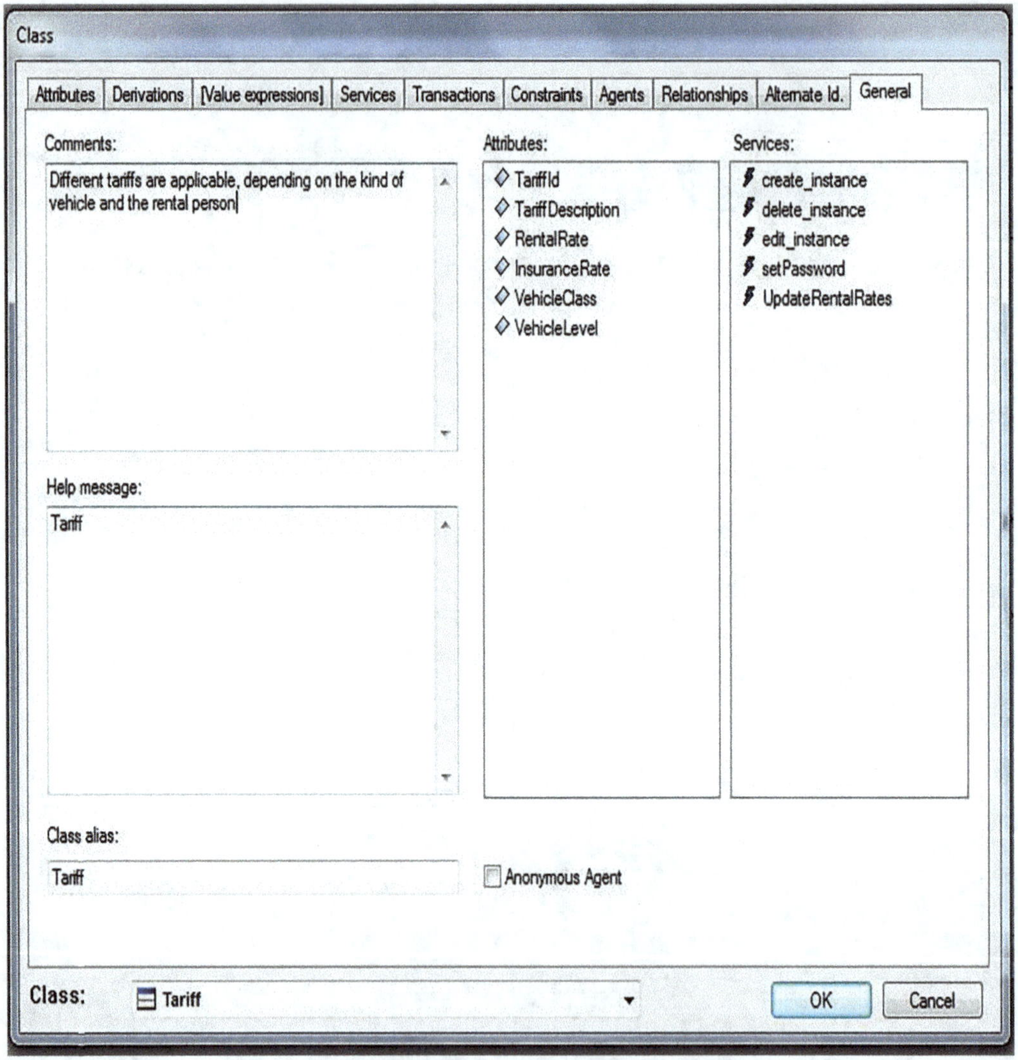

Figure 68 Rent a car Tariff Class

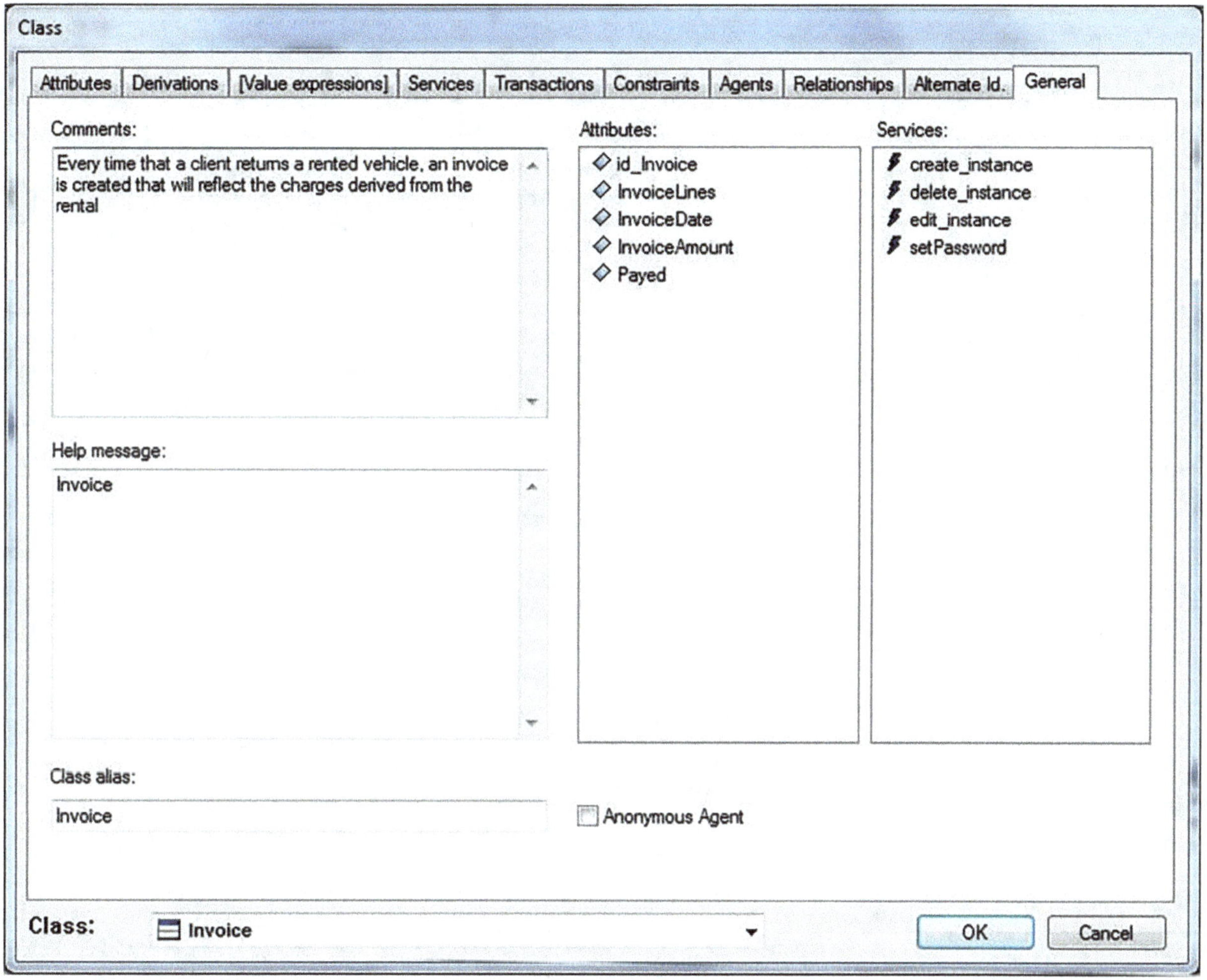

Figure 18 Rent-a-Car Invoice Class

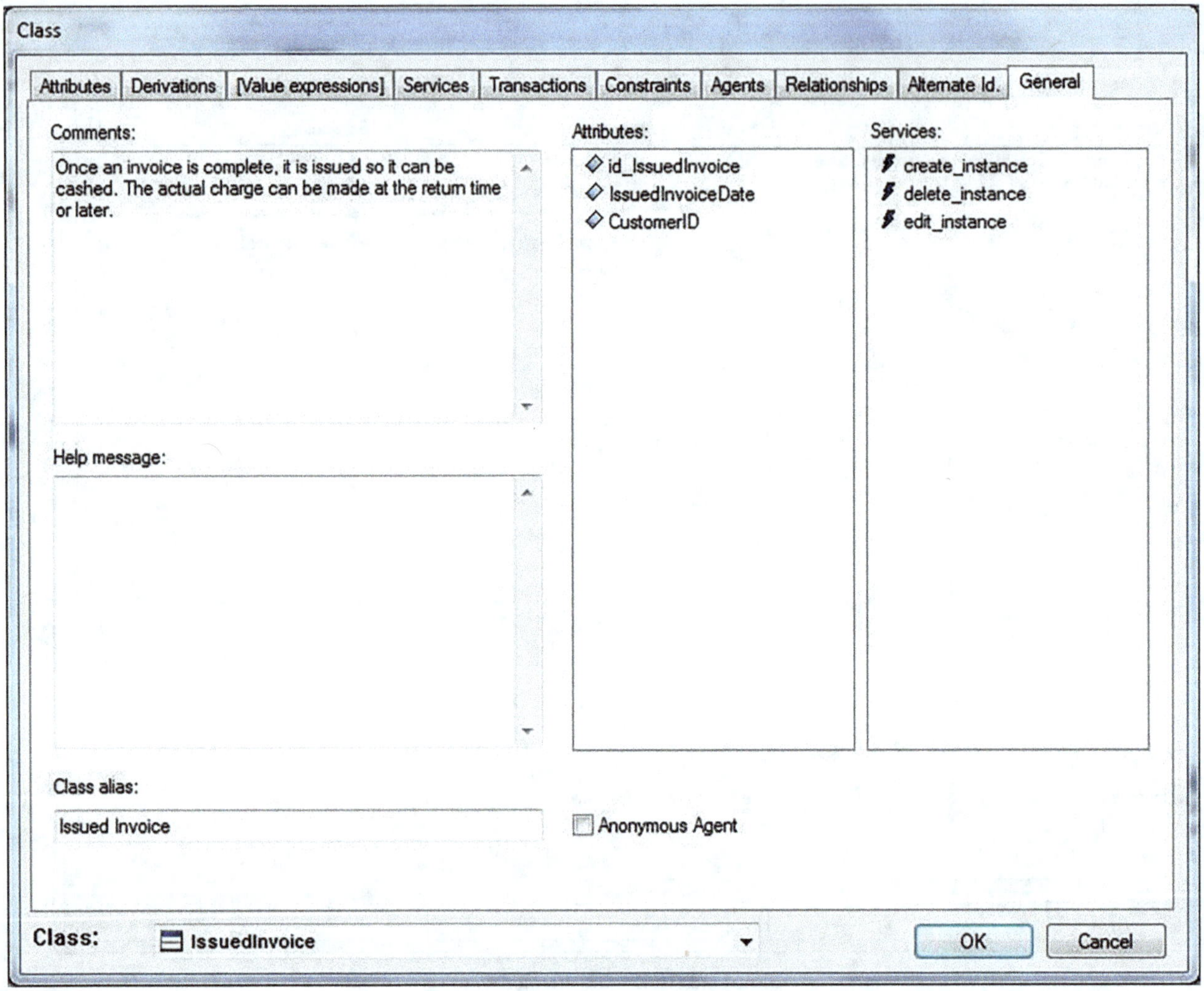

Figure 69 ***Rent-a-Car IssuedInvoice Class***

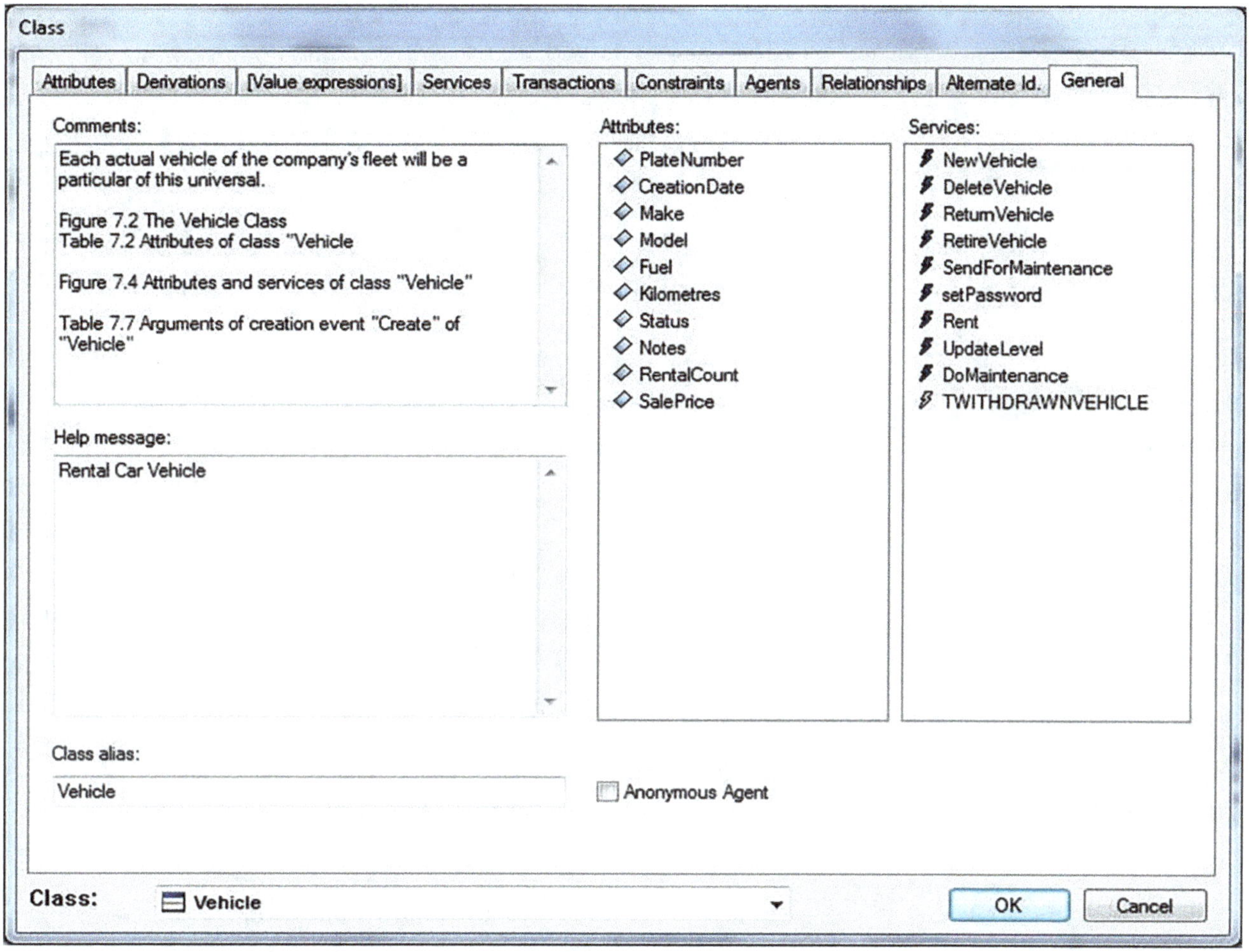

Figure 70 ***Rent-a-Car InvoiceLine Class***

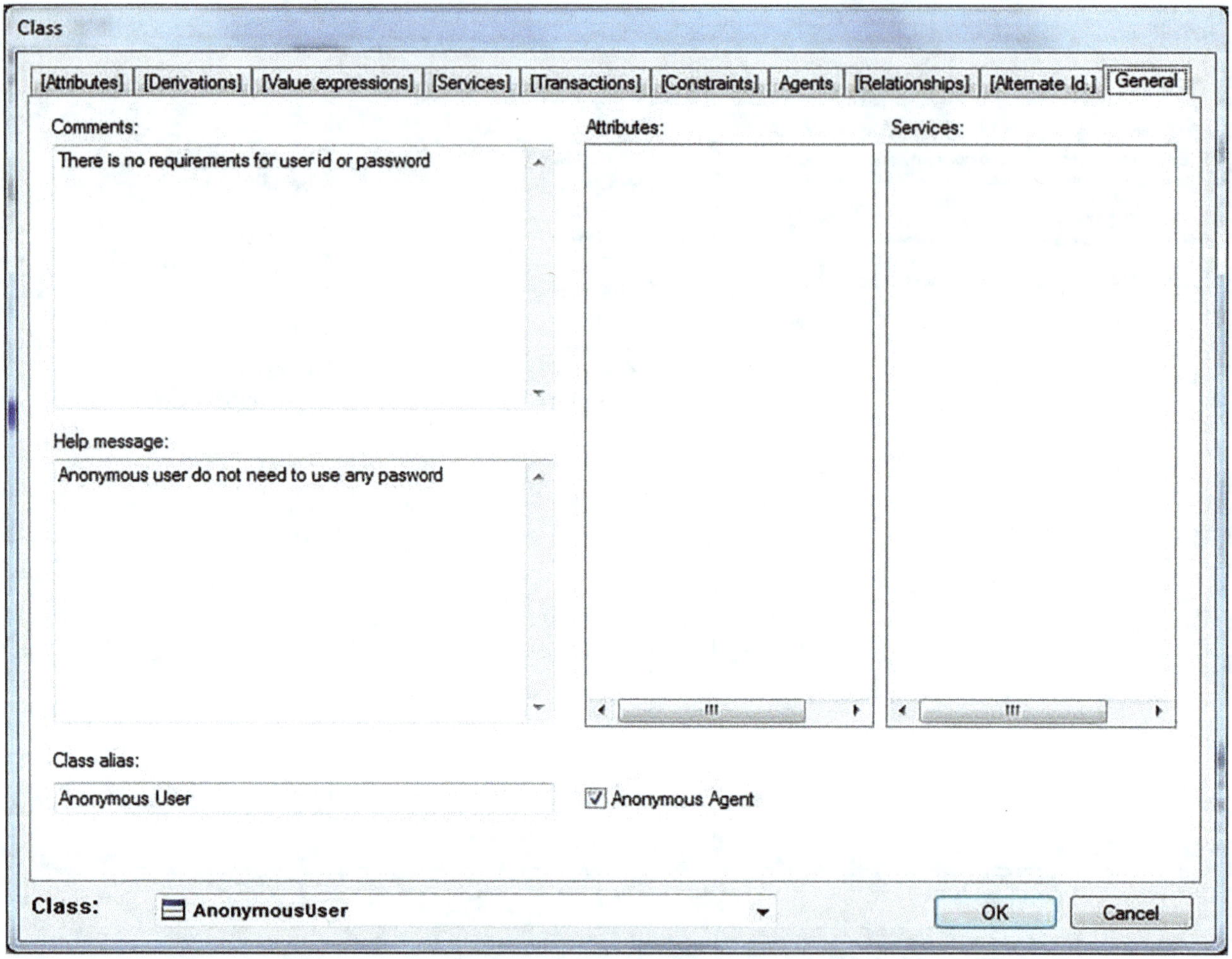

Figure 71 ***Rent-a-Car AnonymousUser Class***

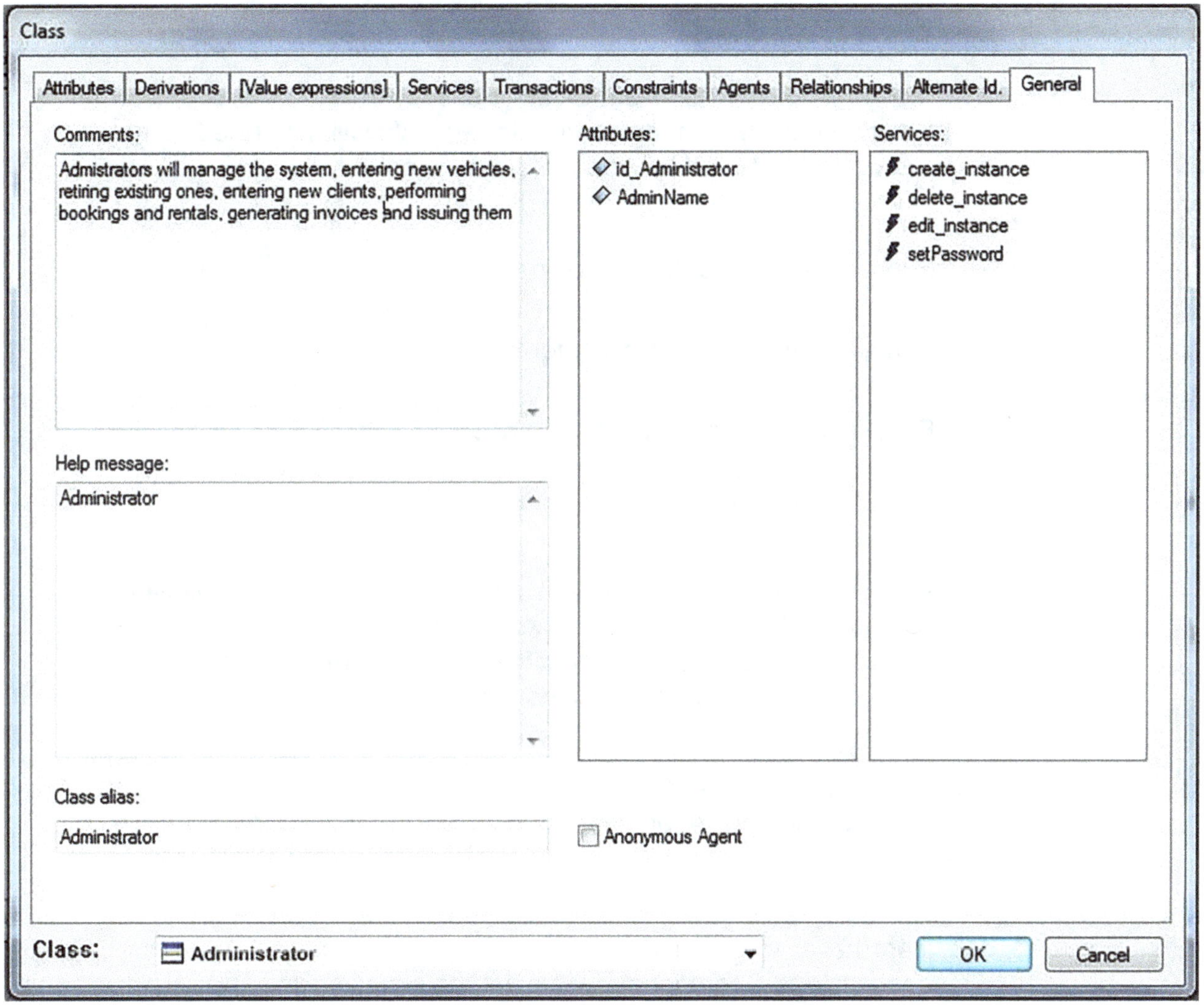

Figure 72 **Rent-a-Car Administrator Class**

Defining basic services and functionality

We have defined the Rent-a-car classes' relevant properties: identification mechanism, creation date, etc. We will also need some basic functionality to manipulate our classes, namely:

- Functionality to create a class instance
- Functionality to edit a class information
- Functionality to delete class instance

We will define this functionality by means of services.

The services of a class are the basic components associated with the specification of the behavior of a class. The concept of service can be defined as a processing unit, which may be atomic (an event) or molecular (a local transaction or local operation).

All services have a Name and, optionally, an Alias, a Help Message and some Comments. In addition to this, service may have a number of arguments.

We can have three kinds of services in our classes: Events, Transactions and Operations. Events are the simplest kind and we will discuss a bit about them here. Further details about events and transactions/operations will be presented later in the series.

If you select the Tools menu item and then the Options sub-menu item, you will see there are three services (specifically events) already in place.

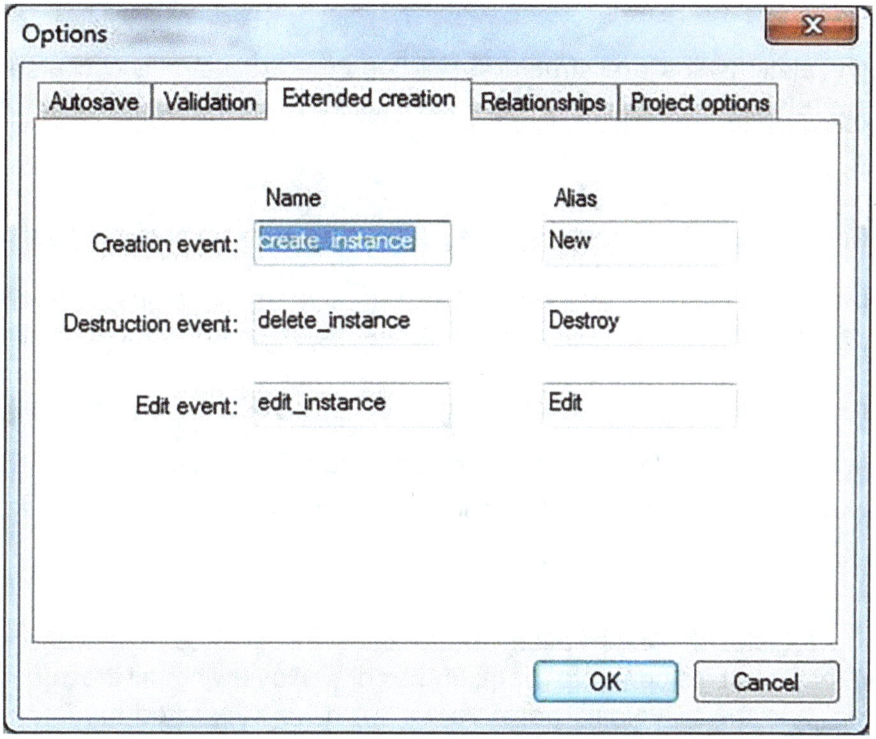

Figure 73 **Extended Services of Rent-a-Car**

These three events were automatically created by the tool when we created a class.

4. Creating relationships

In this example we would require to relate information among different classes. We will need to know the invoice of a client, see the lines added to an invoice line and so on. The way to achieve so, in *Integranova,* is through the definition of aggregation relationships.

The aggregation relationships are structural relationships between two classes. For each class of the relationship, the other class is referred to as a *Role*. The visibility of attributes

and services from each class regarding the other is bi-directional.

We are going to define and create now our first aggregation relationships for our model. Usually, in an aggregation relationship, one of the classes (the dependent class) requires

the other class (the independent class) to be completed.

In the ***Integranova*** **Modeler**, the relationships are drawn from the dependent class to the independent class.

We would like to register the information about client and invoice in terms of which invoice line were ordered by a concrete client, and so on... Reviewing, all the information related with client and their invoice. Therefore, as we have separated the information about client and invoice (each one is a different class) we are going to need and therefore establish an aggregation relationship between both of them as to get this information we have just mentioned.

As we previously said about what aggregation relationships are, we need to decide which of both classes we are going to select first as to draw the relationship. We can ask ourselves about, which of both classes can exist on its own (independent class) or which of both classes is going to need the other one (dependent class), that means, whose objects are going to be aggregated.

In this aggregation relationship between Client and Invoice, when we create an invoice, instance, we will need to tell the system **who** (the client) is requesting the invoice for **what**. Item is requested, Invoice Item, and **when the** item is required and for how long, duration of services. So we need a client prior to an invoice. Then, we know that the relationship is going to be drawn from Invoice class (dependent class) to Client class. Let's create our overall aggregation with the view showing the relationship between pair-wise classes association.

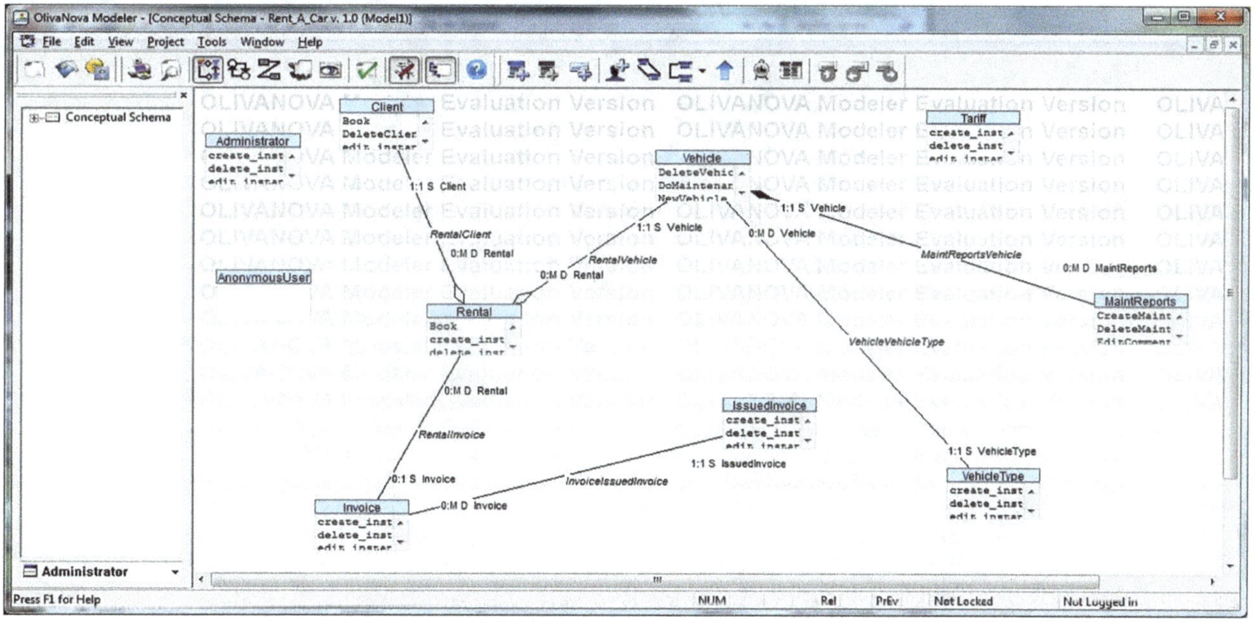

Figure 74 **Relationship between Rent-a-Car Aggregations**

Now we need to define the aggregation relationship properties, to modify if so needed, the properties established by default.

Let's see and edit the aggregation relationship properties. Double click on the line which represents the aggregation relationship and the *Aggregation relationships* dialog will show:

Model-Driven Architecture in Practice Example

The following figure shows the graphical notation used for the aggregation relationship between classes "Rental" and "Client".

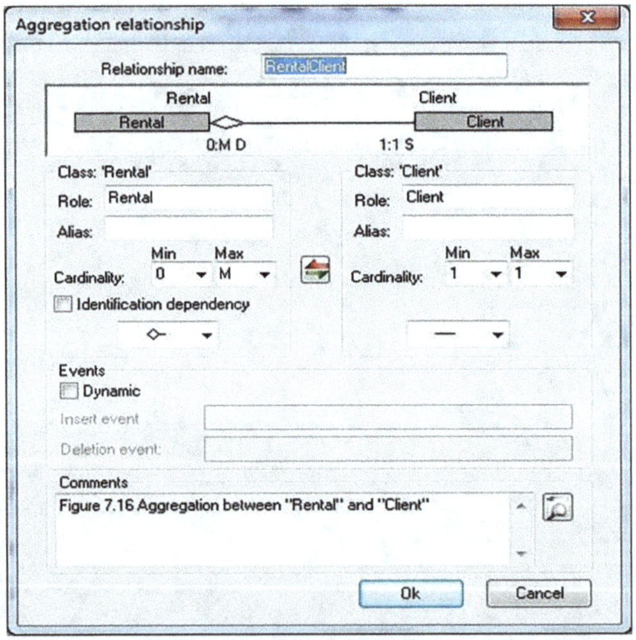

Figure 75 Aggregation relationship Rental-Client dialog

The following figure shows the graphical notation used for the aggregation relationship between classes "Rental" and "Vehicle". A rental has exactly one vehicle (cardinality "1..1), and a vehicle can participate in multiple rentals or none (cardinality of "0..*"). To visualize the "part-of" relationship, an empty (white) diamond is used.

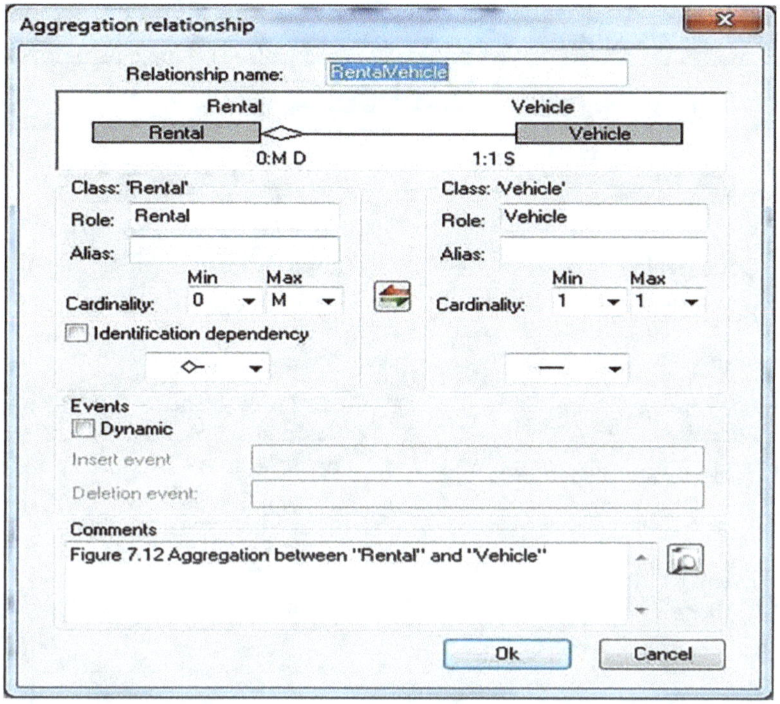

Figure 76 Aggregation relationship Rental-Vehicle dialog

The following figure shows the graphical notation used for the aggregation between classes “Rental” and “Invoice”.

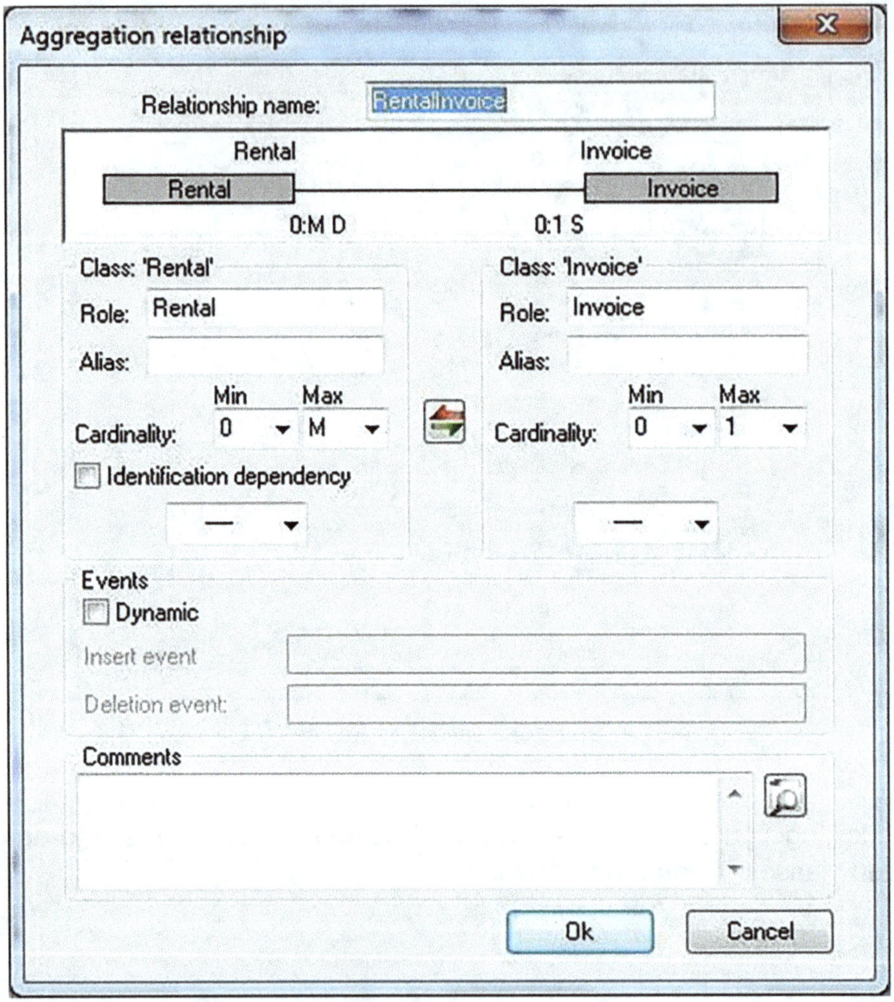

Figure 77 Aggregation relationship Rental Invoice Dialog

The following figure shows the graphical notation used to depict the association between classes "Vehicle" and "VehicleType". The figure shows that every vehicle has one type (cardinality

“1..1” at the “Type” end), whereas a vehicle type can correspond to multiple vehicles (cardinality “*” at the “Vehicle” end).

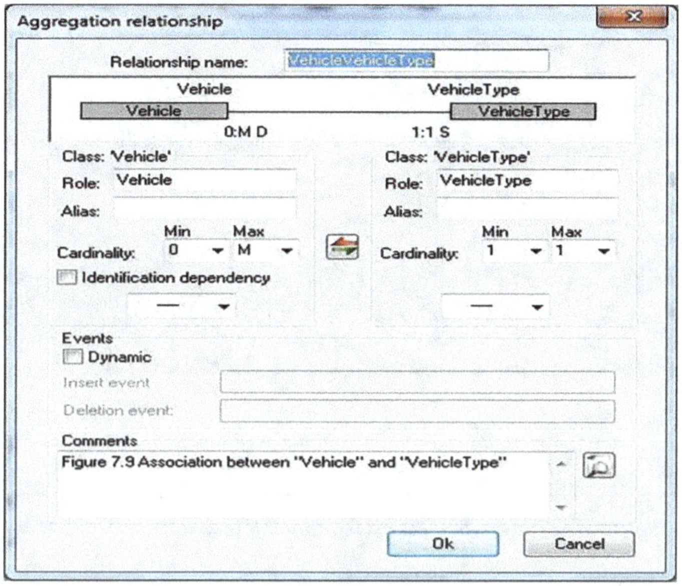

Figure 78 Aggregation relationship Vehicle-VehicleType dialog

The following figure shows the graphical notation used for the aggregation relationship between classes

“Vehicle” and “MaintReports”. Class “Vehicle” participates in the relationship as composite, and “MaintReports” as component. In fact, any vehicle is “made of” zero or more maintenance reports, and each report belongs to one, and only one vehicle to visualize the “composition” relationship, a full (black) diamond is used.

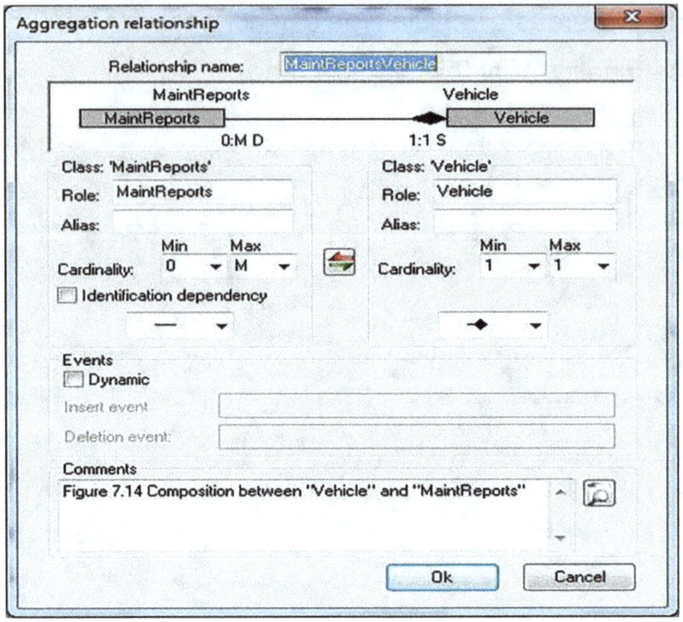

Figure 79 ***Aggregation relationship Vehicle-MaintReports dialog***

The following figure shows the graphical notation used for the aggregation between classes “Vehicle” and “Extra”. “Extra” represent the extras that can be added to a vehicle, e.g. air conditioning, power windows, etc. The “Extra” end is marked as dynamic so that extras can be added to and removed from a vehicle as necessary. The cardinality at the “Vehicle” end is “0..*” to avoid “Extra” to be permanently associated with a vehicle.

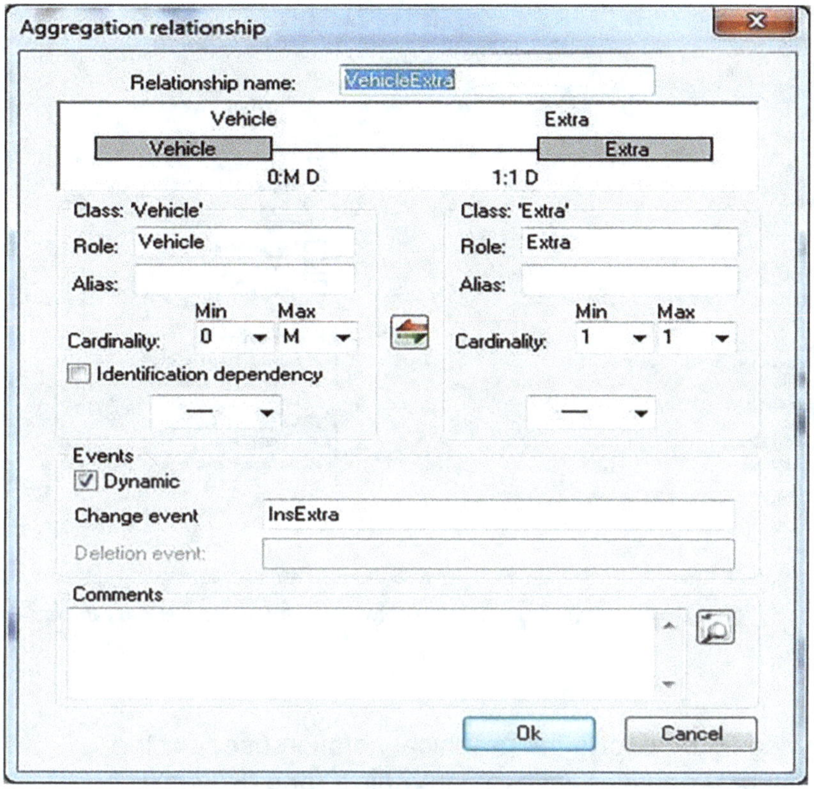

Figure 80 ***Aggregation relationship between Vehicle and Extra***

The following figure shows the graphical notation used for the aggregation between classes “Vehicle” and “RetiredVehicle”.

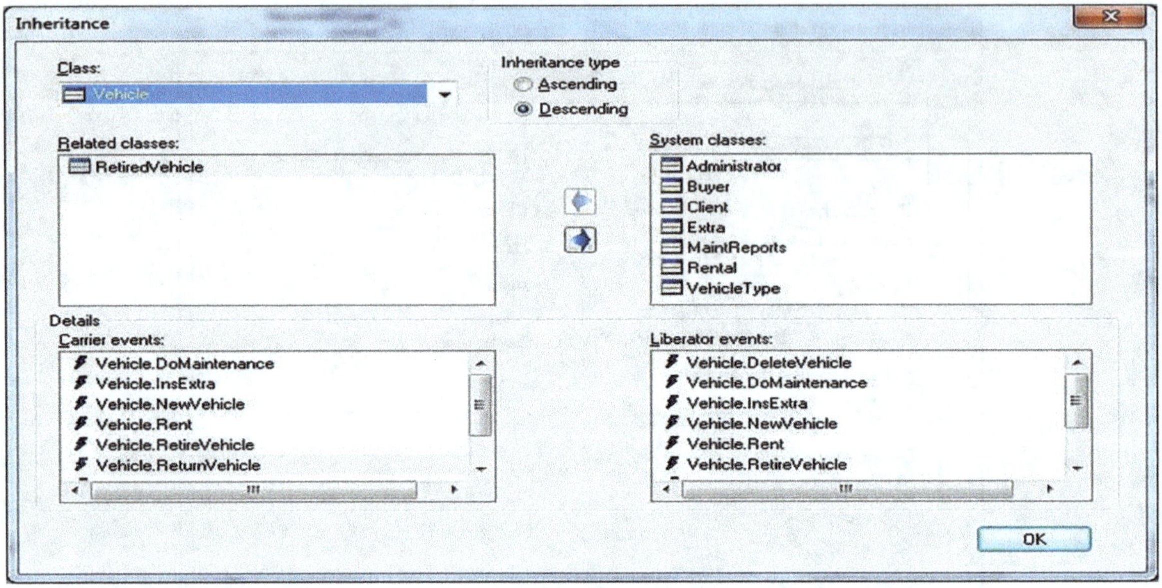

Figure 81 ***Inheritance relationship between Vehicle and RetiredVehicle***

The following figure shows the graphical notation used for the aggregation between classes “RetiredVehicle” and “Buyer”.

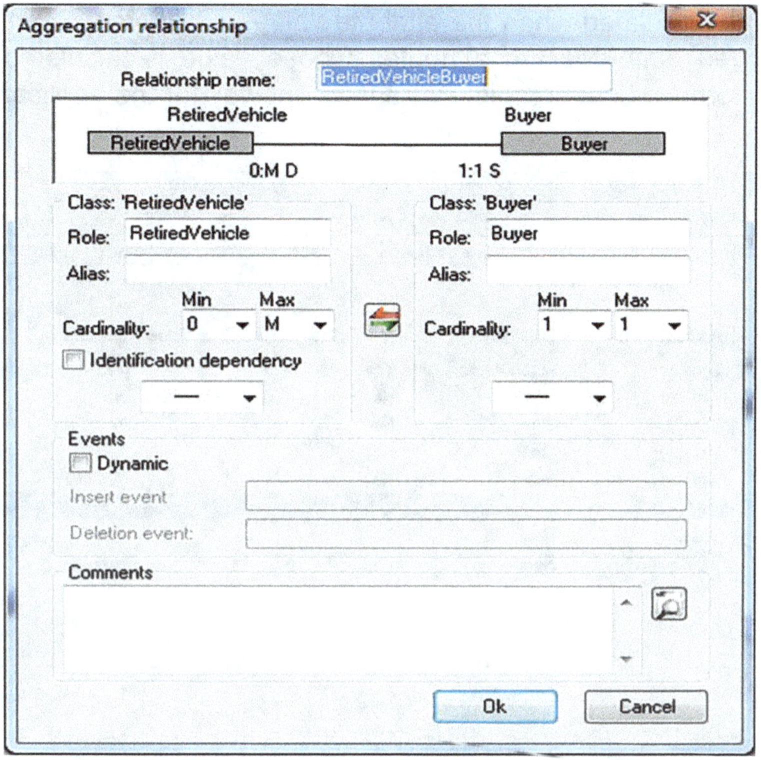

Figure 82 ***Aggregation relationship between RetiredVehicle and Buyer***

Eventually, press on the *OK* button to save the changes.

5. Defining calculated attributes

We are going to need a sort of property in which to save the count of every rental.

Integranova offers a specific type of attributes (Derived attributes), where it is only necessary to write the formula and the value is automatically calculated when the attribute value is required, in other words, derived attributes are attributes whose value is calculated by means of a formula, in a completely transparent way for the application user.

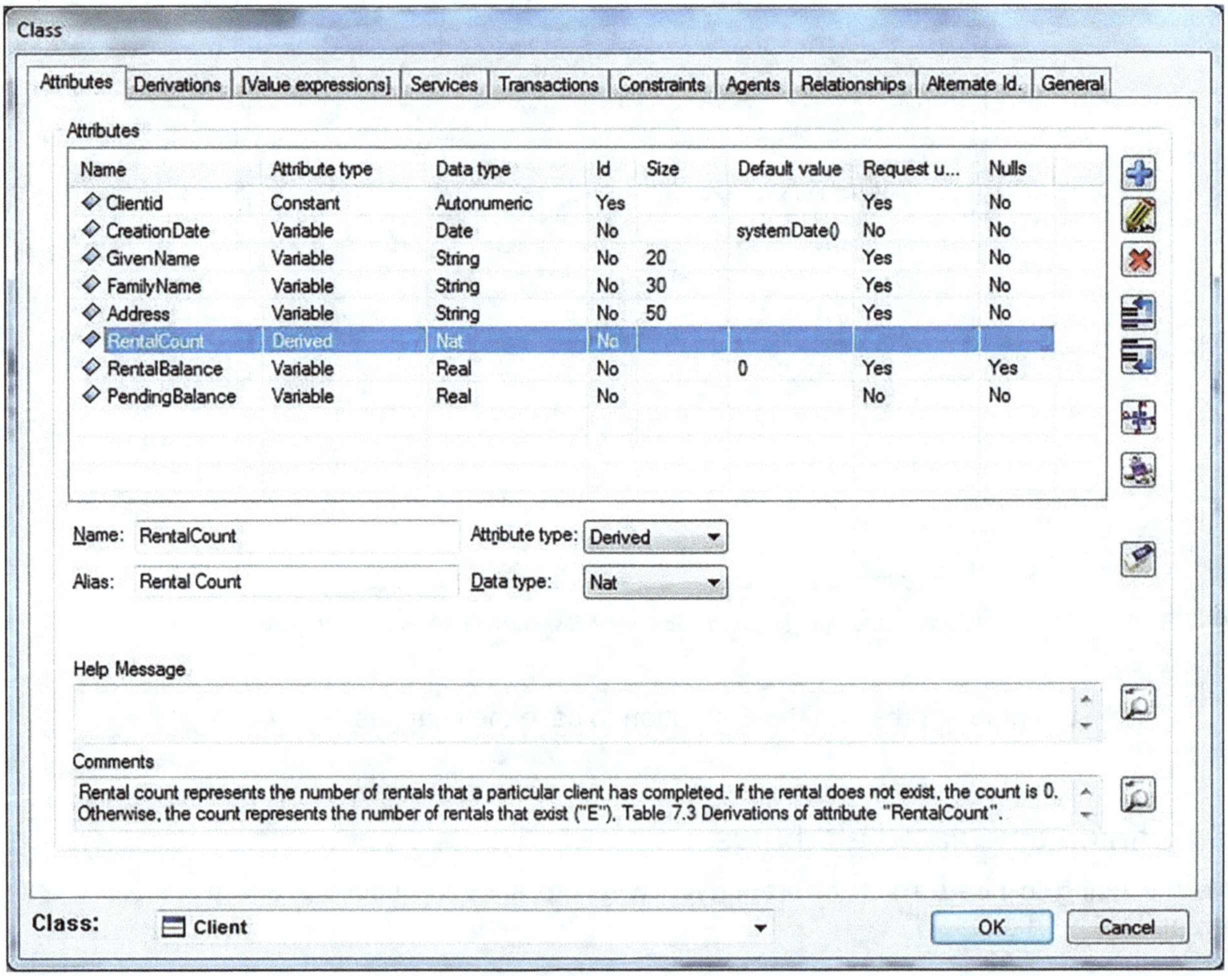

Figure 83 Derived attributes

Now that we have the derived attribute created, we have to add its calculation value formula. From this formula, this attribute is going to get its value. We have said that its value is going to be the purchased article price per the units acquired. Let s then, define such formula. Go to *Derivations* tab, and you will see the following scenario:

The class “Client” has a derived attribute “RentalCount” that represents the number of rentals that a particular client has completed. The derivation formula is:

COUNT (Rental).

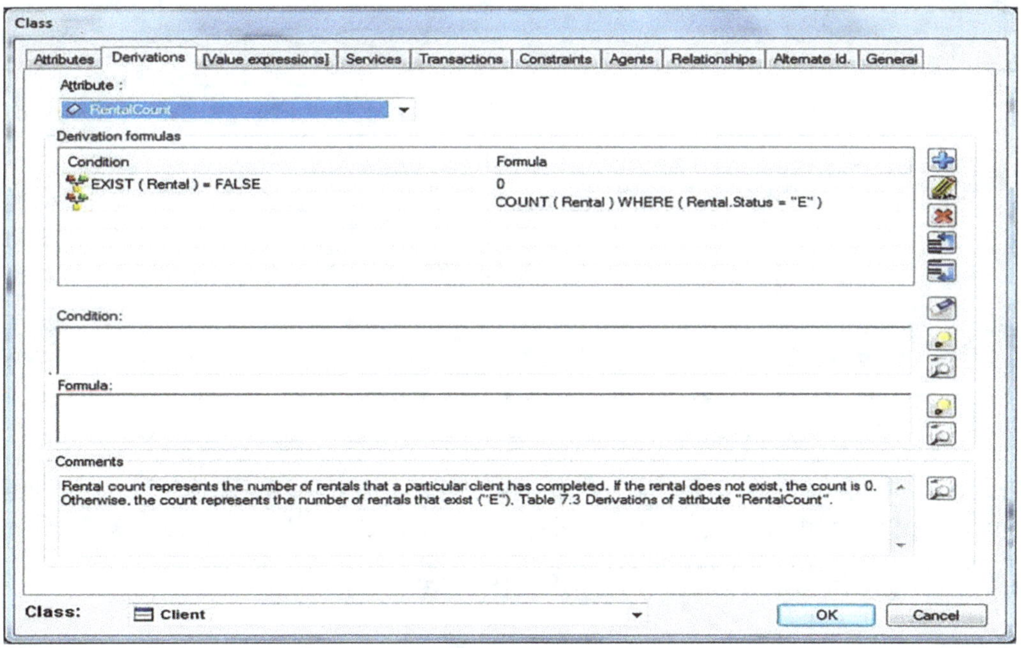

Figure 84 **Derivations tab in Client class**

Class “Vehicle”, for example, contains the derived attribute “RentalCount”, which has the following derivation formula:

COUNT (Rentals).

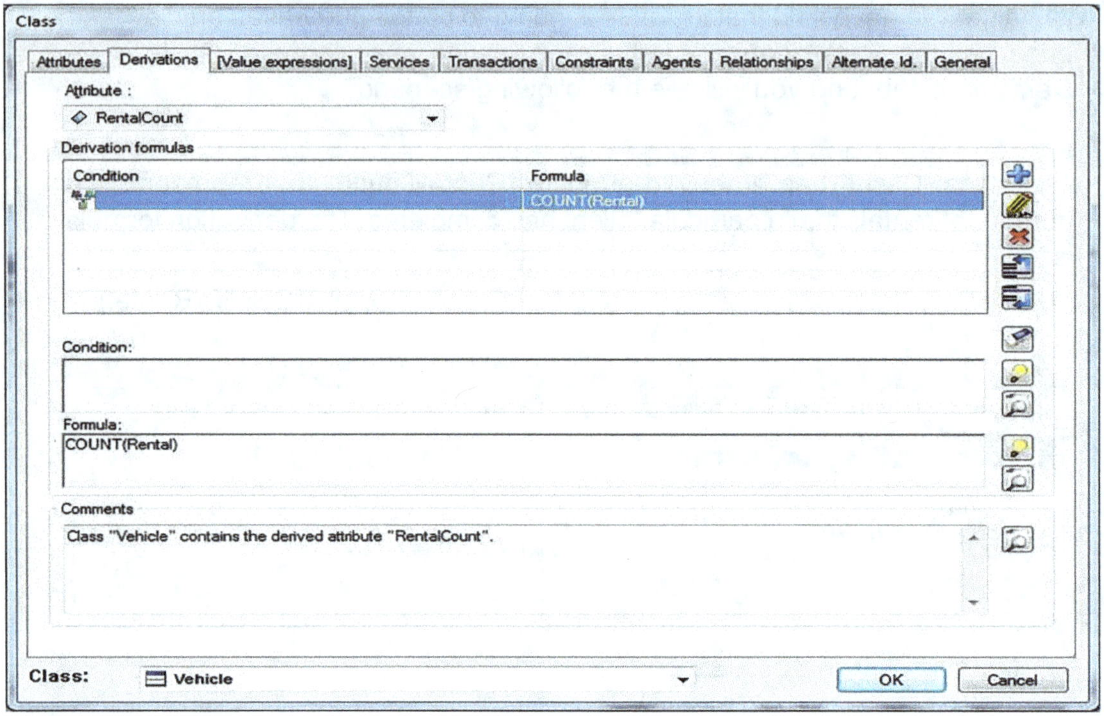

Figure 85 ***Derivations tab in Vehicle class***

The class “Client” has a derived attribute “PendingBalance”, which adds up the amount of money owed by a particular client. The derivation formula is:

SUM (Rentals.Invoice.Amount) WHERE (Rental.Invoice.Payed) = FALSE.

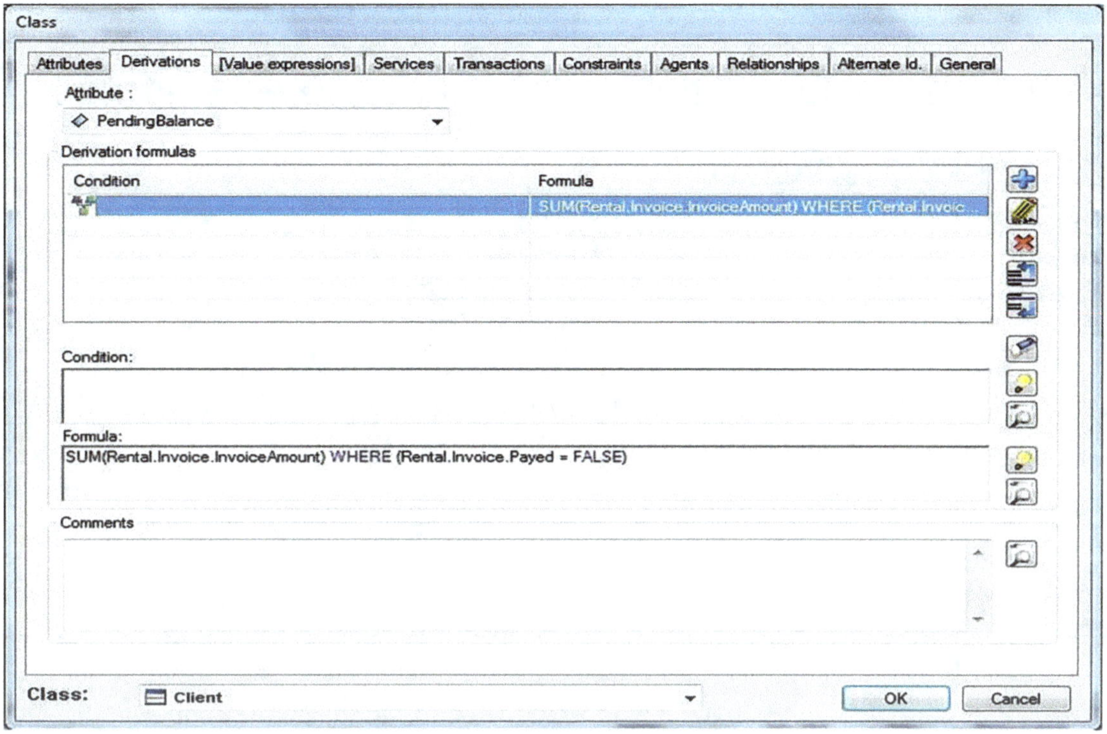

Figure 86 ***Derivations tab in Client class***

A new attribute "InvoiceOn", of type "Date" is added to class "Rental" in order to store the date on which each rental is invoiced, then the derivation such as: Invoice.InvoiceDate could be used.

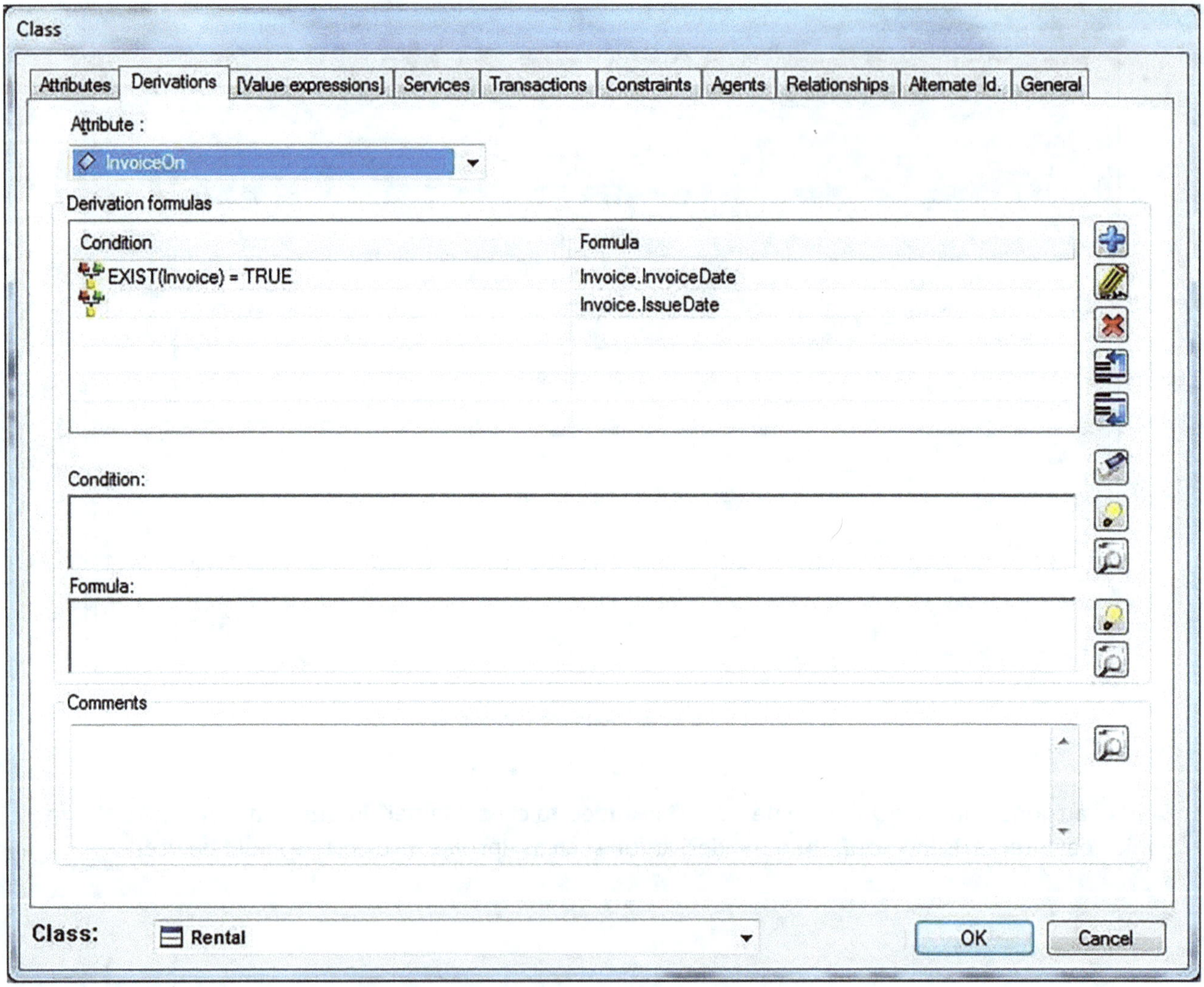

Figure 87 Derivations tab in Rental class

6. Defining more functionality

The specification of the behavior of a class is done by means of the services. We learnt that a class is normally created with three types of events:

l Creation type

l Edit type

l Deletion type

In this section we are going to focus on the Edit type events. This sort of event is in charge of applying value to variable attributes. This is defined by means of the *Valuation* concept.

A *valuation* is the effect of an event of one class on a determined variable attribute of the same class. It determines the value taken by a variable attribute when an event occurs. Let's see how we can define edition events and its valuations.

As you can see, for the class “Client”, we only have the eight created events:

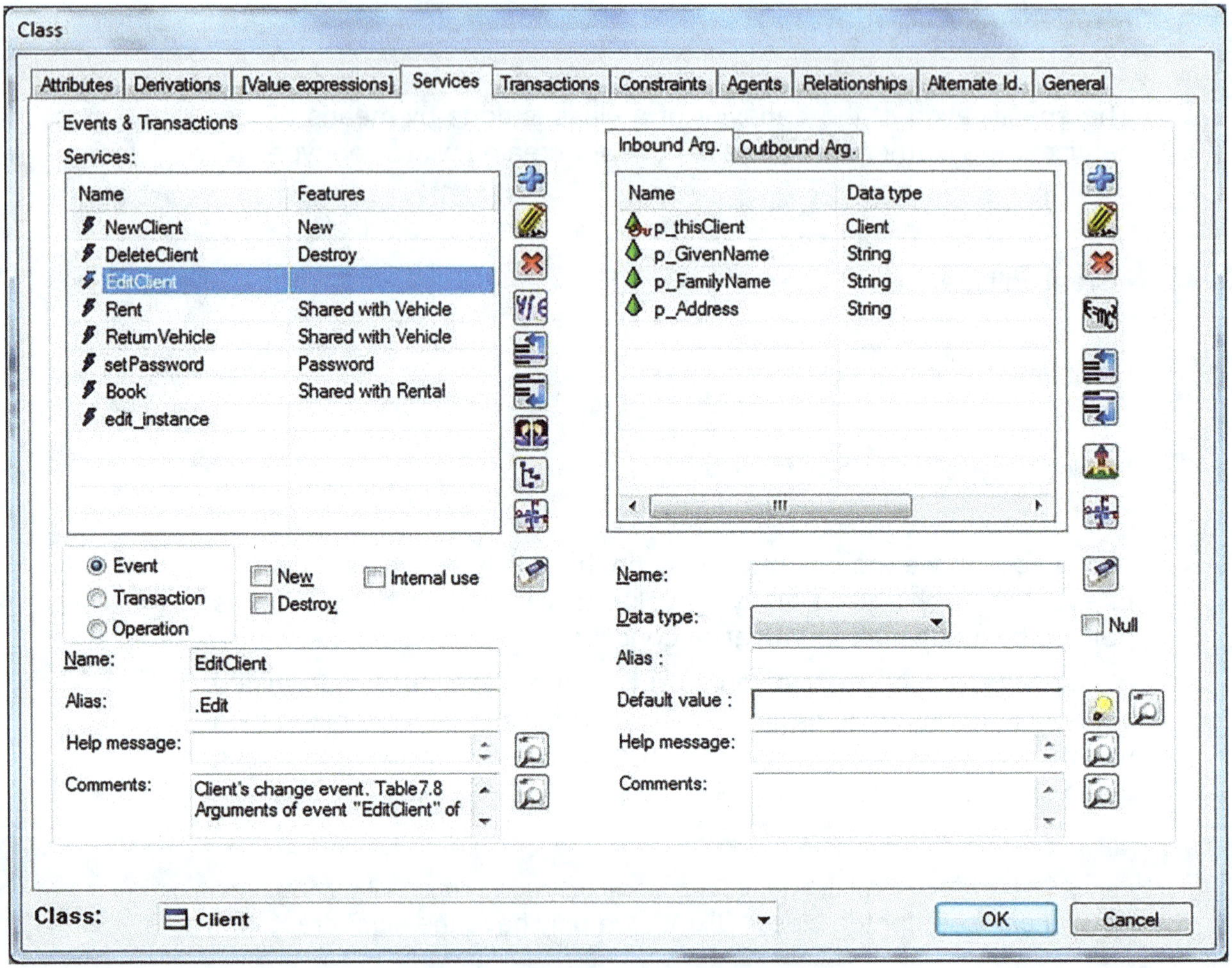

Figure 88 Services tab of the ClientClass

Now, we have our Edit type event created. We are then in need of specifing the effect of the execution of this event. This is the value that one or more attributes may take when this event occurs To do so, we must define valuations for this event Therefore, having selected the event we just created, we press the Goto button and then select the Validations option:

Now, we have our *Edit* type event created. We then need to specify the effect of the execution of this event. This is the value that one or more attributes may take when this event occurs.

To do so, we have to define valuations for this event. Therefore, having selected the event we just created, we press the *Go to*  button and then select *Valuations* option:

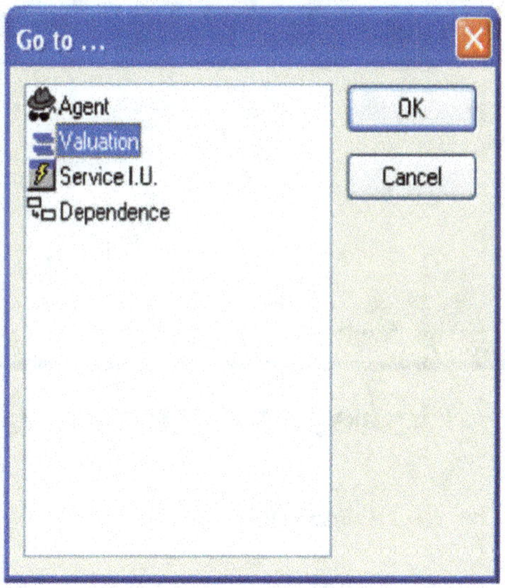

Figure 39 *Go to*dialog

Figure 39 *Go to*dialog

Figure 89 Goto Dialog

Class “Tariff” has an event “UpdateRentalRates” that is used to modify the values of the variable attribute “RentalRate” of a particular “Tariff” instance. The Functional Model shows that the modification done on the value of “RentalRate” depends on the “VehicleClass” to which the tariff applies. Cardinal evaluations of the RentalRate, in which the event has an increment or decrement effect, could also be applied.

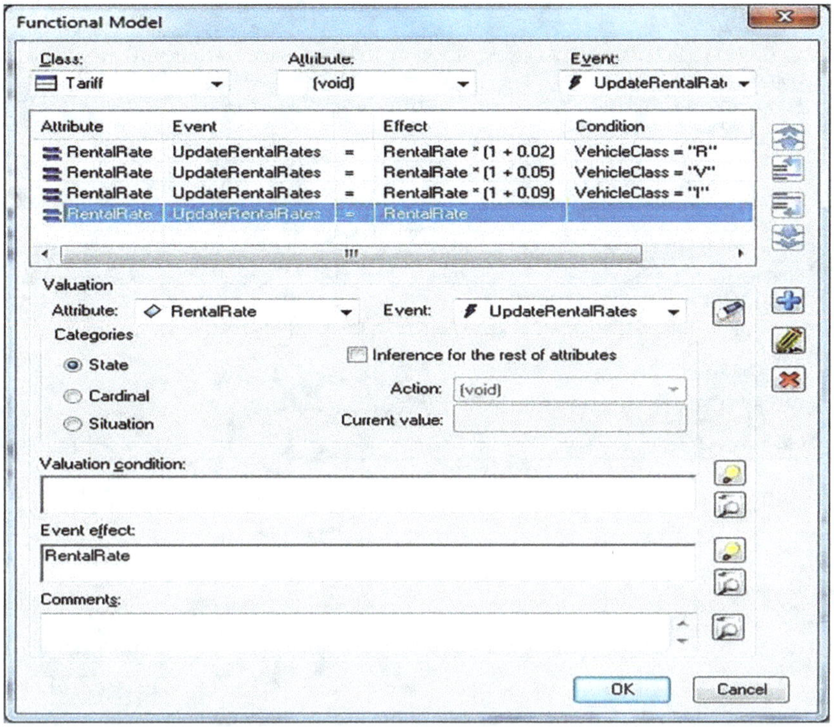

Figure 90 ***Evaluations of event "UpdateRentalRates" of class "Tariff"***

Class "IssuedInvoice" has an event "Pay" that is used to modify the values of the variable attribute "InvoicePayed" of a particular "IssuedInvoice" instance. The Functional Model shows that the modification done on the value of "InvoicePayed" depends on the "Invoice" Agent to which the logic applies.

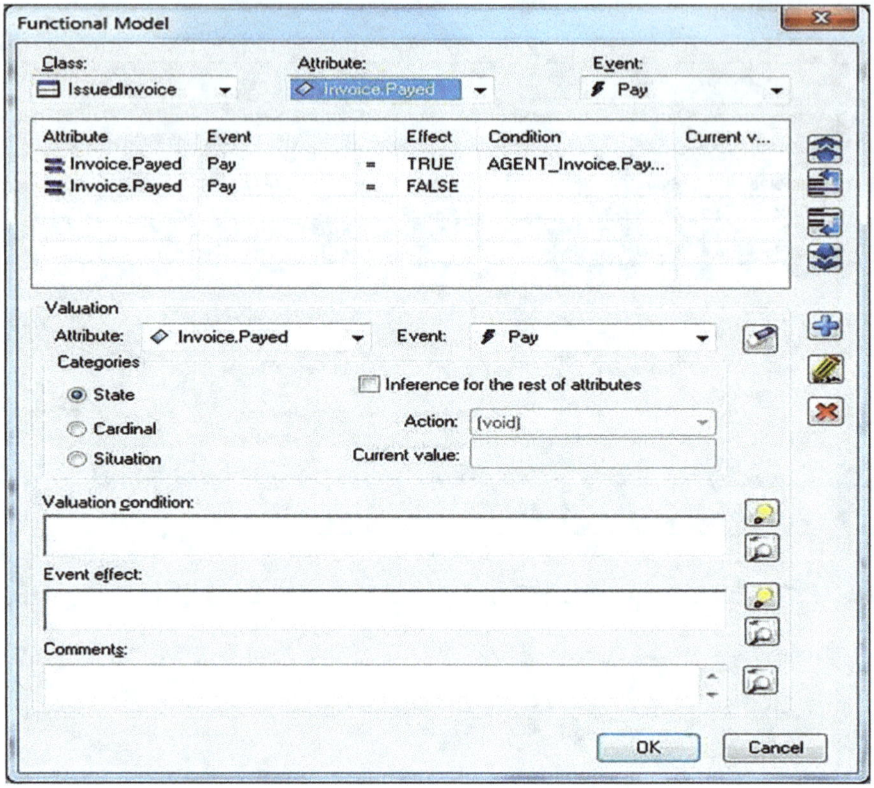

Figure 91 Evaluations of event "Pay" of class Issued Invoice

7. Restricting the information that can be shown

Sometimes it is required or aimed at restricting some information. For instance, a customer only can see those purchase orders that belong to him. It is obvious, for confidential reasons, that any system should not show information about others customers, such us, credit card number, address, and so onto another customer.

In *INTEGRANOVA* we can define these restrictions by means of the *Horizontal Visibility*.

Let's see an example. Let's define restriction through *Horizontal Visibility*, in which we are going to restrict the information a client can access to. In this case we are going to make clients able to see only their own information, such as well as all their personal data (address, phone number).

We are going to define these requirements. These client personal details are saved or defined in the Client class, so we open the Clientclass and go to the *Agents* Tab, and select Customer in the *Server class* dropdown list.

We can see that there are permissions already defined from Client agent class over itself (some items added to the right-side area) that were defined in previous series.

The clue in this example is to define a horizontal visibility formula to restrict the information shown to only the client s own.

Then, we enter the horizontal visibility formula that will be:

Agent = THIS

In this formula, there are two reserved words, which mean:

- AGENT represents the connected client in the system. The client that is logged in

  the application

- THIS represents the client server class. The instance that is offering the

  attributes, services and roles.

So, if we define this formula (AGENT = THIS) we are informing the system to show the information that belongs to the customer which is currently connected in the application,

Let's see the final result of these definitions n *INTEGRANOVA* **Modeler**:

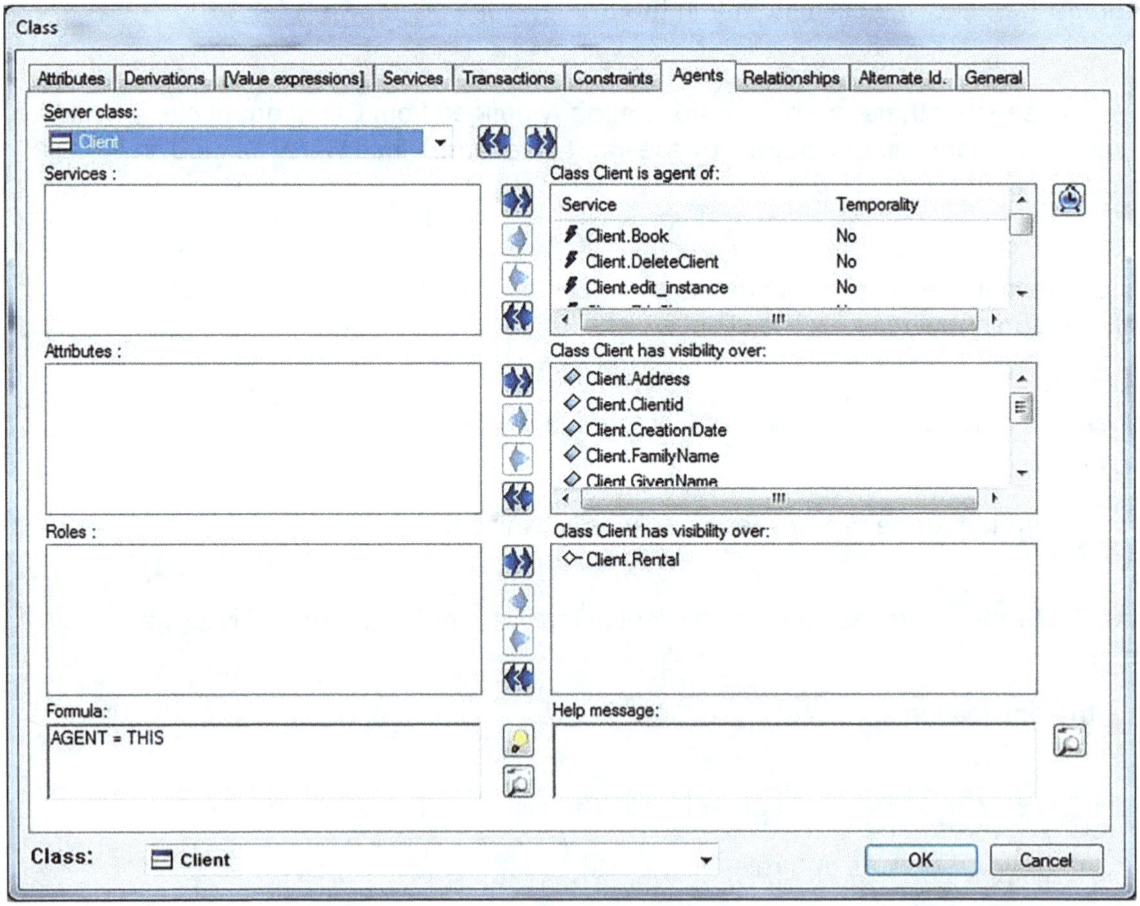

Figure 92 **Client agent permissions**

As we know, clients perform rentals. Logically, and for privacy reasons, each client can access only the information pertaining to his/her own rental contracts, not being able to access rental contract information of other clients.

For this case we are just going to focus on the Horizontal Visibility formula, taking for granted the reader already knows how to define the permissions over the attributes, roles and services if needed.

After that, define the Horizontal visibility formula as follows: Client = AGENT

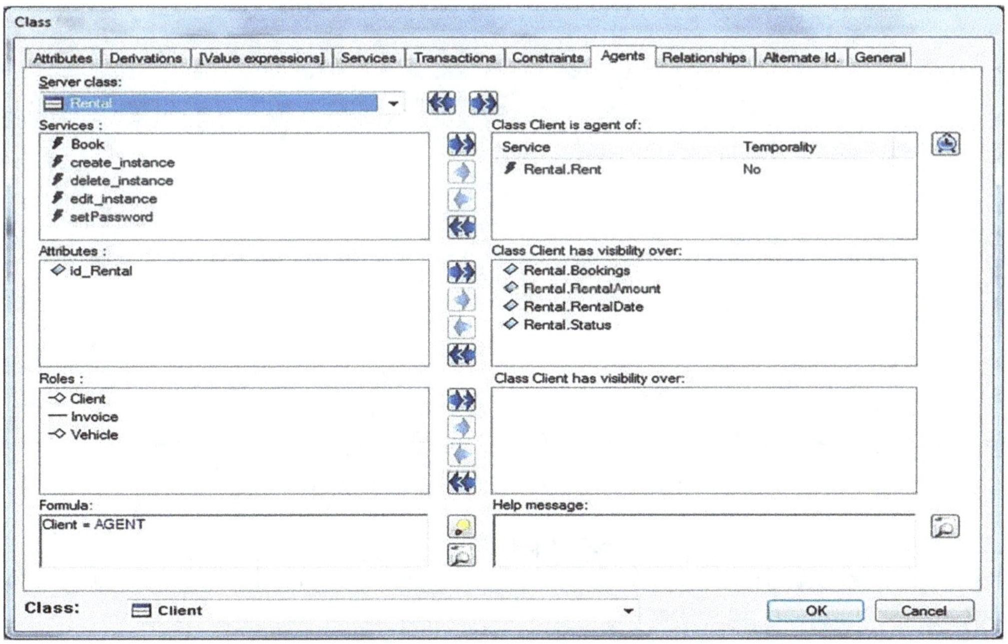

Figure 93 44 Client Class horizontal visibility restriction

8. Defining Preconditions

We would add certain restrictions for our model. To do that, we use *Preconditions*. *Preconditions* are conditions that must be satisfied before executing a service.

Our first precondition in this example must cover the following requirement: “Vehicles must serve for at least 50,000 km before they can be retired (for re-sale or junk), in order to maximize performance”. The precondition formula must be:

Kilometres < 50000.

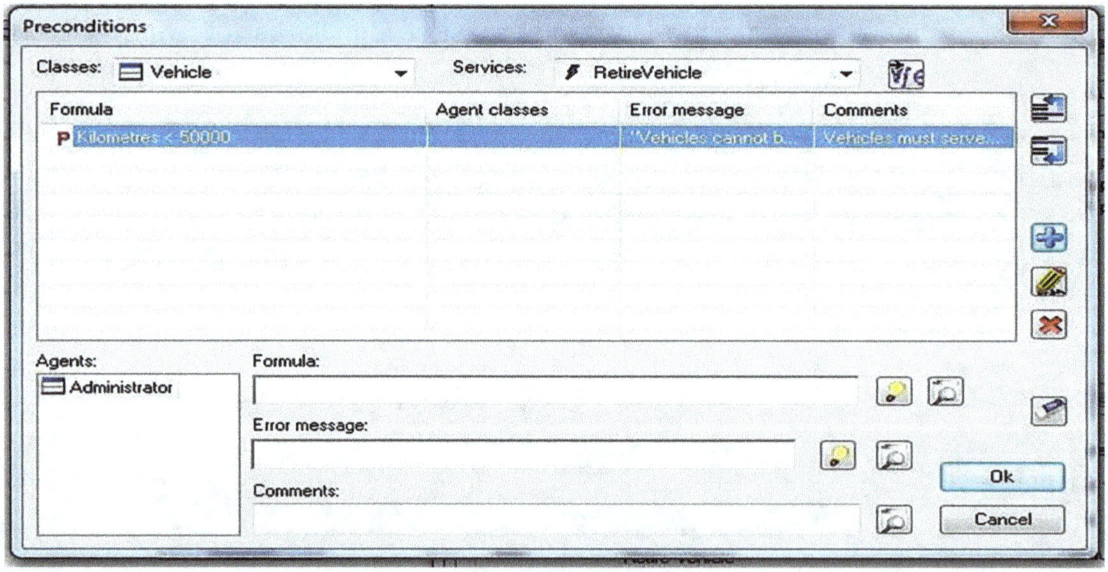

Figure 94 ***Retire Vehicle Precondition***

Our second precondition in this example must cover the following requirement: "The expected return date must be later than or equal to the rental date." The precondition formula must be:

p_atrReturnDate >= p_atrRentalDate.

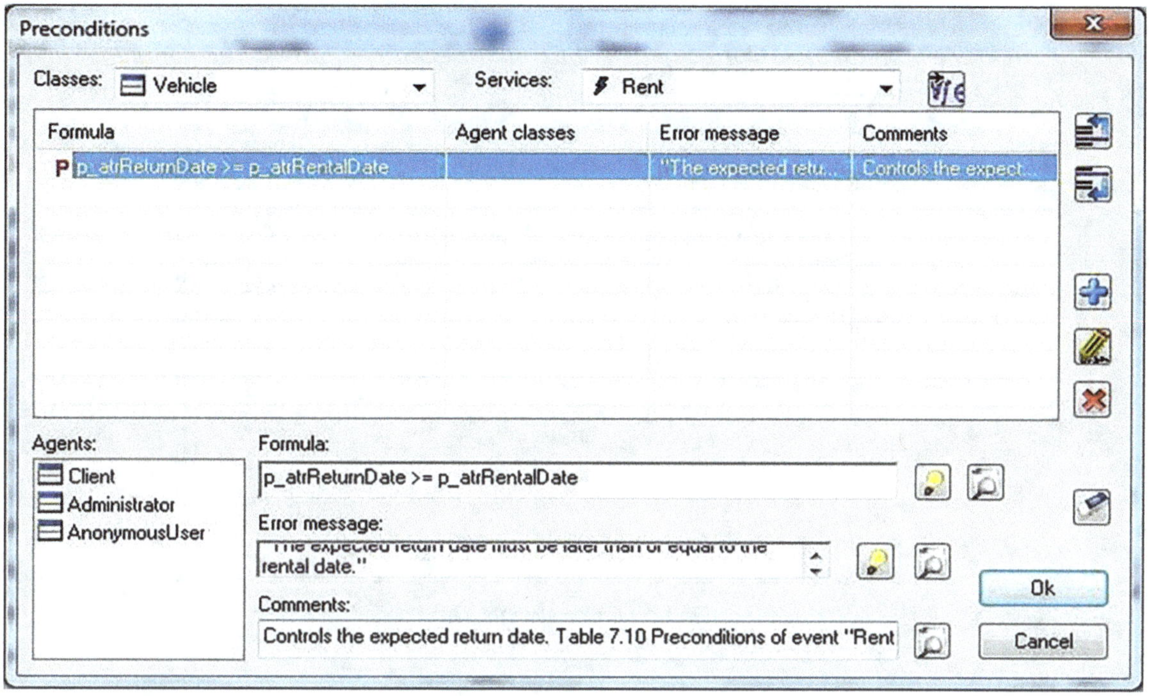

Figure 95 Rent-Vehicle Precondition

9. Defining Integrity Constraints

In this example, the values of the attributes of an object can be restricted by a series of conditions that need to be satisfied at *any time* (= all of the states of the object). These conditions are called *Constraints*.

In objects of class "Vehicle", the kilometer count must be always greater than zero and never above 300,000 km. This is represented in the following integrity constraint:

Kilometres > 0 AND Kilometres <= 300000

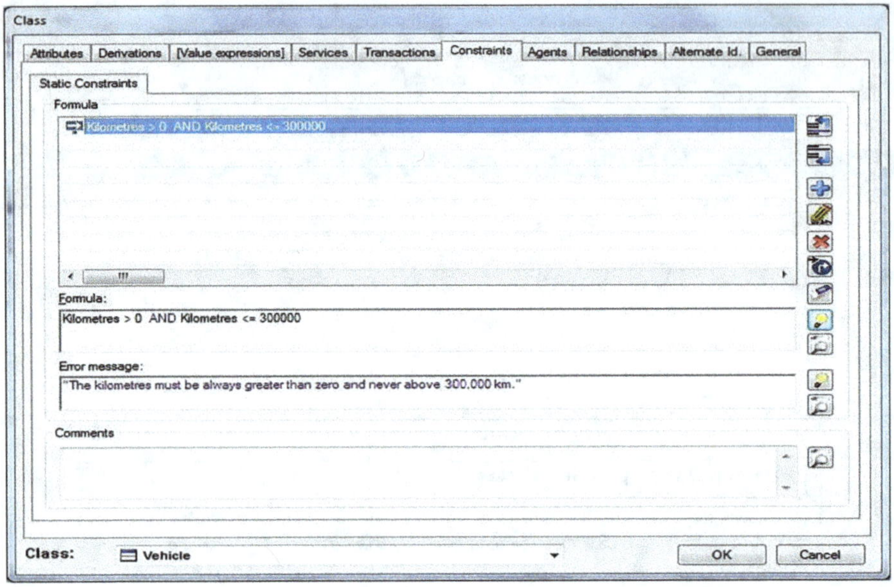

Figure 96 Constraints Tab

10. Agent logged to the application

In this example, the modeling element you will need is the ***AGENT**_ClassName*t allows accessing to the connected agent data. Consequently *ClassName* has to be any agent class defined in the model. In this example, we are going to use:

l***AGENT**_Admin*

l ***AGENT**_Client*

The fact that every service has an associated agent class or classes make it possible that the specification granularity for any particular services is the combined service plus agent. Such a combination of service plus service activating agent is called action. The Administrator as agent, for example has full visibility over all attributes, services and roles associated with the “Vehicle” class.

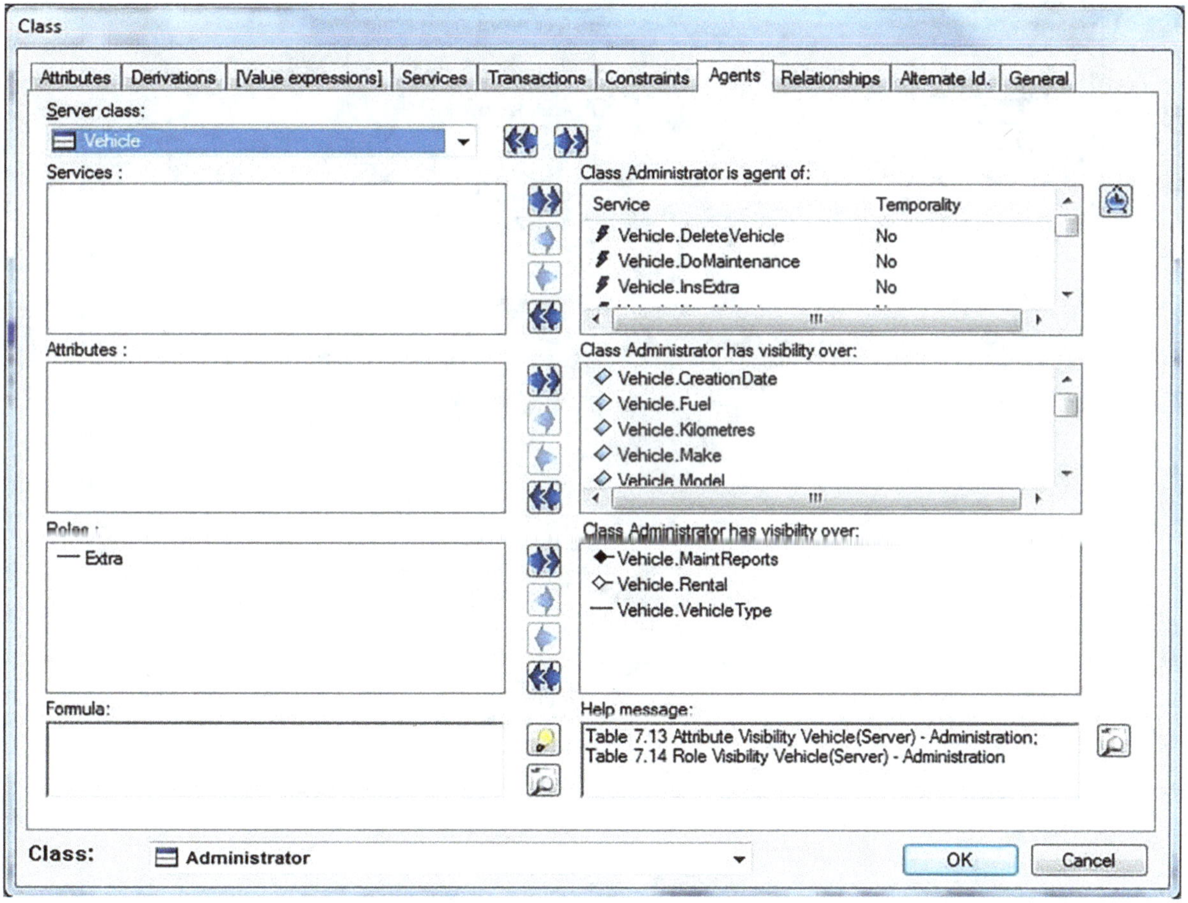

Figure 97 Administrator as Agent

The Client as agent, for example has limited visibility over all attributes, services and roles associated with the "Vehicle" class.

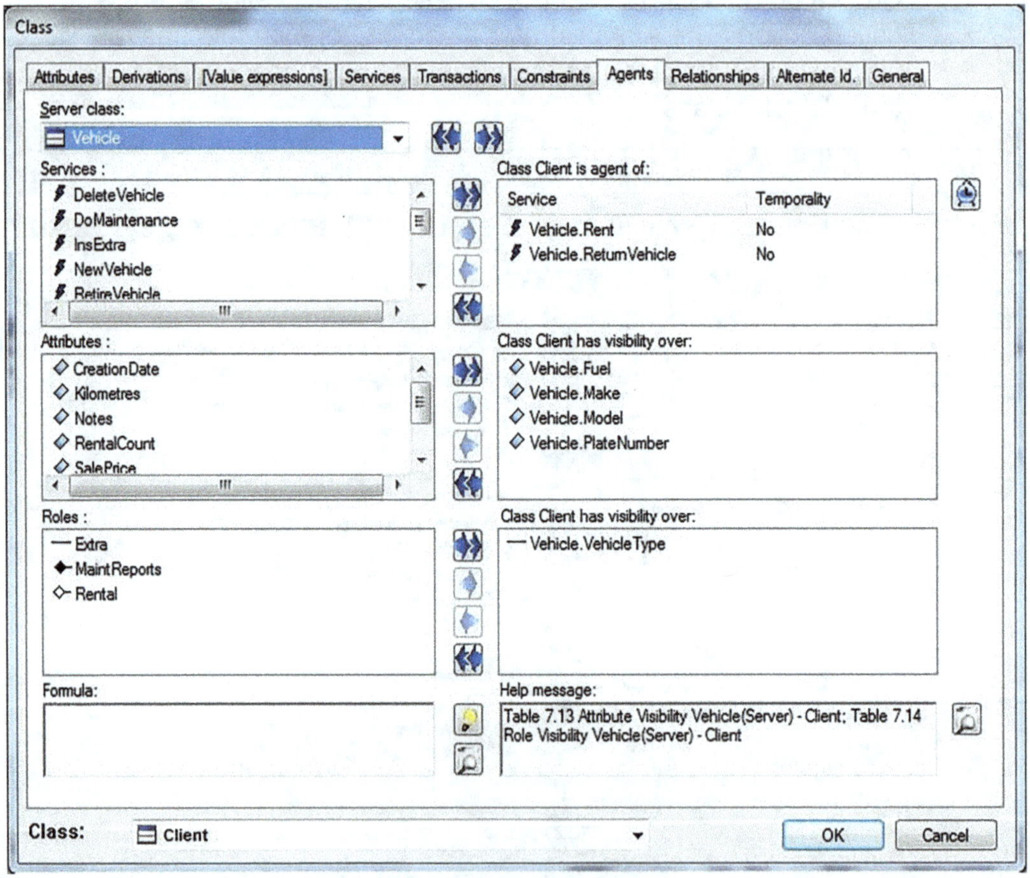

Figure 98 'Client" as Agent

11. Defining complex functionality

In this example we require more functionality for a vehicle rented out. For example when to send to vehicle for maintenance. The way to achieve that in *INTEGRANOVA* is through the definition of *Local Transactions*.

We can have three kinds of services in our classes: Events, Transactions and Operations. Events represent an execution unit. To group several execution units we will need another service type call *Local Transactions*.

Local transactions are defined in a specific class and allow defining complex functionality in a specific formula including events and other transactions in a specific order. At runtime, transactions are executed as **only one processing unit**. If any error occurs, for instance, a precondition is not fulfilled, all the changes that have been made during the execution of the transaction are undone (a roll back is performed) and the affected data remains with their initial values.

Transactions are very similar to events. They are defined in the same tab: *Services.* They have a *Name* (always in capital letters), an *Alias*, a *Help Message*, *Comments* and a list of Arguments. But, instead of having valuations (as events), the way in which they can define its functionality is using *Transaction formula* (in the *Transaction* tab). The *Transaction formula* describes what the transaction must do.

Operations are very similar to *transactions.* The way in which they are defined is the same, but operations are not executed in an all-or-nothing way. That means that when an error occurs during the execution, instead of undoing the changes, the operation follows with the execution of next part of the formula. When the execution is finished, no feedback is given back about the correct or incorrect execution of the operation. In this example, operations will not be defined.

The class “Vehicle” contains the local transaction “WITHDRAWNVEHICLE”, composed of two events of this class:

```
IF ( EXIST ( VehicleType ) = TRUE) { SendForMaintenance(THIS) }.
IF (p_thisVehicle.Kilometres > 50000) {SendForMaintenance(THIS)}.
                    IF ( pt_Km > 10000 ) { SendForMaintenance(THIS) }
```

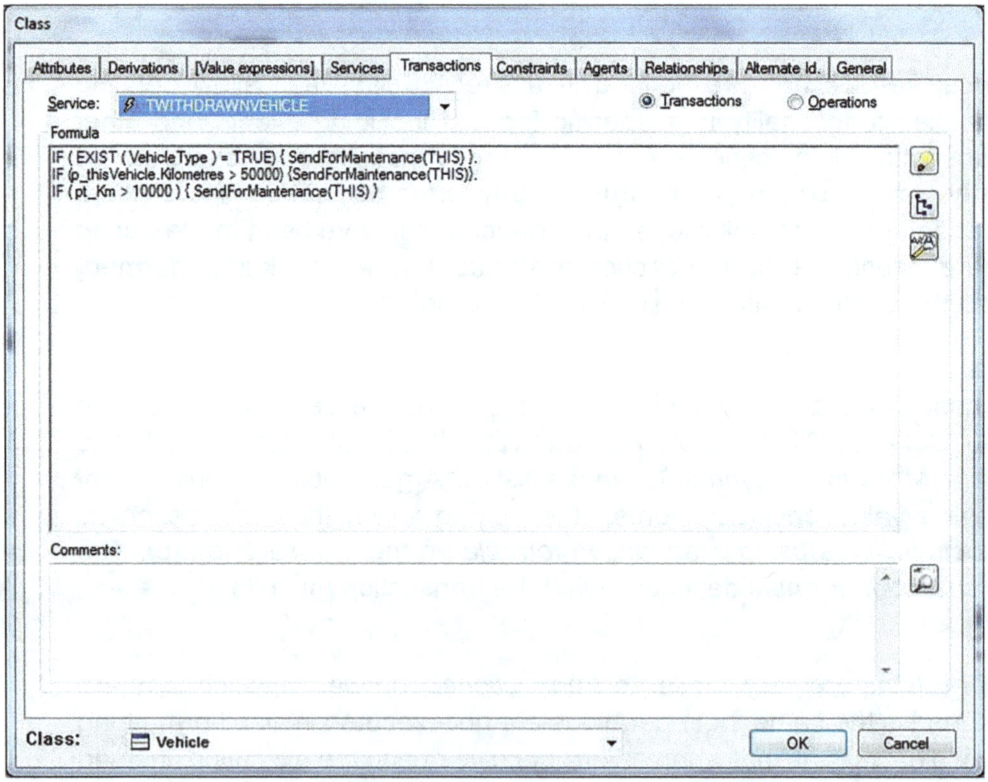

Figure 99 WITHDRAWNVEHICLE Transaction

Car Rental Demo Stats

Table 26 ***Car Rental Demo Stats***

SEEM Parameters

C1	1.3842
C2	1.9684
P1	0.73
P2	0.366
DMF	1
EMF	0.038867

Project Sizes

TotalFPs (Project Size)	841
HighValueFPs	414
CRUD_FPs	245
Data_FPs	182
IFs	26
ClassFPs	32.34615385
TotalRLclassesFPs	355
TotalISclassesFPs	267
TotalERclassesFPs	389
TotalRSclassesFPs	376
TransactionalFPs	659

SEEMestimates

	CarRental	**Roles**	**InvoiceSystem**	**ExpenseReport**	**RentalSystem**
Total Effort	7.343125356	3.91243	3.177847747	4.182568614	4.080064155
Total Duration	4.083436263	3.243014	3.005343143	3.323238584	3.293195213
Total Team Size	1.798271084	1.206418	1.057399304	1.258582106	1.238937837
Total Productivity	114.5288905	90.73645	84.01912906	93.00504926	92.15541366
Total Production	205.9539921	109.4661	88.84176858	117.0544907	114.1748289

Team Roles	PMBOK	FOA	Factor	SEEM Parameter	EFP Ratio	Hourly Rate
QM	Quality Mgmt	Quality Control	QF	C1	7.68%	$32.00
RM	Risk Mgmt	Budget Control	RF	EMF	14.50%	$32.00
PM	ProjectMgmt	Capability Control	CMF	EPML	6.30%	$52.00
SM	IntegrationMgmt	Production Control	AF	P	6.16%	$42.00
SC	Scope Mgmt	Scope Control	IF	P2	30.22%	$32.00
PC	ScheduleMgmt	Schedule Control	EF	DMF	11.90%	$42.00
CE	ResourceMgmt	Confidence Control	CF	C2	4.44%	$42.00
SE	CommMgmt	Complexity Control	CX	C	5.93%	$32.00
SA	ProcurementMgmt	Development Control	DF	SMF	12.87%	$42.00
				TOTAL	100.00%	

Table 27 ***Roles Distribution***

Overhead Ratio Calculation:

1. Development + Integral	SA+ PC + SC + CE + SE =	65.36%
2. Overhead %:	PM + QM + SM + RM =	34.64%
3. Overhead Ratio:	Overhead/Development =	0.52998776
4. Charging Rate:	Development+Overhead =	1.52998776

Table 28 ***Ovehead Calculation***

Appendix O IPALM Work Breakdown Structure

Table 29 IPALM WBS LEVEL

WBS Level	Description	Estimation Factor	Methodology	Assignment Role	Effort Estimation	Schedule Estimation	Team Estimation
5	**ProjectModelFacade**	EFPvalue	**CocomoII/Cosysmo**	PM	EffortFormulaValue	TimeFormulaValue	TeamSizeFormulaValue
"Project" 4	**ProcessModelFacade**		**PMBOK facade**				
"Process"		PF	Costmgmt	DI	PSLEffortAssignment	PSLTimeAssignment	PSLTeamAssignment
		CMF	IntegrationMgmt	PM	CSLEffortAssignment	CSLTimeAssignment	CSLTeamAssignment
		WF	TimeMgmt	SM	WSLEffortAssignment	WSLTimeAssignment	WSLTeamAssignment
		QF	QualityMgmt	QM	QSLEffortAssignment	QSLTimeAssignment	QSLTeamAssignment
		RF	RiskMgmt	RM	RSLEffortAssignment	RSLTimeAssignment	RSLTeamAssignment
		AF	ProductionMgmt	SA	ASLEffortAssignment	ASLTimeAssignment	ASLTeamAssignment
		IF	ScopeMgmt	SC	ISLEffortAssignment	ISLTimeAssignment	ISLTeamAssignment
		EF	OrgMgmt	SE	ESLEffortAssignment	ESLTimeAssignment	ESLTeamAssignment
		CF	GEM_Mmt	CE	PILEffortAssignment	PILTimeAssignment	PILTeamAssignment
3	**ResourceModelFacade**		**OPF façade**	CE			
"Tools"		PF	PSL_PF (Decision Intelligence)	DI			
&			AR - Action Rejected AC -		AReffortfactor	ARtimefactor	ARteamfactor
			Action Changed AP -		ACeffortfactor	ACtimefactor	ACteamfactor
Techniques			Action in Parallel AG -		APeffortfactor	APtimefactor	APteamfactor
			Action Assigned AJ -		AGeffortfactor	AGtimefactor	AGteamfactor
			Action Joint as FS AD -		AJeffortfactor	AJtimefactor	AJteamfactor
			Action Delayed (Lag) AA -		ADeffortfactor	ADtimefactor	ADteamfactor
			Action Automated (Lead)		AAeffortfactor	AAtimefactor	AAteamfactor
			AI - Action Integrated		AIeffortfactor	AItimefactor	AIteamfactor
		CMF	CSL_CMF (Controls)	PM	CFeffortfactor	CFtimefactor	CFteamfactor
			CF - Confidence Control RF		RFeffortfactor	RFtimefactor	RFteamfactor
			- Risk Control EF -		EFeffortfactor	EFtimefactor	EFteamfactor
			Efficiency Control PF -		PFeffortfactor	PFtimefactor	PFteamfactor
			Productivity Control QF -		QFeffortfactor	QFtimefactor	QFteamfactor
			Quality Control WF -		WFeffortfactor	WFtimefactor	WFteamfactor
			Workflow Control IF -		IFeffortfactor	IFtimefactor	IFteamfactor
			Interaction Control AF -		AFeffortfactor	AFtimefactor	AFteamfactor
			Production Control CMF-		CMFeffortfactor	CMFtimefactor	CMFteamfactor
		WF	Capability Maturity	SM			
			WSL_WF (Workflows)		PMeffortfactor	PMtimefactor	PMteamfactor
					SEeffortfactor	SEtimefactor	SEteamfactor
			Project Management		SMeffortfactor	SMtimefactor	SMteamfactor
			Software Engineering		SCeffortfactor	SCtimefactor	SCteamfactor
			System Management		SAeffortfactor	SAtimefactor	SAteamfactor
			System Configuration		SDeffortfactor	SDtimefactor	SDteamfactor
			Software Architecture		RMeffortfactor	RMtimefactor	RMteamfactor
			Software Development		CEeffortfactor	CEtimefactor	CEteamfactor
			Risk Management		QMeffortfactor	QMtimefactor	QMteamfactor
		QF	Cognitive Engineering	QM			

			Complexity Issues		CPLXeffortfactor	CPLXtimefactor	CPLXteamfactor
			Interaces		IFeffortfactor	IFtimefactor	IFteamfactor
			Issues Features		FEAeffortfactor	FEAtimefactor	FEAteamfactor
			Issues		COVeffortfactor	COVtimefactor	COVteamfactor
			Coverage		RELeffortfactor	RELtimefactor	RELteamfactor
			Issues		RCeffortfactor	RCtimefactor	RCteamfactor
		RF	RSL_RF (Differentiators) Reliability	RM			
			PS - Problem Space		PSeffortfactor	PStimefactor	PSteamfactor
			AS - Activity Space		ASeffortfactor	AStimefactor	ASteamfactor
			VS - Validation Space		VSeffortfactor	VStimefactor	VSteamfactor
			SS - Solution Space		SSeffortfactor	SStimefactor	SSteamfactor
			RS - Risk Space		RSeffortfactor	RStimefactor	RSteamfactor
			US - Usability Space		USeffortfactor	UStimefactor	USteamfactor
			VerifS - Verification Space		VerifSeffortfactor	VerifStimefactor	VerifSteamfactor
			Ruse - Reuse Space		RuseSeffortfactor	RuseStimefactor	RuseSteamfactor
		AF	ASL_AF (Seven Schema)	SA			
			OM (Class Structure)		OMeffortfactor	OMtimefactor	OMteamfacto
			FM (Business Logic)		FMeffortfactor	FMtimefactor	FMteamfacto
			PM (User Interface)		PMeffortfactor	PMtimefactor	PMteamfacto
			TM (Dynamic Interaction)		TMeffortfactor	TMtimefactor	TMteamfacto
			CM (Communication)		CMeffortfactor	CMtimefactor	CMteamfacto
			DM (Database)		DMeffortfactor	DMtimefactor	DMteamfacto
			SM (System Clustering)		SMeffortfactor	SMtimefactor	SMteamfacto
		IF	ISL_IF (Triple Constraint)	SC			
			U-CF (Cost)		UCFeffortfactor	UCFtimefactor	UCFteamfactor
			T-CF (Quality)		TCFeffortfactor	TCFtimefactor	TCFteamfactor
			O-CF (Resource)		OCFeffortfactor	OCFtimefactor	OCFteamfactor
			P-CF (Schedule)		PCFeffortfactor	PCFtimefactor	PCFteamfactor
			I-CF (Risk)		ICFeffortfactor	ICFtimefactor	ICFteamfactor
			A-CF (Scope)		ACFeffortfactor	ACFtimefactor	ACFteamfactor
			S-CF (Integration)		SCFeffortfactor	SCFtimefactor	SCFteamfactor
		EF	ESL_EF (GSC)	SE			
			A - Algorithm		Aeffortfactor	Atimefactor	Ateamfactor
			D- Database		Deffortfactor	Dtimefactor	Dteamfactor
			F - Form		Feffortfactor	Ftimefactor	Fteamfactor
			R - Report		Reffortfactor	Rtimefactor	Rteamfactor
			T - Table		Teffortfactor	Ttimefactor	Tteamfactor
			M - Menu		Meffortfactor	Mtimefactor	Mteamfactor
			Q Query		Qeffortfactor	Qtimefactor	Qteamfactor
			P - Prototype		Peffortfactor	Ptimefactor	Pteamfactor
		CF	PIL_CF (GEM)	CE			
			PAMPA		PAMPAeffortfactor	PAMPAtimefactor	PAMPAteamfactor
			JADE		JADEeffortfactor	JADEtimefactor	JADEteamfactor

PICT		PICTeffortfactor	PICTtimefactor	PICTteamfactor
MDA		MDAeffortfactor	MDAtimefactor	MDAteamfactor
HCD		HCDeffortfactor	HCDtimefactor	HCDteamfactor

Appendix P VROOM Language

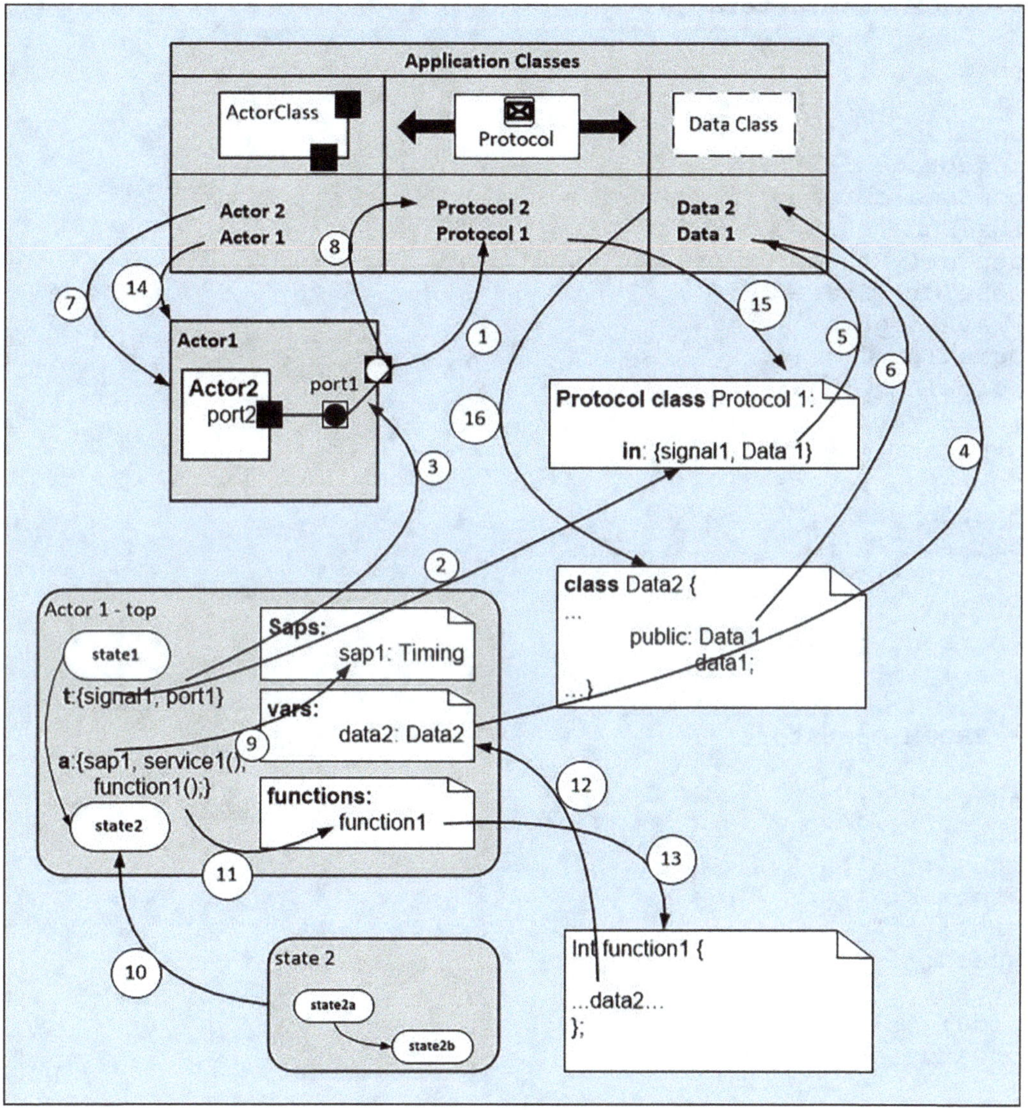

Figure 100 VROOM Modeling Language

```
/* VROOM language tokens */

      /* VROOM Punctuators */

      SemiColon : ';';
      Comma : ',';
      OpenBrace : '(';
      CloseBrace : ')';
      OpenSquareBrace : '[';
      CloseSquareBrace : ']';
      OpenCurlyBrace : '{';
      CloseCurlyBrace : '}';
      ArrayAssign : '=>';
      LogicalOr : '||';
      LogicalAnd : '&&';
      ClassMember : '::';
      InstanceMember : '->';
      SuppressWarnings : '@';
      QuestionMark : '?';
      Dollar : '$';
      Colon : ':';
      Dot : '.';
      Ampersand : '&';
      Pipe : '|';

      /* VROOM Operators */

      Bang : '!';
      Plus : '+';
      Minus : '-';
      Asterisk: '*';
      Caret: '^';
      Equals: '=';
      Percent: '%';
      Tilde: '~';
      Forwardslash: '/';

      /* VROOM Notations */
```

```
Class :'class';
Interface : 'interface';
Extends : 'extends';
Implements : 'implements';
Abstract : 'abstract';
Var : 'var';
Const : 'const';

Modifiers : 'Modifiers';
ClassDefinition : 'ClassDefinition';
Block : 'Block';
Params : 'Params';
Apply : 'Apply';
Member : 'Member';
Reference : 'Reference';
Empty : 'Empty';
Prefix : 'Prefix';
Postfix : 'Postfix';
IfExpression : 'IfExpression';
Label : 'Label';
Cast : 'Cast';
ForInit : 'ForInit';
ForCondition : 'ForCondition';
ForUpdate : 'ForUpdate';
Field : 'Field';
Method : 'Method';


New : 'new';
Clone : 'clone';
Echo : 'echo';
If : 'if';
Else : 'else';
ElseIf : 'elseif';
For : 'for';
Foreach : 'foreach';
While : 'while';
Do : 'do';
Switch : 'switch';
```

```
Case : 'case';
Default : 'default';
Function : 'function';
Break : 'break';
Continue : 'continue';
Goto : 'goto';
Return : 'return';
Global : 'global';
Static : 'static';
And : 'and';
Or : 'or';
Xor : 'xor';
Instanceof : 'instanceof';
Root:'root';
Actor_class:'actor_class';
Derived_from:'derived_from';
Spps:'spps';
Spp:'spp';
Isa:'isa';
Port:'port';
Conjugated:'conjugated';
Implementation:'implementation';
Structure:'structure';
Saps:'saps';
Sap:'sap';
Frame:'frame';
Timing:'timing';
Exception:'exception';
End_ports:'end_ports';
Components:'components';
Actor:'actor';
Substitutable:'substitutable';
Optional:'optional';
Fixed:'fixed';
Imported:'imported';
Contracts:'contracts';
Layer_connections:'layer_connections';
Connection:'connection';
To:'to';
```

```
Bindings:'bindings';
Binding:'binding';
Equivalences:'equivalences';
Set:'set';
Behavior:'behavior';
Language:'language';
Inclusions:'inclusions';
Include:'include';
Functions:'functions';
Code:'code';
Top_fsm:'top_fsm';
Vars:'vars';
Entry_action:'entry_action';
Exit_action:'exit_action';
Substates:'substates';
State:'state';
Choicepoints:'choicepoints';
Choicepoint:'choicepoint';
Transitions:'transitions';
Transition:'transition';
Top:'top';
Source:'source';
Initial_point:'initial_point';
State_border:'state_border';
To_transition:'to_transition';
From_transition:'from_transition';
Destination:'destination';
Triggered_by:'triggered_by';
Events:'events';
Event:'event';
Signals:'signals';
On:'on';
Guard:'guard';
Protocol_class:'protocol_class';
Service:'service';
Message_types:'message_types';
Signal:'signal';
Data_class:'data_class';
In:'in';
```

```
Out:'out';
```

/* VROOM System Class Spec */

```
classSpecification
      :actor_class_spec protocol_class_spec data_class_spec
;
comment: COMMENT
;
className
      :     IDENTIFIER
    ;
rootID      :     Root
        ;
```

/* Actor Class Specification */

```
actor_class_spec
      :     '[' COMMENT ']' Actor_class actor_class_name
Derived_from actor_superclass_id '{' actor_interface_spec '}'
actor_implem_spec '}';
actor_class_name
      :     className;
actor_superclass_id
      :     rootID | actor_class_name;
actor_interface_spec
      :     Interface ':' '{' '[' interf_ref_list ']' '}';
interf_ref_list
      :     (interf_ref_item ';')+;
interf_ref_item
      :     port_ref_item | spp_ref_item;
port_ref_list
      :     (port_ref_item ';')+;
port_ref_item
      :     '[' COMMENT ']' Port port_ref_name '['
replicationFactor ']' Isa '[' Conjugated ']';
```

```
actor_implem_spec
        :     Implementation ':' '{' structure_spec '}' '{'
behavior_spec '}';
```

/* Actor Classes - Structure */

```
structure_spec
        :     Structure ':' '{' '[' end_ports_spec ']' '['
saps_spec ']' '[' spps_spec ']' '[' components_spec ']' '['
contracts_spec ']' '[' equivs_spec ']' '}';
end_ports_spec
        :     End_ports ':' '{' '[' port_ref_list ']' '}';
saps_spec
        :     Saps ':' '{' saps_list '}';

saps_list
        :     (sap_ref_item ';')+;

sap_ref_item
        :     '[' COMMENT ']' Sap sap_ref_name Isa
sap_class_name;
sap_class_name
      : protocol_class_name
;
spps_spec
        :     Spps ':' '{' spps_list '}';
spps_list
        :     (spp_ref_item ';')+;
spp_ref_item
        :     '[' COMMENT ']' Spp spp_ref_name '['
replicationFactor ']' Isa protocol_class_name;
components_spec
        :     Components ':''{' components_list '}';
components_list
        :     (actor_ref_item ';')+;
actor_ref_item
:     '[' COMMENT ']' Actor actor_ref_name '['
replicationFactor ']' Isa dynamics_type;
dynamics_type
```

```
      :     Optional | Fixed | Imported;
contracts_spec
      :     Contracts ':' '{' '[' bindings_spec ']' '['
layer_conns_spec ']' '}';
layer_conns_spec
      :     Layer_connections ':' '{' layer_conns_list '}';
layer_conns_list
      :     (conn_item ';')+;
conn_item
      :     Connection connName Isa protocol_class_name;
connName:   IDENTIFIER;
srce_pt_spec
      :     actor_class_name | sap_ref_name '/' actor_ref_name;
dest_pt_spec
      :     spp_ref_name '/' actor_ref_name;
bindings_spec
      :     Bindings ':' '{' bindings_list '}';
bindings_list
      :     (binding_item ';')+;
binding_item
      :     Binding bindingName ':' '{' end_pt_spec (To
end_pt_spec)+ '}';
bindingName
      :     IDENTIFIER;
end_pt_spec
      :     port_ref_name '/' (actor_ref_name |
actor_class_name);
actor_ref_name
      :     IDENTIFIER;
equivs_spec
      :     Equivalences ':' '{' equivs_list '}';
equivs_list
      :     (equiv_item ';')+;
equiv_item
      :     '[' COMMENT ']' Set equiv_name ':' '{' paths_list
'}';
equiv_name
      :     IDENTIFIER;
paths_list
```

```
        :    actor_path_id (And actor_path_id)+;
    actor_path_id
        :    actor_ref_name ('/' actor_ref_name)*;
```

/* Actor Class Behavior Spec */

```
    behavior_spec
        :    Behavior ':' '{' '[' COMMENT ']' language_spec '['
    inclusions_spec ']' '[' functions_spec ']' fsm_spec;
    language_spec
        :    Language ':' languageName;
    languageName
        :     IDENTIFIER;
    inclusions_spec
        :    Inclusions ':' '{' inclusionsList '}';
    inclusionsList
        :    ( inclusion_spec ';' )+;
    inclusion_spec
        :    Include inclusionName;
    inclusionName
        :    IDENTIFIER;
    functions_spec
        :    Functions ':' '{' functionsList '}';
    functionsList
        :    (function_spec ';')+;
    function_spec
        :    Function functionName ':' '[' functionAttribute ']'
    '{' functionCode '}';

    functionName
        :    IDENTIFIER  '(' ':' IDENTIFIER ':' ')' ;

    functionAttributeList
        :    (functionAttribute ',')+
        ;

    functionAttribute
```

```
    : OpenBrace (attributeDef (Comma paramDef)*)? CloseBrace
InstanceMember (Params attributeDef*)
    ;
paramDef: attributeDef*;
attributeDef
    : attributeName //(Equals^ atom)?
    ;
attributeName
    : Dollar UnquotedString
    | Ampersand Dollar UnquotedString InstanceMember
(Ampersand (Dollar UnquotedString))
    ;
functionCode
      :     Code;
fsm_spec:  '[' COMMENT ']' Top_fsm ':' '{' state_spec '}';
state_spec
      :     '[' vars_spec ']' '[' entry_action_spec ']' '['
exit_action_spec ']' '[' substates_spec ']' '['
choicepoints_spec ']' '[' transitions_spec ']';
entry_action_spec
      :     Entry_action ':' '{' '[' expression ']' '}';
exit_action_spec
      :     Exit_action ':' '{' '[' expression ']' '}';
vars_spec
      :     Vars ':' '{' vars_list '}';

vars_list
      :     (vars_item ';')+;

vars_item
      :      IDENTIFIER ('=' (TEXT|NUMBER|Character))? ';';

substates_spec
      :     Substates ':' '{' statesList '}';

statesList
      :     (stateItem ';')+;

stateItem
```

```
      :     '[' COMMENT ']' State stateName ':' '{' '['
state_spec ']' '}';
stateName
      :     IDENTIFIER;
choicepoints_spec
      :     Choicepoints ':' '{' choicepointList '}';
choicepointList
      :     (choicepointItem ';')+;
choicepointItem
      :     '[' COMMENT ']' Choicepoint choiceptName ':' '{'
(choicepointCase)+ ';' '}';
choicepointCase
      :     caseName ':' '{' booleanExpression '}';
caseName:   IDENTIFIER | Default;
choiceptName
      :     IDENTIFIER;
trans_triggers
      :     Triggered_by ':' '{' '[' eventsList ']' '}';
eventsList
      :     eventItem | eventItem Or eventsList;
eventItem
      :     Event ':' '{' Signals ':' '{' signalsList '}' On
':' '{' interfacesList '}' '[' Guard ':' '{' '['
booleanExpression ']' '}' ']' '}' ;
signalsList
      :     signalLiteral | signalLiteral Or signalsList;
interfacesList
      :     interfaceID | interfaceID Or interfacesList;

interfaceID
      :     port_ref_name | sap_ref_name | spp_ref_name;
port_ref_name
      :     IDENTIFIER;
sap_ref_name
      :     IDENTIFIER;
spp_ref_name
      :     IDENTIFIER;
transitions_spec
      :     Transitions ':' '{'transitionList '}';
```

```
        transitionList
              :      (transition_Item ';')+;
        transition_Item
        :     '[' COMMENT ']' Transition transitionName ':' '{' '['
  trans_triggers ']' '[' trans_code ']' '}';
  transitionName
        :     IDENTIFIER;
  trans_code
        :     Code ':' '{' '[' expression ']' '}';
```

/* Actor Data Class_Spec */

```
  data_class_spec
        : '[' COMMENT ']' data_store_spec entity_class_spec ;
  data_store_spec
        : '[' COMMENT ']' out_data_store in_data_store ;
  in_data_store
        : '[' COMMENT ']' ;
  out_data_store
        : '[' COMMENT ']' ;
  entity_class_spec
        : '[' COMMENT ']' out_data_flow in_data_flow ;
  in_data_flow
        : '[' COMMENT ']' ;
  out_data_flow
        : '[' COMMENT ']' ;
```

/* Protocol Classe spec */

```
  protocol_class_spec
        :     '[' COMMENT ']' Protocol_class protocol_class_name
  Derived_from protocol_superclass_id protocol_spec;

  protocol_superclass_id
        :     ID protocol_class_name;

  protocol_class_name
        :     IDENTIFIER;
```

```
class_name
      :     IDENTIFIER;

protocol_spec
      :     '{' service_spec messages_spec '}';

service_spec
      :     Service ':' service_name;

service_name
      :     IDENTIFIER;

messages_spec
      :     Message_types ':' '{' in_messages_spec out_messages_spec
'}';
in_messages_spec
      :     In ':' '{' message_types_list '}';
out_messages_spec
      :     Out ':' '{' message_types_list '}';

message_types_list
      :     (message_type_spec ';')+
      ;

message_type_spec
      :     '{' Signal ':' signal_identifier Data_class ':'
data_class_name '}';
data_class_name
      :     IDENTIFIER;

signalLiteral
      :     STRING | Integer | HexDigit;
signal_identifier
      :'%' signalLiteral;
variableClass
     :(Real|Character|Boolean|Integer)
     ;
nameOrFunctionCall
```

```
    : name OpenBrace (expression (Comma expression)*)? CloseBrace
InstanceMember (Apply name expression*)
    | name
    ;
reference
    : Ampersand nameOrFunctionCall
    | nameOrFunctionCall
    ;
atom: SingleQuotedString | DoubleQuotedString | Integer | Real |
Boolean
    ;
atomOrReference
    : atom
    | reference
    ;
```

/* Boolean and Miscllaneous Control Functions */

```
booleanExpression
      :     weakLogicalOr | weakLogicalXor | weakLogicalAnd |
logicalNot;
expression
    : weakLogicalOr
    ;
weakLogicalOr
    : weakLogicalXor (Or weakLogicalXor)*
    ;
weakLogicalXor
    : weakLogicalAnd (Xor weakLogicalAnd)*
    ;

weakLogicalAnd
    : assignment (And assignment)*
    ;
assignment
    : name (Equals | AssignmentOperator) assignment
    | ternary
    ;
ternary
```

```
    : logicalOr QuestionMark expression Colon expression
InstanceMember (IfExpression logicalOr expression*)
    | logicalOr
    ;

logicalOr
    : logicalAnd (LogicalOr logicalAnd)*
    ;
logicalAnd
    : bitwiseOr (LogicalAnd bitwiseOr)*
    ;

bitwiseOr
    : bitWiseAnd (Pipe bitWiseAnd)*
    ;
bitWiseAnd
    : equalityCheck (Ampersand equalityCheck)*
    ;
equalityCheck
    : comparisonCheck (EqualityOperator comparisonCheck)?
    ;

comparisonCheck
    : bitWiseShift (ComparisonOperator bitWiseShift)?
    ;
bitWiseShift
    : addition (ShiftOperator addition)*
    ;

addition
    : multiplication ((Plus | Minus | Dot) multiplication)*
    ;
multiplication
    : logicalNot ((Asterisk | Forwardslash | Percent) logicalNot)*
    ;
logicalNot
    : Bang logicalNot
    | instanceOf
    ;
```

```
instanceOf
    : negateOrCast (Instanceof negateOrCast)?
    ;
negateOrCast
    : (Tilde | Minus | SuppressWarnings) increment
    | OpenBrace PrimitiveType CloseBrace increment InstanceMember
(Cast PrimitiveType increment)
    | OpenBrace Bang weakLogicalAnd CloseBrace Bang
    | increment
    ;
increment
    : IncrementOperator name InstanceMember (Prefix
IncrementOperator name)
    | name IncrementOperator InstanceMember (Postfix
IncrementOperator name)
    | newOrClone
    ;
newOrClone
    : New nameOrFunctionCall
    | Clone name
    | atomOrReference
    ;
```

/* Basic data and operator types */

```
HexDigit
      :     ('0'..'9'|'a'..'f'|'A'..'F')
            ;
IntegerTypeSuffix
      :     'u' | 'ul' | 'U' | 'UL' | 'l' | 'L'
            ;
replicationFactor
    : '[' integerLiteral ']'
    ;
integerLiteral
      :Integer
      ;
EqualityOperator
    : '==' | '!=' | '===' | '!=='
```

```
    ;
ComparisonOperator
    : '<' | '<=' | '>' | '>=' | '<>'
    ;

ShiftOperator
    : '<<' | '>>'
    ;
PrimitiveType
   : 'int'|'float'|'string'|'array'|'object'|'bool'
    ;
AssignmentOperator
    : '+='|'-='|'*='|'/='|'.='|'%='|'&='|'|='|'^='|'<<='|'>>='
    ;
IncrementOperator
    : '--'|'++'
    ;
name
    :  IDENTIFIER
        ;
TEXT
    : '\"' ('a'..'z'|'A'..'Z'|'0'..'9'|' ')* '\"'
    ;
Character
    : '\'' ('a'..'z'|'A'..'Z'|'0'..'9'|' ') '\''
    ;
SingleQuotedString
    : '\'' (('\\' '\'') ArrayAssign '\\' '\''
    |          ('\\' '\\') ArrayAssign '\\' '\\'
    |          '\\' | ~ ('\'' | '\\'))*
      '\''
    ;
DoubleQuotedString
: '"'  ( ('\\' EscapeCharacter) ArrayAssign '\\' EscapeCharacter
    | '\\'
    | ~('\\'|'"') )*
      '"'
    ;
Boolean
```

```
    : 'true' | 'false'
    ;
EscapeCharacter
    : 'n' | 'r' | 't' | '\\' | '$' | '"' | 'x' | Digits
    ;
Decimal
:('1'..'9' ('0'..'9')*)|'0'
;
Hexadecimal
      : '0'('x'|'X')('0'..'9'|'a'..'f'|'A'..'F')+
      ;
Octal
      : '0'('0'..'7')+
      ;
Integer
      :Octal|Decimal|Hexadecimal
      ;
DNum
      :(('.' Digits) ArrayAssign ('.' Digits)|(Digits '.' Digits?))
      ;

Exponent_DNum
      :((Digits|DNum)('e'|'E')('+''-')?Digits)
      ;

Real
    : DNum|Exponent_DNum
    ;
Digits
      : '0'..'9'+
      ;
UnquotedString
   : ('a'..'z' | 'A'..'Z' | '_')  ('a'..'z' | 'A'..'Z' | '0'..'9' |
'_')*
   ;
AccessModifier
    : 'public' | 'private' | 'protected'
    ;
ID
```

```
    : ('a'..'z'|'A'..'Z'|'_') ('a'..'z'|'A'..'Z'|'0'..'9'|'_')*
    ;

IDENTIFIER
      :     (('a'..'z')|('A'..'Z'))
(('a'..'z')|('A'..'Z')|'0'..'9')*;
INT
    : '0'..'9'+
    ;
NUMBER
    : ('+'|'-') ? ('0'..'9')+ ('.' '0'..'9')
;
WS
    :      ' '
        | '\t'
        | '\r'
        | '\n'
    ;
COMMENT
    : '/*' STRING '*/'
    | '//' STRING;
STRING
    :  '\'' ( ESC_SEQ | ~('\\'|'\'') )* '\''
    ;
CHAR
    :  '\'' ( ESC_SEQ | ~('\''|'\\') ) '\''
    ;
HEX_DIGIT
    : ('0'..'9'|'a'..'f'|'A'..'F') ;
ESC_SEQ
    :   '\\' ('b'|'t'|'n'|'f'|'r'|'\"'|'\''|'\\')
    |   UNICODE_ESC
    |   OCTAL_ESC
    ;
OCTAL_ESC
    :   '\\' ('0'..'3') ('0'..'7') ('0'..'7')
    |   '\\' ('0'..'7') ('0'..'7')
    |   '\\' ('0'..'7')
    ;
```

```
UNICODE_ESC
    :   '\\' 'u' HEX_DIGIT HEX_DIGIT HEX_DIGIT HEX_DIGIT
    ;
```

Appendix Q IPALM Model-Driven Architecture Implementation

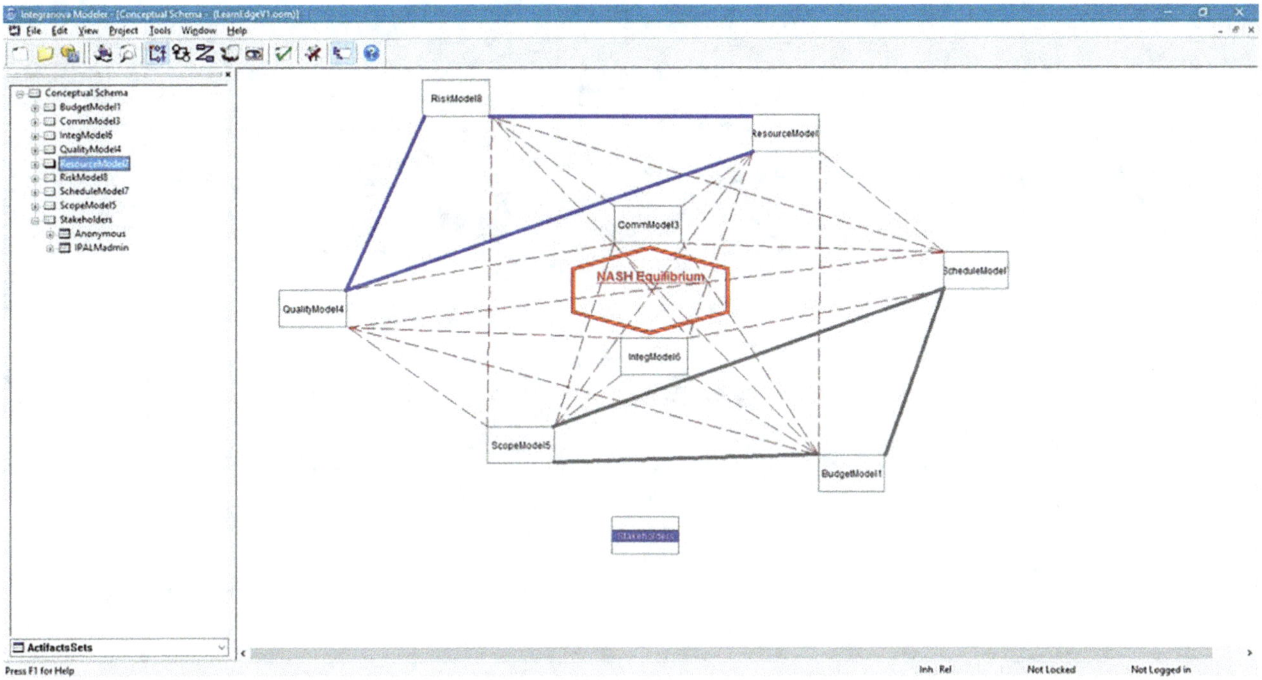

Figure 101 Application Generation in Action Architecture

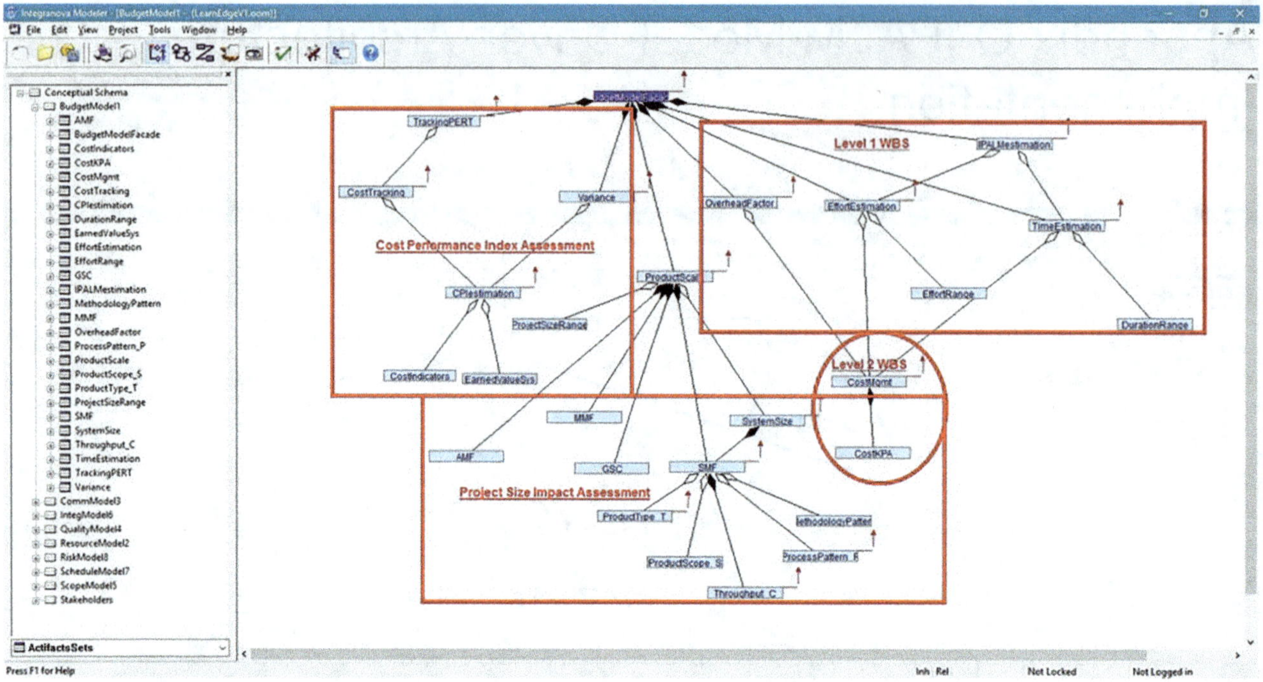

Figure 102 Budget Management Model 1

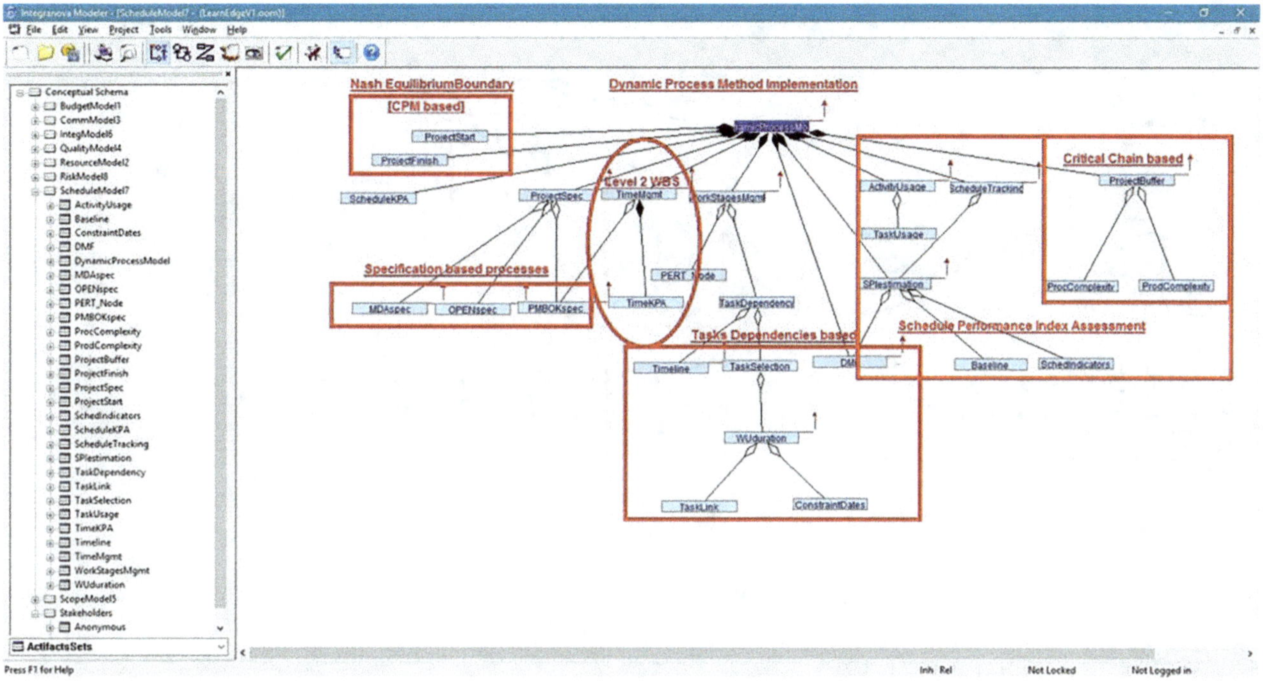

Figure 103 DPM Scheduler Model2

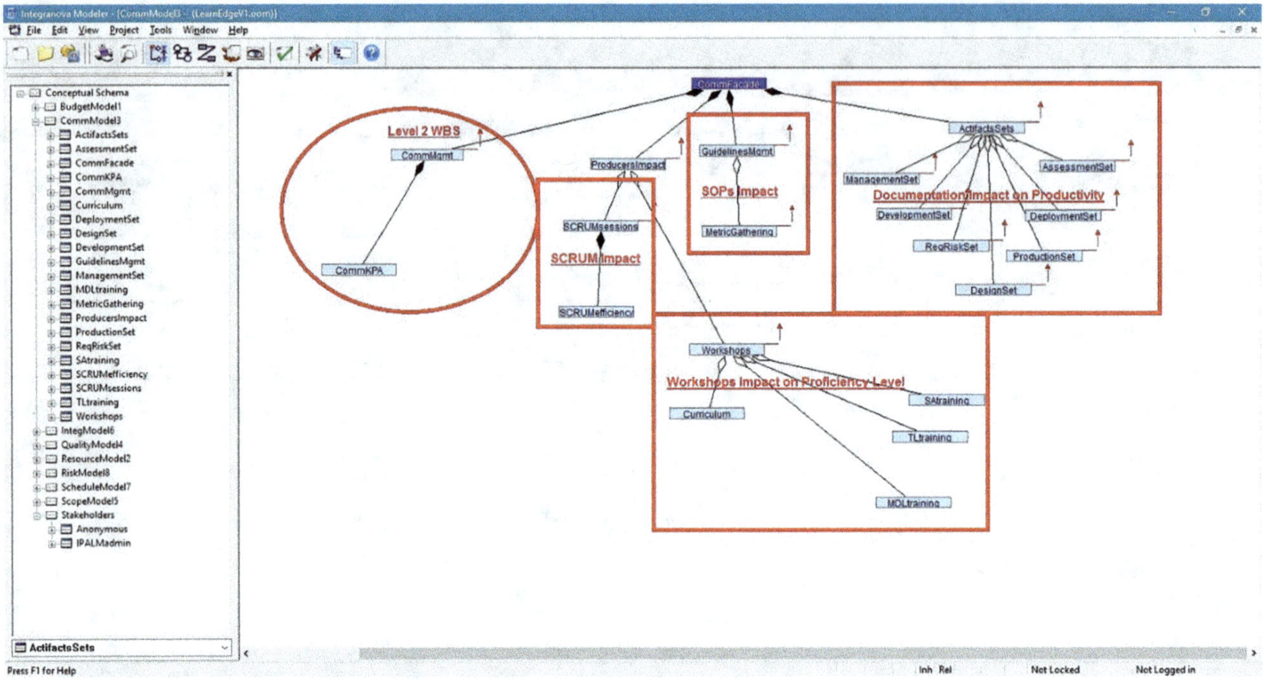

Figure 104 Comm Management Model 3

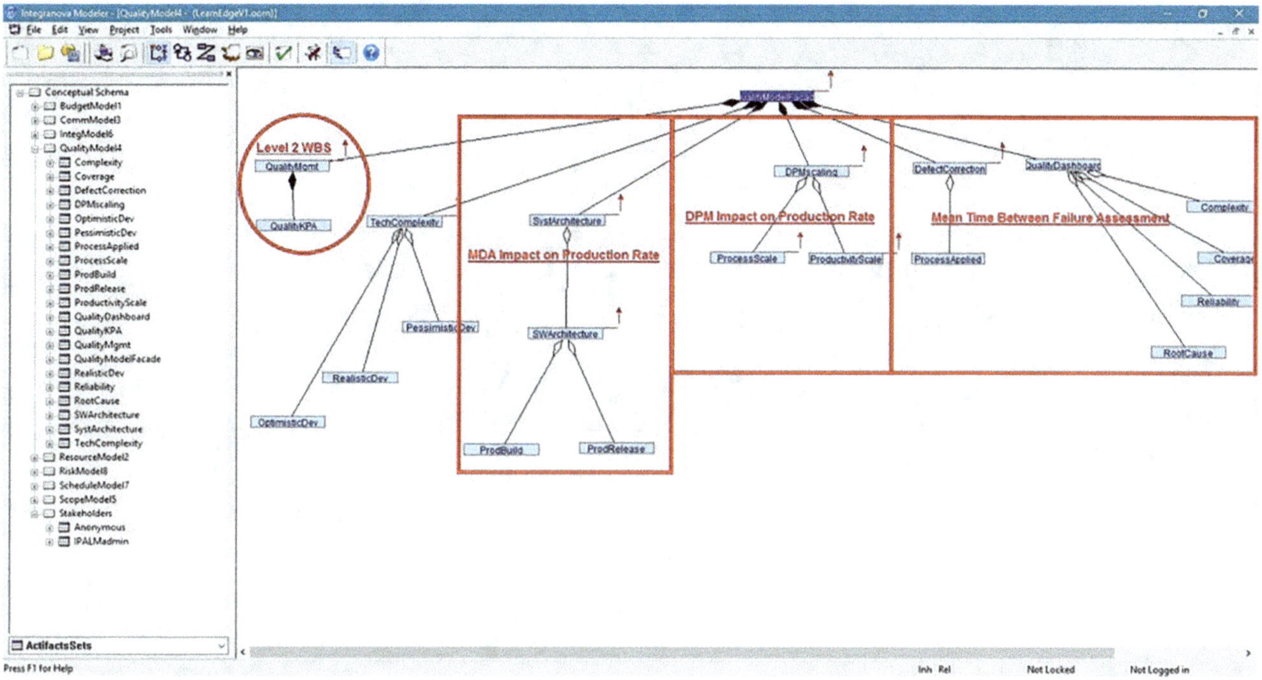

Figure 105 Total Quality Management Model 4

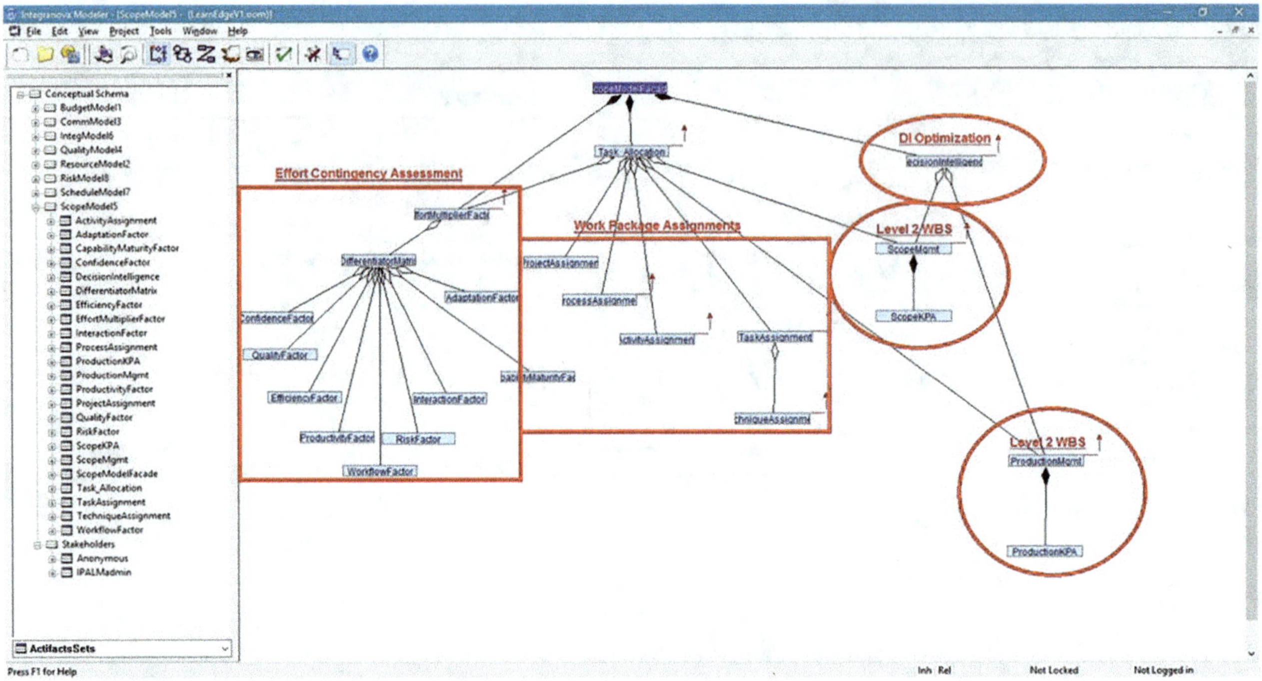

Figure 106 5-WBS Scope Management Model 5

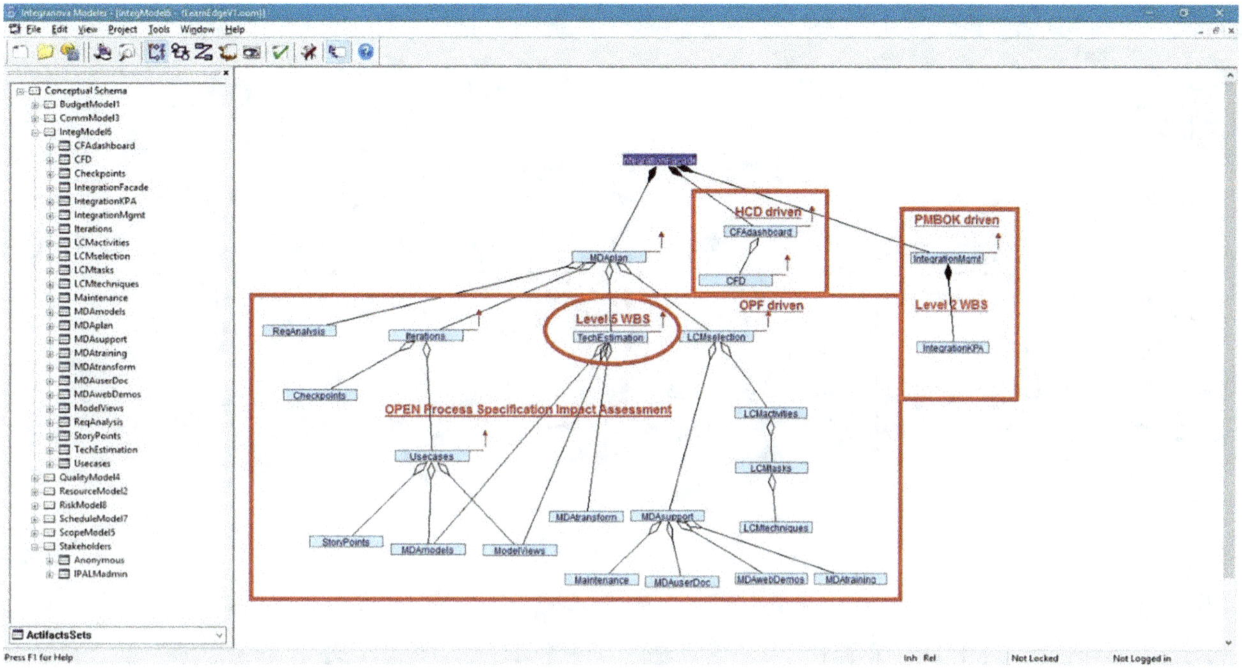

Figure 107 Integration Management Model 6

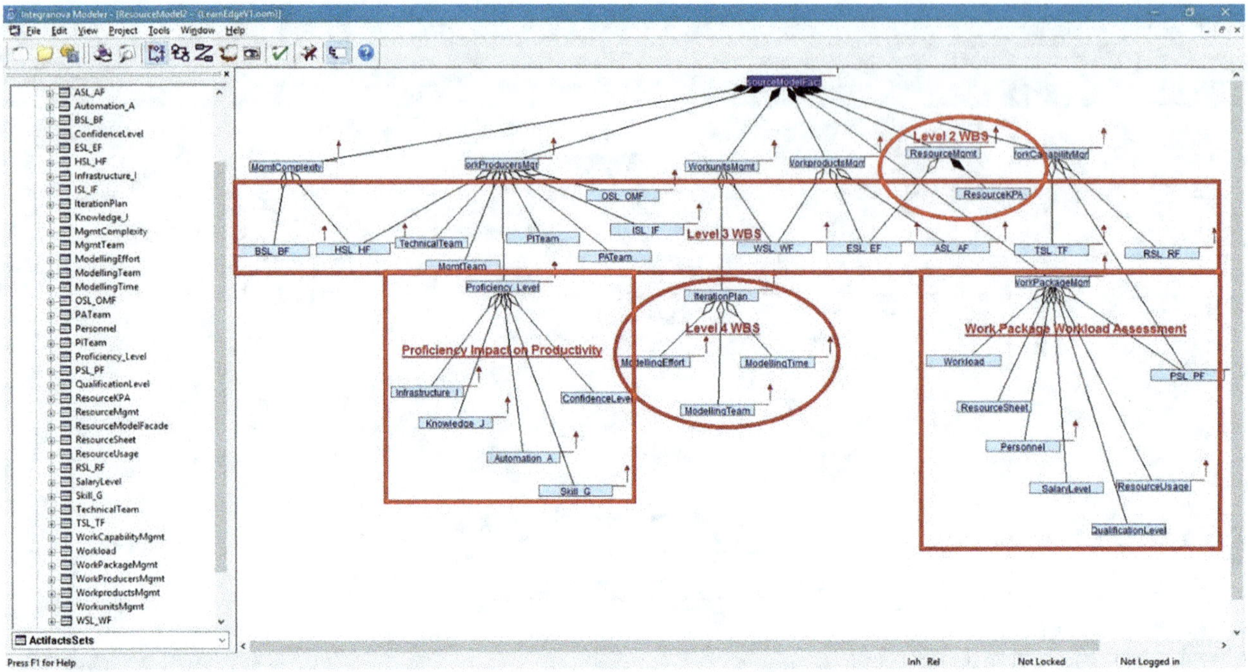

Figure 108 Resource Management Model 7

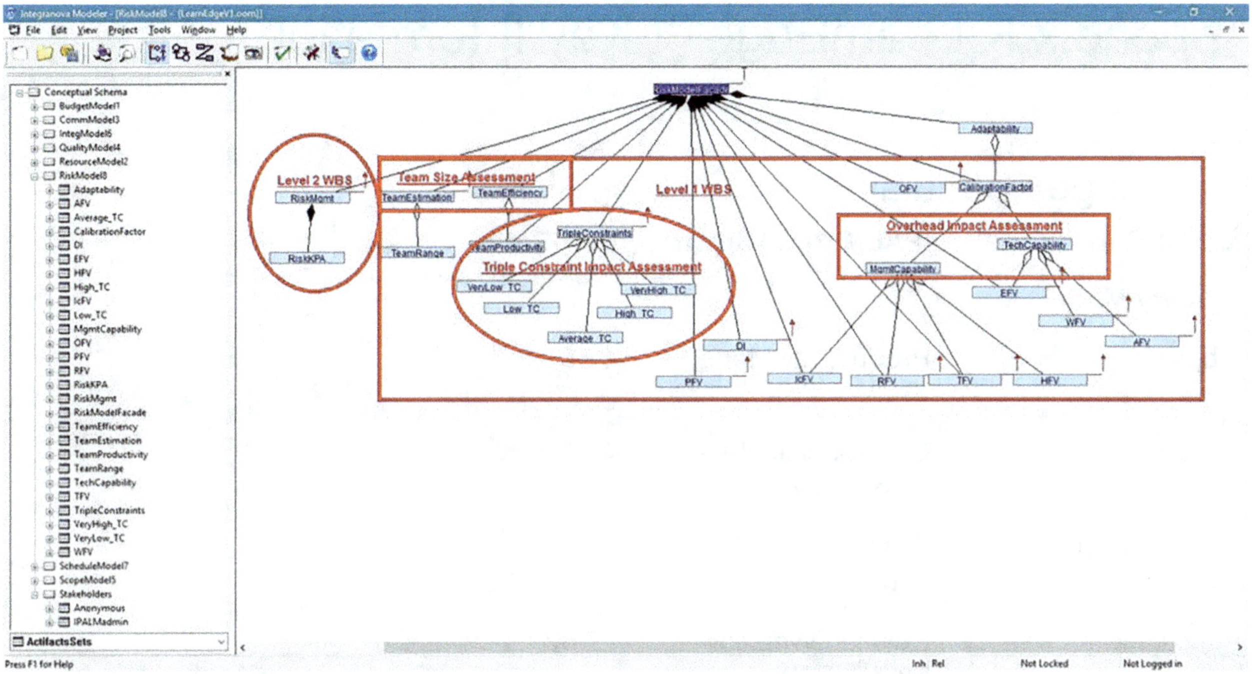

Figure 109 Risk Management Model 8

Appendix R LearnEdge™ Key Information

LearnEdge Formulas

Model Map	**IPALM Breakdown**	**EFP Ratio**
Activity Model		%
Object	Productivity Model (**PM**)	4.65
Object	Open Architecture Model (**OM**)	4.65
Presentation	Cost Data Model (**CM**)	2.32
Functional	Solution Workflow Model (**SM**)	17.42
Presentation	Data Tracking Model (**DM**)	1.16
Functional	Transaction Model (**TM**)	9.29
Functional	Requirement & Risk Model (**RM**)	2.34
Presentation	Usability & Efficiency Model (**UM**)	6.97
Dynamic	Capability Maturity Model (**CMM**)	9.20
Sub-Total		**58.00**

Requirements creep	
Number of iterations (3)	
Implement changes (7% Each)	21.00
Verify changes (7% Each)	21.00
Sub-Total	**42.00**
Project Total	**100.00**

Overhead Ratio Calculation

1. Development %:	SM + SE + CE + SC =	55.00%
2. Overhead %:	PM + QC + PC + RC =	30.00%
3. Overhead Ratio:	Overhead/Development	0.545454545
4. Charging Rate:	Development+Overhead	1.545454545

Where:

A. SM stands for System Management ratio

B. SE stands for Software Engineering ratio

C. CE stands for Cognitive Engineering ratio

D. SC stands for System Control ratio (Configuration Management)

E. PM stands for Project Management ratio

F. QC stands for Quality Control/Management ratio

G. PC stands for Project Control ratio;

H. RC stands for Risk Control ratio

Workflow Distribution by Goals

Focus of Attention (FOA)	Element	Priority Weight(%)	Assignment
Business Management	G&A	15.00%	**BM**
Capability	Project (Mgmt & Admin)	10.00%	**PM**
Process Improvement	Process and V&V (5%) Specification	5.00%	**PC**
Scope	Product Specification	15.00%	**SC**
Quality	Infrastructure (Pragmatics)	10.00%	**QC**
Work	Team Organization (People)	12.00%	**CE**
System	System Management	12.00%	**SM**
Financial Value (Risk)	Performance	5.00%	**RC**
Productivity	Methodology (Practices)	16.00%	**SE**

Eight-Schema Architecture Model

(PRODUCTS) **Model Description**	**GSC**	**Model (PRODUCTS)**
1.System Performance requirements model, is the measurement layer relying on the complexity measure established using a Tree Methodology applicable across all WBS levels of the project and the project sizing measure using an expanded function point based on the established complexity measure.	Perf. Goals	**SM**
2.Operations Rules model, using the predicate calculus and/or declarative language brings out the sets relations between tables identified with the data model. When doing search, tree generation, information grouping or classification, this whole process requires some logical analysis to be conducted using the set theory on tables. **Prolog** is **declarative languages** applied in this case to generate the queries.	Packages	**PM**
3.Facts Reports model, using classes/objects or patterns, bring out the semantic aspect of this communication, a certain degree of abstraction closer to end-user's language. The functions are assigned to a specific class using services in IMES, the data parameters are assigned to attributes and the process model states are assigned to OIDs. Essentially, the IMES model translates the system language into an end-user language using a diagramming technique called **UML**	Class Spec	**UM**
4.Data model, using tables capture the states of system. Data modeling is primarily concerned with the identification of relevant data types (classes for example) and the relationships between entities (1-	Facts&Rules	**OM**

many, for example). This is the **Object Modeling** domain. A common facts & rules repository.

5.Functional model, using service declarations or API
APIs, capture the transformation aspect of the data **RM**
flowing through the system. There is always an input/output relationship between parameters handled by a service. **Visual Prolog libraries** are applied in this case to generate the reports, the formulas, the interactions with the users.

6.Communication model, using protocols and I/F
messages, capture the exchange of information **CM**
between entities. **Message Sequence Charts** are often used to represent such interactions. In essence, an event activates a service which then sends data over the communication medium or path. Events are captured by Process Models. Data are captured by the Data models and Services are captured by the Functional models. The Communication model integrates all those three models using Ports .

PB

7.Process model, using Prolog **Procedure Box** model
coined Horn Clauses, a goal is passed through a “call” **PM**
port, then on an “exit” port upon successful completion. The goal might enter a “redo” port when reactivated
during backtracking. This is the **Inference Engine** IB
domain. This layer provides a platform independence capability.

TM

8.Validation state Inference model, is the functional layer. When making decisions, you have to assert the assumptions made and then validate them through some logic analysis. The constraints also must be asserted and validated using dynamic models. Finally, the expected goals must be asserted and then validated with the **Interaction Box** models. The IPALM dashboard will bring about these models and the interconnectivities between them. This is the **behavior** domain.

Joint Active Design Model

Ac = Time spent on Concurrent Activities

As = Time spent on Serial Activities

Ag = Time spent on GEM Activities

TL = Timeline Count = As + Ac + AG

fc = Concurrent Activities Ratio = Ac / TL

fs = Serial Activities Ratio = As / TL

fg = GEM Activities Ratio = Ag / TL

Tn = Timeline with a team of N persons

T1 = Timeline with a 1 person

RT = Ratio of Timelines = Tn / T1

RT = (fc + fs (N-1) + fg N(N-1))/N [Simmons Communications Model]

NMAX = ((fc - fs) / fg)1/2 [Apply a derivative d/dN and set the results to 0]

fg	fs	fc	NMAX
0.1	0.03	0.875	3

0.058	0.01	0.931	4
0.038	0.0	0.961	5

Where:

fs = 0 is a perfectly partitioned task

fs = 1 is a perfectly atomic task

fc = 0 is a perfectly allocated task

fg = GEM Session Time/Timebox Time (Minutes), e.g. 0.038 x 4800 or 20 Minutes per day.

Maintenance Sizing Rules of Thumb

Maintenance is associated with either the corrective aspect (defects) or the perfective aspect (changes). In either case, the key assessments are conducted or tested under maintenance around the concept of Internal versus External Interfaces. Here is how the total count can be estimated.

Given:

M – The total number of software features (extracted from Use Cases)

N - The total number of designs or tests K - The number of changes or defects

$N = K (M-K) +(K *(K-1))/2$

where the first part of the equation is the External Interfaces Count and

the second part is the Internal Interfaces Count.

$K = (2M-1) \pm ((2M-1)^2 - 8N)^{1/2}$ which requires that $N \leq (2M-1)^2/8 > 0$ (binomial formula).

Logic Operators applied under a Combinational Analysis

P	**Q**	∧ And	**¬∧** **Not And**	∨ Or	**¬∨** Not Or	⊕ XOr	**¬⊕** **Not XOr**	I XAnd	**¬I** Not Xand
T	T	T	F	T	F	F	T	F	T
T	F	F	T	T	F	T	F	T	F
F	T	F	T	T	F	T	F	F	T
F	F	F	T	F	T	F	T	F	T

Where:

1. ⊕ ≡ (P ∨ Q) ∧ (¬(P ∧ Q))

2. ¬⊕ ≡ (¬(P ∨ Q))) ∧ (P ∧ Q)

3. I ≡ P ∧ (¬Q)

4. ¬I ≡ ¬ (P ∧ (¬Q)) or (¬ P) ∨ Q

5. **And** , **NotAnd**, **XAnd** and **NotXAnd**, represents an **Additive** operator for pairwise association

6. **Or , NotOr**, **XOr** and **NotXOr** represents a **Multiplicative** operator for pairwise association

There are three logic operators added: XAnd, Infers and Not Infers. XAnd is the complement to XOr. Infers only gets

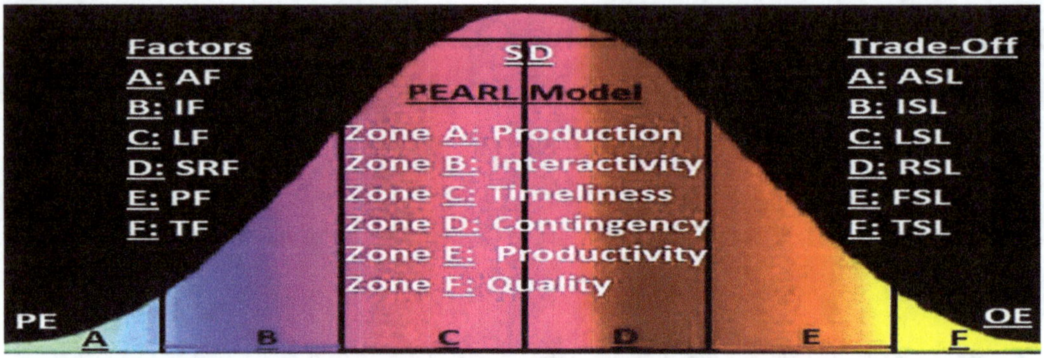

Figure 110 Optimistic to Pessimistic Scenarios Evaluation

Project Evaluation Analysis and Review over the Life cycle Formulas for each node

Optimistic Estimates (OE) represent the management estimates based on: OE = (CMF+SF+SRF+PF+LF) * SEEMduration.

Pessimistic Estimates (PE) represent the technical estimates based on: PE = (AF+IF+TF+CF) * SEEMduration.

Overhead Estimates (OH) represent the following estimates: OH = (1+OE/PE) * 100.

Variance Estimates (VE) represent the following estimates: VE = (OE – PE) / 6.

Realistic Estimates (RE) represent the median estimates based on RE = (OE-PE)/2 = 3 * VE.

Targeted Estimates (TE) represent the following estimates: TE = (OE + 4RE + PE) / 6.

Workload Estimates (WL) represent the following estimates: WL = (1 – TE / RE) * 100.

Appendix S LearnEdge™ Proof of Concept

OVERVIEW

VIP is an Object-Oriented Programming Language (OOPL for short) that can be used to create programs that run under MS Windows GUI, Graphical User Interface. You will need to learn about these three subjects (programming in VIP, programming the GUI and object-oriented programming) in the following sequence:

a. This manual will start by explaining what you see when you start Visual Prolog. What you see is the Integrated Development Environment, the IDE.

b. Then This manual should like to extend your knowledge to the basics of Console and Graphical User Interface (GUI) interactions in programming under MS Windows.

c. Then we go back to Visual Prolog as an Object-Oriented Programming language, using VIP sections syntax.

d. We look at well-known data structures such as stacks, queues and trees.

e. There is a chapter on how to decently handle stream input and output to communicate with the Message Window.

IDE Interactions

When you start Visual Prolog, what is really started is the Integrated Development Environment, the IDE. It looks more or less like figure 1.12

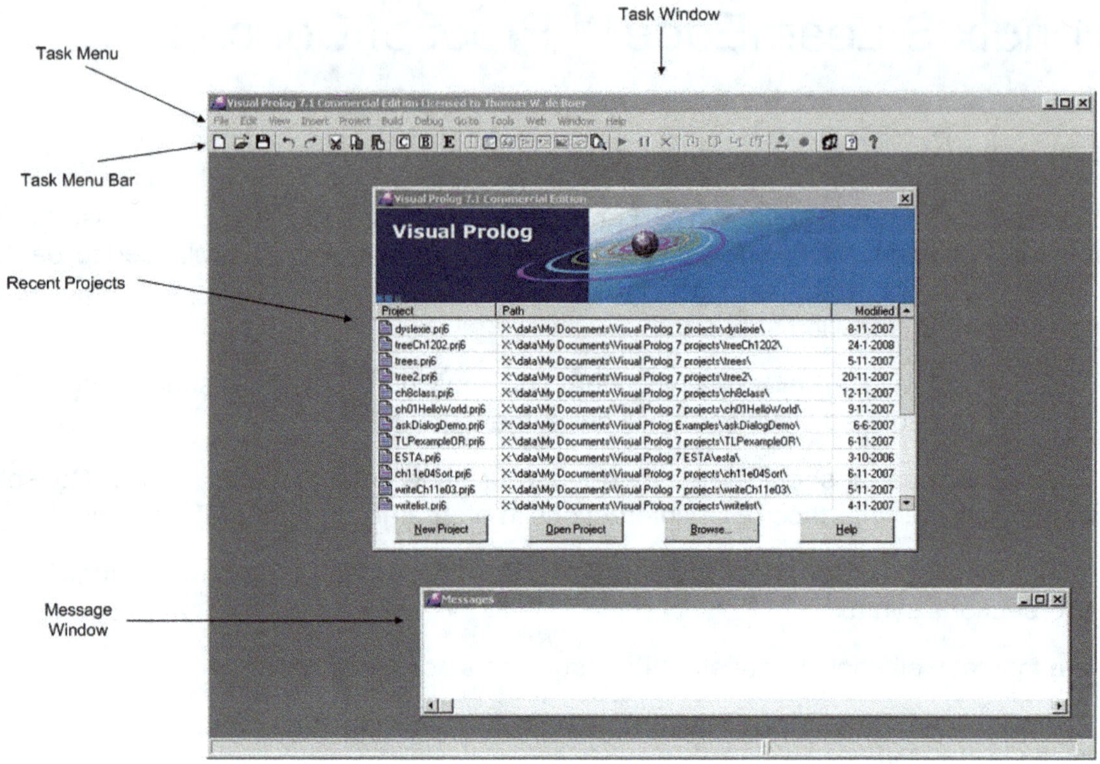

Figure 111 The Integrated Development Environment of Visual Prolog

The IDE shows the usual parts of a Windows program. In the rest of this book we will refer to several

parts of the IDE. These parts are marked in figure 1.1 with the names that are used within Visual Prolog. They are:

• The Task Window. In the IDE the Task Window is the window that is shown when you start a program. You could also call it the “Main Window”. This window usually shows the menu options “File, Edit, View, ..., Windows, Help” on top.

• The Task Menu. It is the menu that will be familiar to you as it contains options like “File”, “Edit”, and the other well-known Windows menu options. This menu will also be referred to as “Main Menu”.

• The Task Menu Bar. It contains icons for the most used options in the Task Menu.

• The Project Overview. It lists the names of the projects that have been processed in the IDE. When you start Visual Prolog for the first time, there probably will be no recent projects.

• The Message Window. This window is typical for Visual Prolog and the IDE. Here you will find the messages from the IDE and later on you are going to write short messages in the Message Window yourself.

PIE Interactions (no GUI or OO interactions) (Example : Fundamental Prolog)

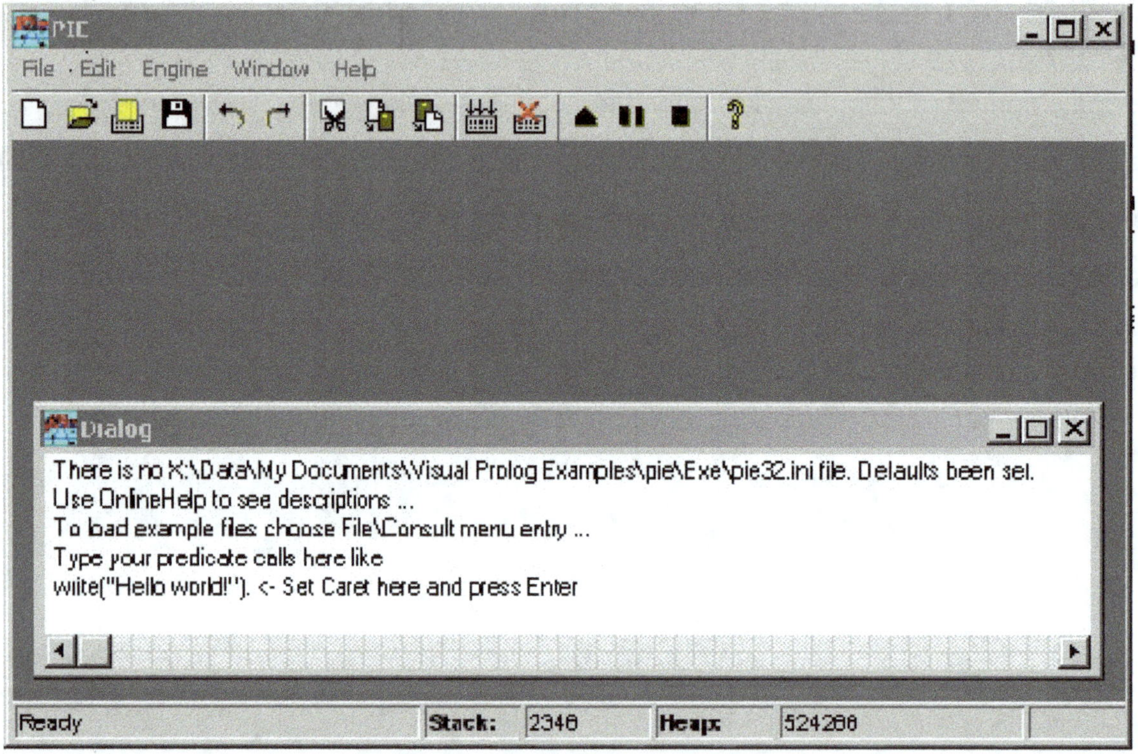

Figure 112 PIE and the dialog window

Console Interactions (no GUI interactions) (Example : Family 1)

In VIP there is a special class of procedures to read from and write to the console. Think of a VIP

program as a process. Then you can imagine that when you work with a few programs at the same

time, there are many processes going on at the same time. Each of these processes has a connection to a console and at the same time each process has no more then one console. For input and output the console supports three streams: an input stream where it reads characters, an output stream where it writes characters and an error stream where it writes special messages in case of errors.

DATA (Model) Interactions (Example : Family 4)

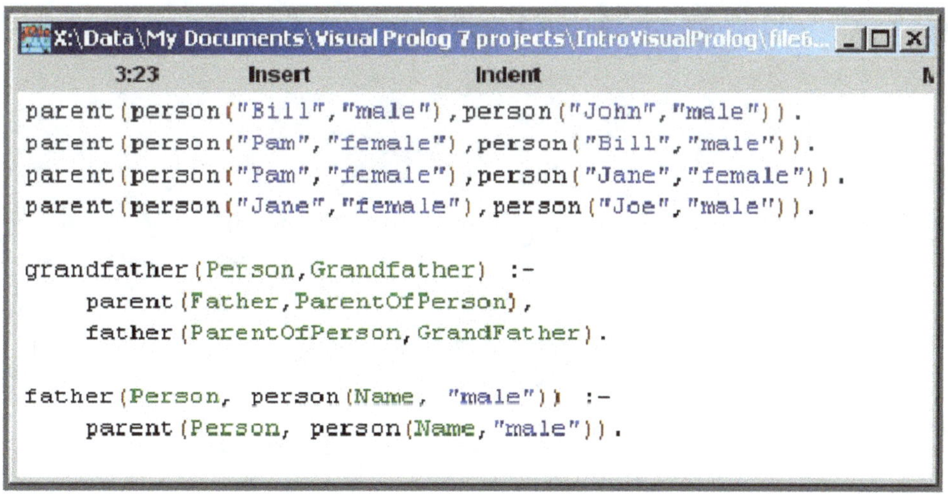


```
parent(person("Bill","male"),person("John","male")).
parent(person("Pam","female"),person("Bill","male")).
parent(person("Pam","female"),person("Jane","female")).
parent(person("Jane","female"),person("Joe","male")).

grandfather(Person,Grandfather) :-
    parent(Father,ParentOfPerson),
    father(ParentOfPerson,GrandFather).

father(Person, person(Name, "male")) :-
    parent(Person, person(Name,"male")).
```

Figure 113 Another family theory

GUI (View) Interactions (Example : Family 2)

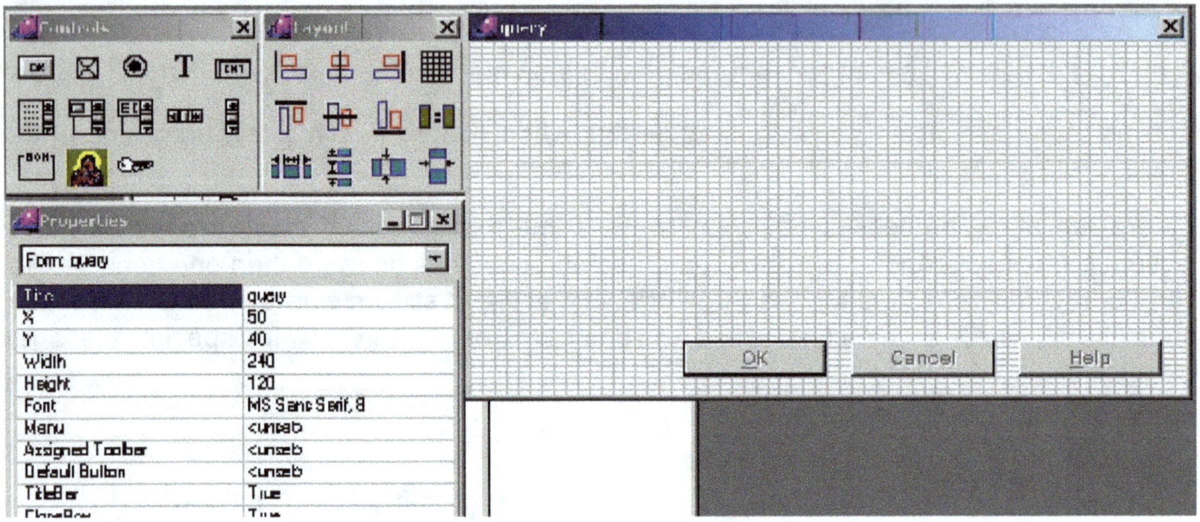

Figure 114 The forms editor with controls and layout toolbars and properties window

Business Logic (Control) Interactions (if …then…else) (Example Family 3)

```
implement person
   open core

class facts
   createdCount : unsigned := 0.

clauses
   getCreatedCount() = createdCount.

facts
   name : string.

constants
   className = "person/person".
   classVersion = "".

clauses
   classInfo(className, classVersion).

clauses
   new(Name) :-
      name := Name,
      createdCount := createdCount + 1,
      stdIO::write("Hello world, I'm a new object. My name is ", name),
      stdIO::nl,
      stdIO::write("I am object number ", createdCount),
      stdIO::nl.

clauses
   getName() = name.

clauses
   setName(Name) :-
      name := Name.

end implement person
```

Facts and Rules Interactions

fact declaration is ...	public fact	private fact
for an object member	in class interface "facts"	in implementation "facts"
for a class member	in class declaration "facts"	in implementation "class facts"

Table 9.2 declarations of facts

Predicate declaration is ...	public predicate	private predicate
for an object member	in class interface "predicates"	in implementation "predicates"
for a class member	in class declaration "predicates"	in implementation "class predicate"

Table 9.3 declarations of predicates

Goal and Constructor Interactions (Example Person)

The goal section defines the main entry point into a Visual Prolog program.

In order to obtain a compiled program, there is a special section that starts with the keyword "goal". This section contains a special predicate "run" that is used without arguments. That predicate is the one from which the entire program execution will start. So the goal section is the entry to a program. It starts with the word "goal", followed by a clause body. An example:

```
goal

mainExe::run(main::run).
```

When you enter the data of a new person, your OO information system literally creates a new object that represents the new person. Every class in a OO program has a method called *new()*. That method is called the constructor of the class; it creates new instances. In the example the new object will contain the data of the new person. An example:

```
class person : person

open core

predicates

classInfo : core::classInfo.

% @short Class information predicate.

% @detail This predicate represents information predicate of this class.

% @end

constructors

new : (string Name).

end class person
```

Domain and ADT Interactions (Example Stack, Queue, Tree)

List Structure (Head|Tail)

```
    list
   /    \
  a     list
       /    \
      b     list
           /    \
          c     list
               /    \
              d      []
```

List	Head	Tail
['a', 'b', 'c']	‘a’	['b', 'c']
['a']	'a'	[] /* an empty list */
[ ]	undefined	undefined
[[1, 2, 3], [2, 3, 4], []]	[1, 2, 3]	[[2, 3, 4], []]

Table 1: Heads and Tails of Lists

Tree Structure Traversal

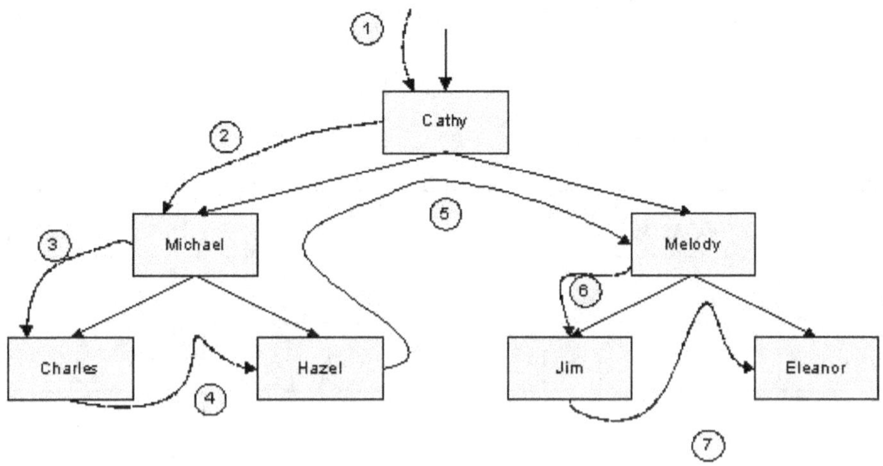

Figure 115 depth-first tree traversal

Horn Clauses Interactions (Example drawMap, mapDatabase)

Horn Clause logic is a formal system for reasoning about things and the way these things are related to each other. An example: in natural language I can express a statement like:

John is the father of Bill.

Here I have two "things": John and Bill, and a "relation" between these, namely that one is the father of the other. In Horn Clause Logic I can formalize this statement in the following way:

father("Bill", "John").

In this rule we use, next to the predicates two so called logical operators: the words “if” and the word “and”. In this formalization the word “if” is replaced by the symbol “:-“ and the word “and” is replaced by a comma “,”. For Example:

In Horn Clause Logic I can formalize this rule as:

```
grandFather(Person1, Person3) :-
father(Person1, Person2), father(Person2, Person3).
```

Predicate Modes Interactions

predicate mode	succeeds or fails	# solutions	backtrackpoint?
fail	always fails	none	no
procedure	always succeeds	one	no
determ	can fail or succeed	none or one	no
multi	always succeeds	one or more	yes
nondeterm	can fail or succeed	none, one or more	yes

Table 9.1 Predicate modi

Interfaces Interactions

The file that you don't know of is the file "person.i". It is the so-called interface to the class person. The interface is like a counter where you can get information. In this case, the interface is what the outside world sees of the objects that are generated. The public class predicates are in "person.cl".

Now you can imagine what that means: in the files "person.cl" and "person.i" are the declarations of public methods. In Prolog methods are performed by predicates. Predicates that are declared here, are callable by other objects and classes.

The IDE has already put some code in the file "person.i". Here it is.

```
interface person
```


open core

end interface person

As you can see, there are not yet any public predicates in the class person. Next to methods, the objects of class person will have attributes. Here I shall confine the attributes to a single one, the name of the object. As said in the previous section, when an object has an attribute, it can (and often will) have a get- and set-method for it that are callable publicly. So in the class person we want two predicates, getName and setName. When you call the first one, the object sends its name to you, with the second one you can enter (or change) the name of the object. So now change the contents of "person.i" into:

interface person

open core

predicates

getName: () -> string Name.

setName : (string Name).

end interface person

Class and Object Interactions

To illustrate the difference between class and object predicates, let us extend the example above with

code that counts the number of person objects that are created. This count will increase every time an

object is created and never decrease. I will extend the declaration of the class with a predicate (i.e.

getCreatedCount) that can return the current count. So please now change the file person.cl into:

class person : person

```
open core

predicates

classInfo : core::classInfo.

constructors

new : (string Name).

predicates

getCreatedCount : () -> unsigned Count.

end class person
```

Why do we declare this predicate in the class declaration “person.cl”? Well, think of this. Each object that is generated, knows everything about itself. But it doesn’t know anything about other objects. Especially in this case, it doesn’t know if it is the latest object generated or even if there are other objects at all. But the class knows! Because the class generates the objects, it can count them and retain the number. You may think of a class as an umbrella covering the objects (or maybe as an mother duck covering little ducks). So when you want to know the number of objects created, you have to ask the class, not any object. So this is a class predicate and it must be declared in the class declaration. This is a strict rule with no exceptions. Public predicates are declared in both the interface and in the class declaration. The class predicates (performed by the class) are declared in the class declaration. The object predicates (performed by any of the objects) are declared in the interface declaration. It is not allowed to declare object predicates in a class declaration, and it is not allowed to declare class predicates in an interface.

Scope Interactions

The keyword “open” is used to extend the *scope visibility* of the class. In this section you specify the names of other classes.

A domain definition defines a domain in the current scope, that is in the current file (class, module), that is the file in which the domain is defined.

A constants section defines one or more constants in the current scope. It starts with the keyword constants.

A facts section declares the facts that are contained in a fact database. The fact database and the facts belong to the current scope.

The section "predicates" declares a set of object or class predicates in the current scope. The section begins with the word predicates that is followed by one or more predicate declarations. A file can contain more than one section "predicates".

Conditional Interactions

A compilation item is an interface, a class declaration, a class implementation, the goal section or it can be a conditional compilation item, which are described in Conditional Compilation.

CompilationItem :

Directive

NamespaceEntrance

ConditionalItem

InterfaceDefinition

ClassDeclaration

ClassImplementation

GoalSection

Each compiler directive starts from the **#** character. The following directives are supported:

- **#include**, **#bininclude**, **#stringinclude** - file inclusion.
- **#if**, **#then**, **#else**, **#elseif**, **#endif** - conditional statements.
- **#export**, **#externally** - exporting and importing classes.

- **#message**, **#error**, **#requires**, **#orrequires** - compilation time information.
- **#options** - compiler options.

Stream I/O Message Interactions

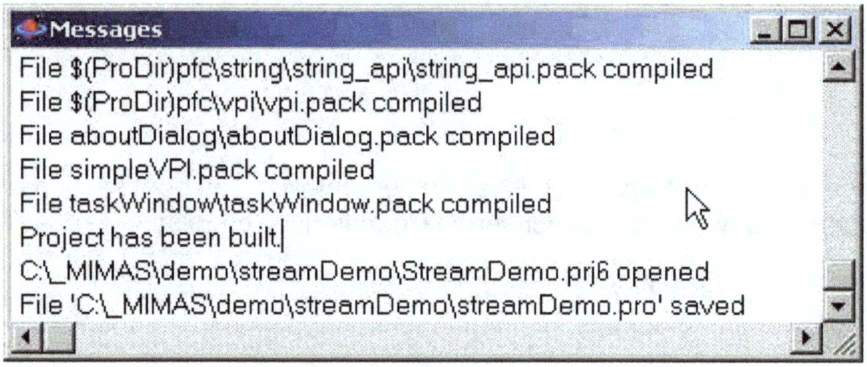

Figure 116 The Messages Window in the IDE

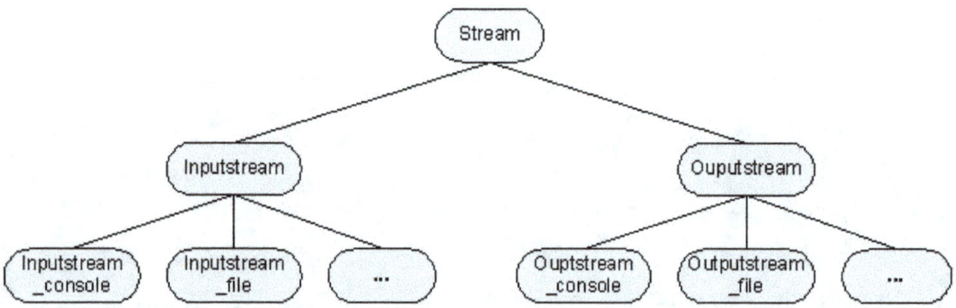

Figure 117 The class hierarchy of Stream

Three-Way Independent Combinational KPUs Interactions: 741 decision elements

a. Mapping prototype demonstrators: 243 decision elements
    - **i.** mapDataBase project: Select the option “Form” called mapCity in Plotter class.
    - **ii.** draw MapObj project: Create a GDIObject called mapCity in Plotter class.
    - **iii.** draw Map project: Apply Paint Responder on mapCity in Plotter class.

b. Tailor the map techniques per prototype: 81 decision elements

c. Select the IDE: 27 decision elements

d. Tailor the application window: 9 decision elements

e. Transform the drawing functions: 3 decision elements

The resolution rate is 92 decision elements per hour.

Continuous Process Improvement: A Canonical Model

- Levers prioritization: Effective Process Management Level modeling.
- External modelization: Cognitive Function Evaluation Matrix modeling.
- Transformations optimization: Verifiable Requirements in OO Methodology modeling.
- Outcomes verification & validation: Pair-wise Independent Combinational KPUs modeling.
- Earned Value Management integration: EVMS modeling.
- Schedule management integration: Project Evaluation & Analysis and Review of the LCM.
- Risk management integration: System Architecture Features Evaluation modeling.
- Quality management integration: Changes and Defects Modeling.

Continuous Process Traceability: Verifiable Requirements in OO Model

- Lexical Elements: Keywords, operators, punctuation. [TOM]
- Syntactic Elements: Interfaces, Declarations, Implementations. [OOM]
- Semantic Elements: Objects, Object Types, Value Types, Classes. [SOM]
- Discourse Elements: Dialogs, Forms, Menus, Windows, Taskbars. [UOM]
- Content Elements: Compound Domains, Lists, Facts, Scopes. [DOM]
- Context Elements : Predicates, Interfaces, Classes, Facts. [ROM]

Capability Maturity Integrated Process Observability: System Eng. Economics Model

- Decision Elements: Rules, Goals, Constructors. [COM]
- Situation Elements: Actors, Events, Actions. [POM]
- Application Elements: Prolog Foundation Classes, Libraries, Packs. [AGIA]

Dynamic Progress Method Model Measurement Analysis

GOAL	MODEL	SERVICE	VROOM MODEL	EFP ratio	ROLE	FACTOR	Appendix	Paragraph
Capability	BEF	AGIA	Application Model	21 %: 7*3	PM	CMF	C, F, G, M	9
Proficiency	UOM	JADE	User Interaction Model	6%	CE	CF	H,I, J	5
Efficiency	DOM	SEEM	Decision Model	8%	DI	SF	E	4

Contingency	ROM	SAFE	Complexity Model	10%	RM	SRF	K, L	8
Quality	TOM	PICK	Transformation Model	21%: 7*3	QM	TF	S	11
Productivity	POM	PAMPA	Process Improvement Model	11%	PI	PF	S	10
Adaptability	OOM	VROOM	Open Architecture Model	8%	SA	AF	P	6
Dependency	SOM	PEARL	Dynamic Progress Model	6%	SM	LF	S	12
Interactivity	COM	IPALM	Communication Model	9%	SE	IF	O, Q	7

Note: EFP ratio for Capability and Quality spread over 3 iterations at 7% ratio each.

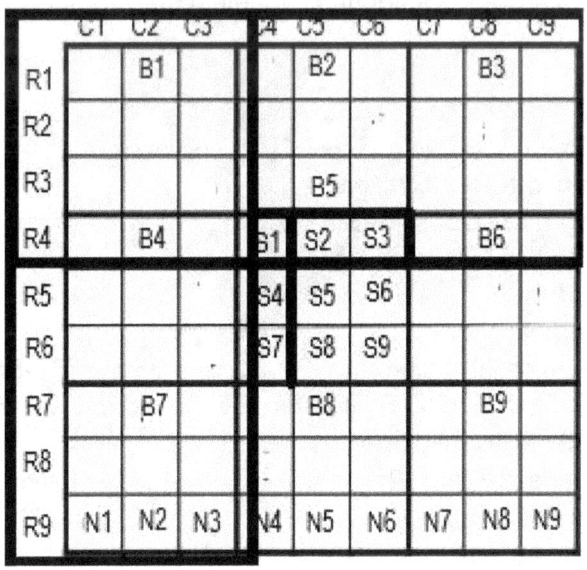

Sudoku Strategies and Nomenclature for Self-Learning

The Mobius strip illustrates very well the concept of the Power of Habit.

What is most fascinating, it's the association between the competency level reached by the user and the Sudoku Level that can be reached.

For example, a junior engineer would be mapped against the EASY level of Sudoku puzzle. The team leader would be mapped against the expert level. In total, LearnEdge™ explores 5 levels of competency. The Sudoku Level accommodates 5 levels of proficiency.

LearnEdge™ is designed around the concept of predicate to elaborate hypothesis testing and theory exploration. What a predicate implies is that the assertion is either True or False.

Each cell on a Sudoku grid requires a 1 to 9 response to a cell entry, non-duplicated on the row, column or block associated with that cell. Now you can devise rules for validating the cell entry, you can devise patterns related to rows, columns and blocks and you can devise the user proficiency by selecting the initial states of the puzzle.

For example:

- **Two Canonical Coordinates System**
    - Row-Column (RC) Coordinate.
    - Block-Square (BS) Coordinate.
- **3-Way Solution Chain**
    - Opposite Adjacent
    - Opposite Horizontal Blocks: B1-B2-B3; B4-B5-B6; B7-B8-B9.
    - Opposite Vertical Blocks: B1-B4-B7; B2-B5-B8; B3-B6-B9.
- **Rows & Columns Solution Strategies**
    - Opposite indices: + 2 or -2.
    - Adjacent indices: +1 or -1.
- **Symmetries with Row, Column and Diagonal per block**

- On any block, two spaces pair NX-NY generate symmetries, including diagonal.
- Two spaces pair on adjacent or opposite rows or columns generate symmetries, when on the same horizontal or vertical block axis.
- Opposite Row, Column, of different block, *on the same horizontal or vertical block axis* When two opposite rows or columns contain the same number(s), apply complements on third row or column of the third block. When a number sits on the intermediate row or column and one of the opposite blocks, apply complements on related opposite block.
- Adjacent Row, Column, of different block, *on the same horizontal or vertical block axis* When two opposite rows or columns contain the same number(s), apply complements on adjacent row or column of the third block. When a number sits on one of the adjacent blocks, apply complements on the other opposite blocks.
- Filled Row, Column Spaces of different block *on the same horizontal or vertical block axis.* When an adjacent row or column spaces are filled/even partially, apply complements on another opposite column or row spaces. When an opposite row or column spaces are filled/even partially, apply complements on adjacent column or row spaces

Appendix T LearnEdge™ Natural Language Processing

OVERVIEW

LearnEdge™ applies a Unification-Based Grammar (UBG) to explore Natural Language Processing. The language is based on the following Phrase Structure rules (terminals and non-terminals), for example from Covington "Natural Language Processing for Prolog Programmers":

S -> NP VP % A sentence is based on Noun Phrase and Verb Phrase

VP -> V (NP) % A verb phrase is based on a Verb accompanied by a Noun Phrase

NP-> D (P | I)% Pronoun or an Identifier

D-> the, a, two, three

P-> he, she, it, they, them

I-> class, predicate, interface, clause, domain, fact, property

V-> consult, reconsult, compile, run

The Lexical analysis stage captures the Lexical Entries: P, I, D, V % terminals

There are five features to enforce five constraints:

1. Number agreement of subject and verb.
2. Number agreement of determiner and Identifier.
3. Assignment of nominative cases to subjects.
4. Assignment to restrictive cases to subjects.
5. Subcategorization to distinguish verbs that do and do not take objects

Unification rules work equally well when applied either bottom-up or top-down scanning.

A feature structure is applied consisting in a set of FEATURES (ATTRIBUTES) and VALUES.

Car RentalExample: The reader is invited to explore the work of Meinte Boersma “Domain-Specific Languages Made Easy”.

References and Bibliography

[PDC] Visual Prolog Development Center (PDC) Tutorials – Appendix S

[Ambler] Scott W. Ambler "Process Patterns", SIGS Books

[Ambler] Scott W. Ambler "More Process Patterns", SIGS Books

[Boehm] Barry W. Boehm "Software Engineering Economics", Prentice Hall

[Boehm] Barry W. Boehm et al "Software Cost Estimation with COCOMOII", Prentice Hall

[Boersma] Meinte Boersma "Domain-Specific Languages Made Easy", Manning

[Booch] Grady Booch "Object-Oriented Analysis and Design with Applications, Addison-Wesley

[Buschmann] Frank Buschmann et al "A System of Patterns - Pattern- Oriented Software Architecture", Wiley

[Cantor] Murray R. Cantor "Object-Oriented Project Management with UML", Wiley

[Caputo] Kim Caputo "CMM Implementation Guide", Addison-Wesley

[Covington] Michael A. Covington "Natural Language Processing for Prolog Programmers", Prentice Hall

[Douglass] Bruce Powel Douglass "Doing Hard time developing Real- Time systems with UML, Addison-Wesley

[Eriksson] Hans-Erik Eriksson et al "The UML Toolkit", Wiley

[Fowler] Martin Fowler "Analysis Patterns - Reusable Object Models", Addison-Wesley

[Frakes] William B. Frakes et al "Software Engineering in the Unix/C Environment", Prentice Hall

[Gilb] Tom Gilb, Dorothy Graham "Software Inspection", Addison- Wesley

[Graham] Ian Graham, Brian Henderson-Seller et al "The OPEN Process Specification", Addison-Wesley

[Hatley] Derek J. Hatley, Imtiaz A. Pirbhai "Strategies for Real-Time System Specification", Dorset House

[Henderson] Brian Henderson-Sellers et al "The OPEN Toolbox of Techniques", Addison-Wesley

[Jones] T. Caper Jones "Software Assessments, Benchmarks, and Best Practices", Addison-Wesley

[Jones] T. Caper Jones "Estimating Software Costs", Mc Graw Hill

[Pressman] "Software Engineering - A Practitioner's Approach", Mc Graw Hill,

[Royce] Walker Royce "Software Project Management - A Unified Framework", Addison-Wesley

[Rumbaugh] James Rumbaugh, Michael Blaha, et al "Object-Oriented Modeling and Design", Prentice Hall

[Selic] Brian Selic, Garth Gullekson, Paul T. Ward "Real-Time Object- Oriented Modeling", Wiley

[Shlaer] Sally Shlaer, Stephen J. Mellor "Object Lifecycles - Modeling the world in states", Yourdon Press

[Simmons] Dick B. Simmons et al "Software Measurement - A Visualization Toolkit", Prentice Hall

[Texel] Putnam P. Texel, Charles B. Williams "Use Cases combined with Booch, OMT, UML Process and Products", Prentice Hall

[Pastor] Oscar Pastor, Juan Carlos Molina "Model-Driven Architecture in Practice", Springer

[Boy] Guy André Boy "Orchestrating Human-Centered Design", Springer

[EVMS] https://en.wikipedia.org/wiki/Earned_value_management

www.ingramcontent.com/pod-product-compliance
Lightning Source LLC
LaVergne TN
LVHW080018210926
848481LV00011B/3054